SCOTLAND'S GARDENS

SCOTLAND'S GARDENS

Edited by G. Allan Little

SPURBOOKS
in association with
THE SCOTLAND'S GARDENS SCHEME

1981

Published by

SPURBOOKS
(A Division of Holmes McDougall Ltd)
137-141 Leith Walk
Edinburgh EH6 8NS

in association with
The Scotland's Gardens Scheme
26 Castle Terrace
Edinburgh EH1 2EL

Part 1 © Spurbooks, 1981
Part 2 © G. Allan Little, 1981

ISBN 0 7157 2091 0

Designed by Pat Macdonald

Typeset in 10/12pt & 9/10pt Bembo

Printed in Great Britain by
Holmes McDougall Ltd
Edinburgh

Frontispiece
The Rose Arch, Hilton
House

CONTENTS

ACKNOWLEDGEMENTS

The publishers and editor gratefully acknowledge the collaboration of the Scotland's Gardens Scheme in the compilation of this book; the helpful assistance of all the garden owners who provided information; and the co-operation of all those who have kindly provided photographs.

ABBREVIATIONS

N.T.S.	National Trust for Scotland
R.B.G.	Royal Botanic Garden, Edinburgh
R.C.A.H.M.S.	Royal Commission on the Ancient & Historical Monuments of Scotland
S.G.S.	Scotland's Gardens Scheme
S.R.O.	Scottish Record Office, Register House
S.T.B.	Scottish Tourist Board

LIST OF ILLUSTRATIONS

Small illustrations in margins are from the *Historia Generalis Plantarum* of Dalechamps (Lyon, 1586-7), courtesy R.B.G. Library, Edinburgh; photographed by Kenneth Grant. Decorated initial letters & tailpiece illustrations by Pat Macdonald.

FOREWORD

Sᴄᴏᴛᴛɪsʜ ɢᴀʀᴅᴇɴs ᴀʀᴇ ᴀᴍᴏɴɢsᴛ ᴛʜᴇ ɢʀᴇᴀᴛᴇsᴛ ɪɴ ᴛʜᴇ world and this book indicates why this is so. Gardens are monuments to their creators and caretakers, to those who had the love and devotion to seize upon an idea of beauty and then fought the elements to establish it. Unlike some monuments, a garden, once created, cannot be left unattended for a decade while ownership changes hands. The very fact that it is alive means it must be continually pruned, weeded and repropagated to remain within its original concept. Many of the gardens listed in this book are opened to the public under 'Scotland's Gardens Scheme' to raise money for charity. How long the majority can exist in their present form is a disturbing question.

In this book the reader can entertain his own curiosity, delve into a part of history and read detailed descriptions of some of the great gardens and the cost of running them today.

I hope that others will enjoy reading these pages as much as I have.

The Countess of Minto
Chairman
Scotland's Gardens Scheme

Summer 1981

PART ONE

SOME ASPECTS OF SCOTLAND'S GARDENS

FIGURE 1
*Kinross House, showing
Leven Castle 'placed' on the
principal axis of the garden
(altered in other respects)*

CHAPTER I

THE HISTORY OF GARDEN DESIGN IN SCOTLAND

William Brogden

NY HISTORY OF ARTS IN SCOTLAND CAN, AND PERHAPS, should, begin with an observation on the vanity of human productions. Gardeners, whether in Scotland or elsewhere, do not need to be reminded of this. It would be well, however, for visitors to gardens to bear always in mind that all arts are ephemeral, and that of these, gardening is the most fleeting. Literature and architecture, which can include sculpture, are the most enduring of human productions. Architecture and sculpture, at least in the past, were hard edged, highly artificial, made of the best and most long-lasting materials, so that even in ruin they retain some of the qualities their makers gave them. Literature with all its allusive and imaginative power survives too, so long as some of the symbols which record it can be found. Gardening is rather more like music, a thing always of the present, whose past, while usually pleasing, is always imprecise.

For gardening to flourish as an art, as opposed to grubbing for food and medicines on the level of subsistence, requires domestic peace and orderly government, a good measure of prosperity, and a temperate climate. Every schoolboy knows to what extent these factors are to be found, all together, in Scottish history. For gardens to survive, or strictly speaking, for gardening to survive requires that continuing care, attention and money are expended. It is therefore rather remarkable that any garden site can survive through more than two generations in anything like its 'original' form, and it is even more remarkable that this should occur in Scotland. But despite all difficulties, there is a garden history in Scotland, and a distinguished one, but to recover it, reference has often to be made to 'architectural' remains, and, of course to literature, either for the *idea* of the garden at any particular time, or as evidence of its actual state, as well as to the too rare paintings of, or plans for, gardens.

Any planting for purpose whether for food, for herbal remedy, or for pelasure had, even in the remotest past a measure of design in it: shall there be a row of cabbages, or shall we broadcast seed and let them grow where they will? Rudimentary garden design of this king has always been with us, but design in the modern sense — that is relatively large areas set aside for pleasure began, or was revived, like so much else, in the sixteenth century. In conscious imitation of what they thought were the pleasure grounds of Hadrian, or the sacred sites of Fortuna at Palestrina, Pope Julius and later Cardinal d'Este created at the Vatican and at Tivoli very large gardens famous for plants certainly, but as importantly

FIGURE 2
Old Yester House Gardens, from the south (oil painting by de Witt, c. 1700)

FIGURE 3
Stirling Castle, with what remains of the King's Knot to the right

famous for the stories they told — the symbol of sculpture, of place, and of allusion. And above all they were manifestations of order, and of power.

Very soon other princes began to emulate this new kind of art: du Perac sent drawings of the Villa d'Este to Germany and France in the 1570s; engravings then appeared, and at some time before his accession to the English crown James VI and his Queen were infected with the itch to garden grandly, and they did so at Stirling. Queen Anne already had a garden just south of the Palace. Its form is unknown, but its character must have been 'medieval' — that is, it was a sequestered garden set within an impregnable castle, and being presided over by a Queen was, at least by metaphor, the setting for courtly love.

The King's Knot is entirely different. It is well outside the castle in the ample flat ground to the west. It is not defended; but rather it is open, confident, perhaps even thrusting. The King's Knot is formed of a series of geometric terraces of banked earth, and like its Italian contemporaries it is as much 'architecture' as it is garden. Of the original furnishings we can only guess, but they would have included fruit trees, ornamental shrubs, vases of flowers according to season, very likely figurative sculpture, and at the centre of the Knot an ornamental building surrounded by its own tiny moat.

But gardening on a princely scale is rare outside Italy at so early a date. Naturally with the removal of the prince in 1603 gardening in Scotland was confined within less extensive bounds, and it was the end of the seventeenth century before the amplitude of the King's Knot, or its use of sculpture and fine plants within an 'architectural' setting was to any significant extent employed in Scottish gardens. The seventeenth century generally introduces, and witnesses the perfection, of what is often thought of as the national type — the walled garden of limited extent ornamented by renaissance architectural detail perhaps but otherwise rather plain, possessing little sculpture, beyond the odd sundial, and relying on homely plants for pot, apothecary, or nosegay for its furnishing. How just such an assessment this is, in fact, is really beside the point: since the turn of the nineteenth and twentieth centuries it has been accepted as true, and has been the spur for recreated gardens by men of considerable skill and finesse such as Sir Robert Lorimer, beginning at Earlshall, Fife, and followed by other professionals, and perhaps more importantly by many amateur garden makers of less than princely means.

Gardens of this type continued to be made throughout the seventeenth century, and even the eighteenth century. But by as early as the 1660s, echoing, but only just, the advances being made by André Le Nôtre for Fouquet and the King of France, there is evidence of a desire for orderly arrangement of parts, of extent, and even grandeur in Scottish gardens. This desire is codified by one John Reid, gardener to Sir George MacKenzie of Rosehaugh, Ross-shire, in his *The Scots Gardener* of 1683, the first book on gardening published in Scotland. It is really a handbook of gardening prepared for the climate of Scotland, in itself an indication of a growing interest in gardening; but layout of gardens was very

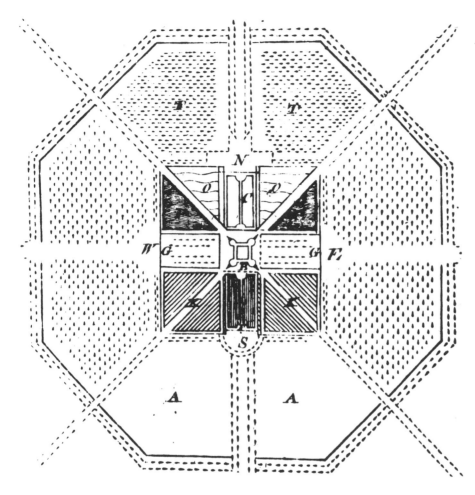

FIGURE 4
*John Reid's ideal garden
(plate from The Scots
Gardener, 1683)*

important to Reid, and he devoted a large section of his book to 'contrivance and design'.

To him the greatest calamity was irregularity and all means were to be employed to avoid this. His easiest prescription runs thus:

In a confined situation of ground, I add what I can but diminish nothing. I take a survey of the work and when I find several regular and irregular things done on one side of the house, and nothing correspondent on the other, I mark the very same on the opposite side, and this I continue to do, till two irregularities produce one uniformity.

There were more ingenious ways of obtaining the impression of extent, if not actually producing a uniform symmetry, and Reid's passion for regularity was not shared by many of his countrymen. One such device was employed by Andrew Fletcher of Saltoun, East Lothian, often surnamed the patriot for his

FIGURE 5
*Fletcher of Saltoun's plan
for the garden at Saltoun
Hall, East Lothian*

honourable, but predictably unsuccessful counsel against self-interest in the negotiations for the Second Act of Union. Fletcher's gardens were a 'typical' collection of rectangular enclosures, without any sense of 'design' such as symmetry or correspondence of parts. His method to supply this deficiency was simply to connect the centres of all his 'gardens', and where the connecting 'lines' crossed intervening walls he constructed *clairvoyées*.

This meant he could both throw all parts of the garden 'open' without losing the benefit of the enclosing walls, and also, the resultant correspondence of parts was surprising, and at the same time 'irregular'. This seeming paradox was exploited also in France in the early eighteenth century, in England by Charles Bridgeman, especially at Stowe, Buckinghamshire, and in Scotland on a much larger scale by Lord Mar.

Sir William Bruce of Kinross, like Reid, sought a regularity of design, and like Fletcher a correspondence of parts, but his means of attaining these ideals were those of architecture. First at Balcaskie, Fife, from 1663 onwards Bruce exploited an 'ideal' site: fairly steeply sloping south-facing ground with the significant foreground of the Forth and a background of East Lothian beyond. He regularised the house in Reid's fashion — by balancing irregularities and, further, by the very early employment in Britain of the Palladian device of equal but symmetrically disposed pavilions or dependencies. By these means he formed a regular and somewhat grand 'court' to the north of Balcaskie. The south side was arranged as a series of three terraces, one below the other, and taken all together formed a large enclosed rectangle. Bruce pointed the symmetry of the scheme — house, garden, court — by exploiting the feature of the Bass Rock. This, by design, he 'placed' on the centre line of the scheme — all parts were equally disposed to right and left of the imaginary line. The device allowed him both regularity and variety: regularity was obtained by the very obvious attunement of his scheme to 'nature', so surprising, pleasing and satisfying that very little further regularity was called for, leaving the disposition of plantings and other furnishings to display intricacy and variety — the lesson learnt and demonstrated by the great French schemes at Vaux-le-Vicomte, recently seen by Bruce.

The use of a great natural feature such as the Bass Rock or a ruin was repeatedly used by Bruce and is a feature of his work — at Kinross, he uses the ruin of Level Castle in Loch Leven, whereas at Hopetoun it is North Berwick Law (on a very clear day!) or closer at hand Blackness Castle, again a ruin. Bruce is amongst the earliest, if not the earliest, designer to employ this device and he has not received the credit due him. It not only allows his designs to have the grand rather Baroque simplicity of French gardens but it also exploits some of the joys of Scottish topography — curiously abrupt hills, and ruined castles — in a fashion of landscape pictures, thus predating the Picturesque by roughly one hundred years.

Bruce usually had one point of view only, and it was central to his scheme.

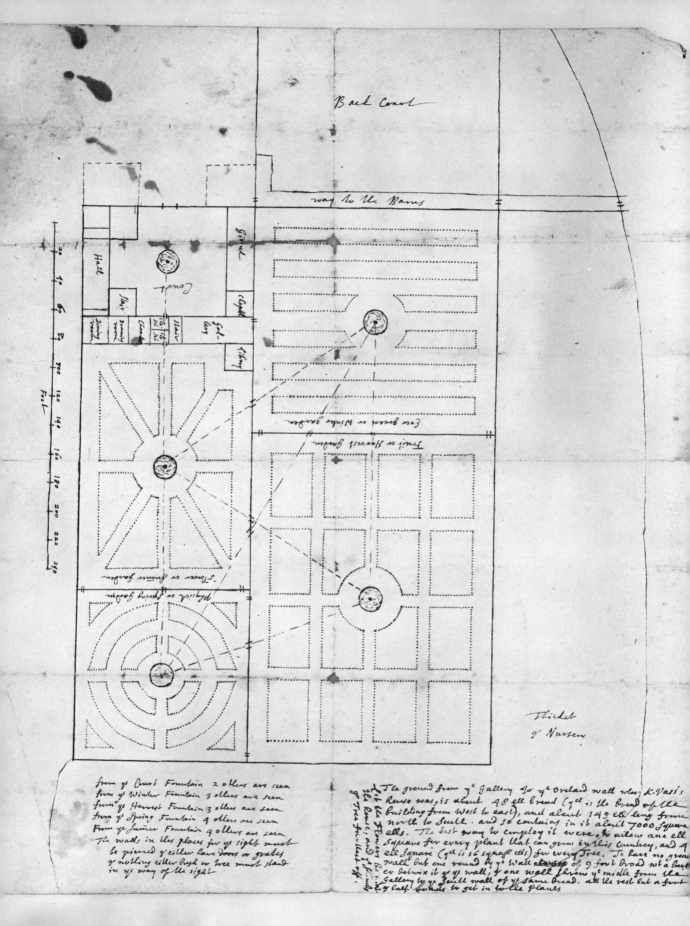

With the turn of the eighteenth century it is apparent that more complexity was wanted by gardeners, and also a greater sense of extent. These were of profound significance in the development of garden design in Scotland — much more significant than the necessary first steps taken by Bruce, for they resulted in a new kind of gardening — gardening or improvement of whole stretches of countryside. This change was brought about in several ways, and although it was closely related to similar developments in England it produced significantly different results.

As in the seventeenth century the way forward was led by those with wealth, leisure and the wit to do so, generally from the nobility. Chief among these was

> the late Earl of Mar that first introduced the wilderness way of planting amongst us, and very much improved the taste of our gentlemen, who very soon followed his example.

'The Wilderness Way of Planting' was a restatement of Fletcher of Saltoun's method of turning the various divisions of a garden into a kind of 'happy confusion' allied to the scale, extent and employment of terminations introduced by Bruce. John Erskine, 11th Earl of Mar, is remembered for his unsuccessful backing of the Pretender in 1715, but he was also an amateur architect and garden designer of considerable skill. His greatest work was his own estate of Alloa, Clackmannanshire in the early eighteenth century.

His achievement is shown in an engraved plan of the town, gardens and parks of Alloa dated 1710, an enormous layout which, according to the travel writer John Macky contained forty-two acres of gardens and one hundred and fifty acres of woodland. The house and town of Alloa are on the flat land just north of the Forth with the gardens laid out in front. Behind, on the steeply sloping hill, were the woodlands. Like Bruce and other designers typical of the age, Mar laid out his main garden symmetrically about the main axis through the south front of the house. But he added complexity to this by taking axes from the other fronts of his house, perhaps in imitation of John Reid, as well as the diagonal lines which recalled the *pate d'oie*, a favourite French device.

To this basically architectural scheme Mar added the prospects of neighbouring castles or mountains just as Bruce had done, but Mar had

> thirty-two different vistoes, each ending on some remarkable seat or mountain, at some miles distance; one of them shows you Sterling Castle, at four miles distance; another the Palace of Elphinstone, on the other Side of the River; a Third the Castle of Clacmanning; and so the rest
>
> (John Macky, *Journey Through Scotland*)

All these lines or 'Vistoes' criss-crossed Alloa, and formed a large series of apparently irregular spaces, which were laid out as gardens, woodlands, or parks.

Lord Mar's ambitions as a designer far outstripped his means, and it was partly to mend his fortune that he dabbled in dangerous politics. But his inclination to garden on the grand scale, and to plant his estate, was not so

FIGURE 6
Balcaskie, view from the house looking southwards towards the Firth of Forth, with the Bass Rock (partly obscured by sea haar) occupying a central position in the vista

megalomaniac as it might seem today. Planting and improvement of land was
seen from the 1690s onwards as a means to personal and national wealth, and
insofar as forests furnished the navy it was to be the basis of international
prestige also. Scientific husbandry had begun with the enclosures of common
land in parts of England in the late sixteenth century, but there was little
advancement in the seventeenth century and in Scotland there was practically no
improvement. The crown and court had departed; something like a small
'ice-age' had perceptibibly changed the Scottish climate and seriously affected
horticulture and husbandry; there was general economic malaise and decline;
and there was also fierce religious dispute and Civil War. Any of these could
have been the inducement to lie low and put off schemes for improvement. But
towards the end of the century confidence began to return, and at first in the
Lothians and subsequently in the rest of the country there were systematic
schemes for drainage, enclosure, and above all, planting of forest trees both in
woodland, and in the essential shelter belts. These early improvements were
arranged in rectangular blocks, and laid out by surveyors' instruments, and
usually they were the business of the landowners, and not of agents. Therefore
what happened in the field and in the garden came to be seen as the same kind of
activity, and carried on with the same geometrical rules. John Reid's *Scots
Gardener* made little distinction between horticulture and agriculture, and
indeed appears to have established the pattern for estate improvement carried on
by both the professional surveyors and countless amateurs in the eighteenth
century.

After the Second Act of Union the pace of planting and improvement quick-
ened, and by 1724 the very lively and influential Society of Scotch Improvers
had been established under the leadership of the Duke of Atholl. In the very early
days improvers sometimes imported Devonshire farmers, but the eighteenth
century saw steady and remarkable advances in Scottish agriculture and horticulture, and from mid-century onwards there began the soon-to-be-famous
export of gardeners.

A desire to plant and improve, coupled with the prevalent taste for gardening
on the grand scale, led to such gardens as Alloa, but more typical, perhaps, was
the experience of the Haddingtons at Tyninghame, East Lothian — experience
instantly recognisable by anyone who had laid out a garden.

The Haddingtons moved to Tyninghame at the beginning of the eighteenth
century, and found that previous attempts to plant, drain and enclose had come
to little good purpose, and most of these plantations had been destroyed by the
tenants. It was thought that the exposed, marine situation rendered planting
impossible, but through the persuasion of Lady Haddington an attempt was
made which succeeded. This was followed by a small wilderness which Lord
Haddington laid out in a centre with fourteen walks from it, most of them
having 'tolerable good terminations'.

After this Lady Haddington proposed they should enclose the muir of

FIGURE 7
*John Erskine, 11th Earl of
Mar's plan of his estate at
Alloa, 1710*

Tyninghame and plant its 360 acres; he was against it but she proceeded anyway.

> After she had begun to plant it, I thought it would be a pity not to have a centre in it, and walks from it, with the best terminations we could find.

He walked over the area and found a suitable centre which Lady Haddington liked, 'but walking about, lighted on a spot of ground she thought more proper'. They were expecting some friends to visit and decided, therefore, to leave the choice to them. They all went to the muir, and Lady Haddington spoke in favour of her choice; Lord Haddington was keen to move on to his choice but one of the friends,

> Lord Marchmont said it would be best to set up the instruments and to take the views and walks, when that was done he would go forward, and do the like at mine; and when both were laid down upon paper, it might be judged which was best. In the meantime, Sir John Bruce had straggled from us, and sent to tell, he had lighted upon a finer spot of ground for a centre, than either of the two we were contending for. My Lord Marchmont sent him the same answer he had given me.

When the three centres with their various walks and terminations were drawn up it was decided, perhaps not unreasonably, to use all three. The only change from this was the addition of serpentine walks and 'some figures' by their teenage son Lord Binning.

Free advice from friends is usually very easily obtained, but what of professional advice about laying out gardens? There were skilled gardeners who also wrote, like John Reid, and there were also surveyors whose skills might be extended to include advice on layout, but generally speaking these matters were thought of in terms of taste, and reference to existing gardens or, when in doubt, to friends was the normal procedure. There were exceptions, however. William Boutcher and William Adam both gave designs for gardens, but their principal businesses were those of nurseryman and architect/builder respectively. Adam remodelled Hopetoun, West Lothian in the 1720s and extended the design of Bruce and Alexander Edward, and he acted in a similar capacity at Hamilton Palace, Lanarkshire, where he made a garden near his new kennels — but his design was first shown to Charles Bridgeman, the royal gardener, and it was laid out within the pre-existing landscape designed by Edward.

Both Adam and Boutcher were employed at Sir John Clerk of Penicuik's 'Villa' at Mavisbank, Midlothian in the early 1720s, but the real force behind that design was its owner. Indeed Clerk is a considerable character in the history of gardening, and of architecture. Grandson of a merchant and picture dealer, cousin to a priest in Rome, adviser to the Hopes on the building, furnishing and grounds of Hopetoun, Baron of Exchequer and Commissioner for Union, Clerk built and planted Mavisbank, Cammo and Penicuik, and he oversaw and made additions to Drumlanrig, Dumfriesshire for his friend the Duke of Queensberry. Although Clerk started gardening about 1700 his achievement is more characteristic of the middle of the century, and through him we can see the transition from baroque grandeur, complexity and extent to the pastoral and poetic ideas manifested in the landscape style of the later eighteenth and nineteenth centuries.

He improved Penicuik house and grounds by stages, beginning before his father's death, when he planted to a scheme prepared by William Adair. After building and planting Mavisbank, Clerk seems to have lost interest in relating grounds to architecture, and although the gardens at Penicuik were composed of typical elements — avenues with suitable terminations, parterres, walled gardens, etc. — it appears that it was their effect within the particular topography of the place that pleased more and more. In his maturity Clerk responded not so much to a garden and improved estate, but to the landscape as a whole.

This is illustrated by one of the most interesting and most forward-looking parts of Penicuik, Hurley Cave and Pond, which were completed in 1742. According to Clerk, Hurley Pond was

> noteworthy for its position and solitude, which a poet only could describe. It is surrounded by hills and steep rocks, and no one can get access to it but by the mouth of a frightful cave. To those who enter, therefore, first occurs the memory of the cave of the Cuman Sibyl, for the ruinous aperture, blocked up with stones and briars, strikes the eye. Then there comes upon the wayfarers a shudder, as they stand in doubt whether they are coming among the living or the dead. As, indeed, certain discords set off give finish to musical cadences in such a way as to render the subsequent harmony grateful to the ear, so does the form of this mournful cave, with its long and shady path followed by the light and prospect, make the exit more delightful. For suddenly the darkness disappears, and as it were at the creation of a new world.

It is clear that here, and perhaps elsewhere at Penicuik, Clerk was relying on the association and contrast of ideas and sensations to give his garden structure and a sense of form, and no longer on architectural composition however complex or extended. In order to 'civilize the prospect' to the south from Hurley Pond, Clerk built two small houses and planted gardens around each. He later planted oaks nearby at Clermon Hill and finished a summer house at Hurley to

> entice my friends . . . to walk for their diversion, and in this I myself have found great advantage. The natural beauty of the place, and the solitude which one finds here, are a great help to studies and meditation.

Clerk's early and somewhat tentative steps towards landscape gardening were contemporary with other amateurs such as Philip Soutcote and Thomas Hamilton in Surrey, or with the professional garden designers such as Kent or Switzer, also working in England. There is little to distinguish his efforts from theirs in terms of quality, and the naturally increasing communication between the various parts of England and Scotland would lead us to expect a development towards a truly national style. But the landscape garden is essentially English, and basically was unsuitable to the topography of Scotland: indeed, it was also

unsuitable to much of the topography of England. The landscape style of gardening sought to imitate nature, but rather a special kind of nature — the gently rolling hills of Worcestershire or perhaps Hampshire, planted partly with deciduous woods but mostly undulating grassland ornamented with buildings, and always allusive of the classical past, or of poetic feeling.

The style was established by its greatest practitioner, Launcelot Brown, and he judged a site not so much in its own terms, but rather according to whether it had 'capabilities of improvement' to his ideal. Brown's career was confined to the gentler parts of England. However, the style was widely imitated by his *élèves* and the highly regularised pastoral quality of the pure landscape style was employed at places such as Duddingston near Edinburgh, and Williamston, Aberdeenshire.

Later exponents of the landscape garden such as Humphry Repton and J. C. Loudon 'consulted the genius of the place' more fully and more sincerely and were thus able to exploit Scottish topography. But towards the end of the eighteenth century the copying of beautiful nature had become predictable and not only had its freshness passed but the landscape style was increasingly seen as destructive — destructive of ancient 'regular or formal' gardens, destructive of stately avenues and groves (because they had not been considered 'natural'), but most importantly destructive of a sense of the past — of history.

Without yet wishing to return to the ancient styles — though this does happen from about 1835 onwards — a bolder and more extensive expression was desired, a kind of gardening that could appeal directly to the senses and to the emotions. Such was the kind of gardening practised by Sir John Clerk of Penicuik at Hurley; and his younger contemporary and colleague Henry Home, better known by his legal title, Lord Kames, made this kind of gardening philosophically accessible to a wide public in *Elements of Criticism* of 1763. Kames' *Elements* were a part, and not the most distinguished part, of a school of philosophy centred on Edinburgh and the other university towns of Scotland. This school sought, among other things, to account for and explain the role of the senses in thinking. Kames took the notion of the association of ideas and applied it to garden design. Clerk, and others, had already done this, of course, but Kames' exposition was systematic and reached a very wide public.

> Architecture and gardening cannot otherwise entertain the mind, than by raising certain agreeable emotions or feelings . . . Gardening, besides the emotions of beauty by means of regularity, order, proportion, colour, and utility, can raise emotions of grandeur, of sweetness, of gaiety, melancholy, wildness, and even surprise or wonder.

To Kames this was the highest form of gardening, the most perfect idea, and was a positive advance on gardens which contained natural objects, trees, flowers, statues and buildings only. But how does such a garden work?

Like the landscape style, it follows nature, but unlike it Kames would have every part of a large garden assigned some quality which by judicious planting

FIGURE 8
*Hurley Pond, Penicuik,
now very much overgrown*

FIGURE 9
*General view of
Duddingston House
(engraving by Scott after
A. Wilson,
Edinburgh Magazine,
1800)*

and ornamentation could be enhanced. For instance, an open, sunny and gently undulating park would arouse sensations of beauty and might, therefore, be finished as a pastoral landscape with clumped trees, perhaps a serpentine stream, and a flock of sheep. However, a rocky ridge overlooking a ravine would conjure up, by its nature, another emotional response; perhaps wildness or melancholy. Scots pines, rustic or even 'ruined' buildings, and turbulent streams or falls of water would be appropriate to such a situation. A gloomy place could be enhanced by planting yews and by erecting a memorial either to a dead loved one, or to an ancient lost cause; either would incline the visitor to sad reflection.

Kames assumed an extensive layout. Those with small gardens had to content themselves with 'one form of expression'. Otherwise the garden should be

so contrived, as in various scenes to raise successively all its different emotions.

This was achieved by grouping the areas which raised emotions best seen in conjunction, such as gaiety and sweetness or motion and grandeur, whereas gaiety and gloominess were best arranged so as to follow in succession.

For that reason, a ruin, affording a sort of melancholy pleasure, ought not to be seen from a flower-parterre, which is gay and cheerful. But to pass immediately from an exhilarating object to a ruin, has a glorious effect.

Kames and Brown were contemporary and both owed considerable debts to their predecessors, but Kames' method was much more suited to the varied topography of Scotland, and with its explicit poetic overtones was more suited to romance and the darker passions, and a fond evocation of history. And by simple extension Kames' ideas permitted the kind of eclectic and dotty richness both in horticulture and ornamentation which is characteristic of the mid-nineteenth century.

His ideas are important also in that they could be employed on a small scale as well as on the estate scale for which they were originally proposed. A suburban garden could be, and often was, laid out in a series of imaginative scenes, taking their character from a fragment of sculpture acquired in Italy, or a fine botanical specimen, or whatever — the possibilities were limitless.

Kames' 'most perfect idea of a garden' remained pertinent throughout the nineteenth century, and remains so today. It survived and, in a sense, encouraged the revival of various historic styles such as the Italian gardens which began to appear in the 1840s; and it survived the purer revival of seventeenth-century Scottish gardens by Lorimer at the beginning of the present century.

An even greater systematiser, and equally great Scot was J. C. Loudon, quintessentially Victorian, but actually earlier. Loudon produced a truly prodigious body of works on gardening and related subjects, but perhaps his greatest contribution to garden design was to take Kames' 'most perfect idea' and make it particularly suitable for the display of plants. In the eighteenth century plants were used in mass, as a kind of architecture — they formed or enclosed scenes, and rarely ornamented them. The nineteenth century saw not only a 'rapid progress in gardening as an Art of Culture' but also an extra-ordinary widening of interest in gardening so that Mawe and Abercrombie's *Everyman His Own Gardener* became literally true.

In Loudon's scheme — he called it the Gardenesque — trees and shrubs were planted with greater regard to their botanical qualities. Plants were treated as specimens, and as ornaments in themselves. Some nineteenth-century gardeners followed this scheme fully and created effectively botanical gardens, but of more interest were those which added a glen of rhododendrons, a ridge of Chilean monkey puzzles to the Kames type. It is this kind of garden whose form and character varies with its owner's knowledge and taste, varies too with the local topography, which is such a delight in Scotland.

SOME SCOTTISH PLANT COLLECTORS

Brinsley Burbidge

T THE BEGINNING OF MAY 1772 A CONVERTED WHITBY collier, the *Resolution*, set sail from Woolwich on the way to Sheerness. Her Captain was James Cook. Even with her hold empty she could barely manage more than a snail's pace and was in continual danger of capsizing despite an almost flat calm in the Thames. Captain Cook, one of the greatest mariners of all time was not to blame. Only eleven months before he had returned triumphant from his three year voyage round the world. The culprit was Joseph Banks who had been the naturalist on Cook's first voyage and was determined that the second voyage should provide every facility for collecting and studying plants and animals. To Cook's dismay Banks had ordered the Captain's cabin to be torn apart and converted into a laboratory, relegating the Captain to a small round cabin above the poop deck. A new deck had been added above the main deck to provide more accommodation for the scientists, and the officers were to be crammed into a dingy space between decks.

Joseph Banks, later to become Sir Joseph, had spent £5000 of his own money on the conversion, but it was all to be wasted as Cook refused to move any further in this top-heavy one-knot ship. The First Lord of the Admiralty intervened, and between 18 May and 13 June when the *Resolution* finally set sail, every one of Banks' additions was removed. Banks was angry in the extreme, and neither he, nor any of his team of scientists, was aboard and all his supplies and equipment, which had cost an additional £10,000, had been withdrawn. He was, however, represented by a young Aberdeen gardener, Francis Masson, who had been working for several years at Kew Gardens. Banks, the Director of Kew, kept in the background, but paid Masson's bills and received the many parcels of plants he was to send to Kew during his lifetime. Thus began the career of the first official plant collector sent out from Kew, the first of a long line of hardy explorers who were to change the appearance of our gardens.

Masson arrived at the Cape at the end of October, little knowing that he was to spend a total of ten years in Southern Africa. It took him until the end of December to familiarise himself with the country around Cape Town and to organise the first shipments of plants back to Banks at Kew. Very few members of the extraordinarily rich Cape flora were then cultivated in Britain. The country was in the control of the Dutch East India Company and the few bulbs and living plants which had reached Britain had come by way of Holland. Banks had spent some time at the Cape, and from his own observations knew that there

FIGURE 10
Rhododendron
frictolacteum *on the Sun
Kwei Pass (photographed
by George Forrest)*

FIGURE 11
Francis Masson

were some treasures which would do well in our gardens. He also knew that many others would need the protection of a glasshouse. The Cape area is hot with infrequent rainfall, in parts similar to the Mediterranean, but elsewhere much drier. Forests are rare and most of the vegetation consists of scrubby bushes, succulents able to withstand aridity, bulbs and annuals, each in their own way able to cope with long periods without rain.

Of great importance was the fact that most of these plants would travel well. Any plant able to remain dormant during a long dry period would also be comparatively happy with the neglect of a long sea voyage back to Europe. Bulbs could simply be harvested during the dry season and sent back in sacks. Seeds were easy to transport and only the odd, delicate plant would need care and attention. In fact the Cape was one of the world's better areas from which to send plants to Europe. The proportion of hardy plants in any consignment, compared with collections from more temperate or more mountainous areas, was obviously lower and the impact of Masson's work was more on the specialist grower than on the average gardener. Much was quickly lost to cultivation either due to the cool, wet British climate or to the gardeners' inexperience with plants from hot dry areas. Much also survived.

After two preliminary excursions Masson met up with Carl Thunberg, the Swedish botanist and a pupil of the great Carl Linnaeus himself. Thunberg was on his way to Japan but spent some five years at the Cape, much of it collecting with Masson.

Masson and Thunberg were a curious mixture of personalities, Masson the burly, dependable but slow gardener and Thunberg the small, assertive, egocentric, academic botanist and doctor. They had no language in common with the exception of a few words of botanical Latin and yet the partnership appeared to work. They both left detailed accounts of their journey together and a comparison makes fascinating reading. When crossing the Duyvenhoeks River Thunberg relates, 'I, who was the most courageous of the company and consequently always in the lead had the misfortune to plunge into a deep hippopottamus-wallow, which might have proved fatal if I, who have always had the good fortune to possess myself in the greatest dangers, had not with the greatest calm and composure guided the animal and kept myself in the saddle'. Masson's account of the incident is different: 'The doctor imprudently took the ford without the least enquiry, when on a sudden he, and his horse, plunged head over ears into a pit made by a hippo, deep and steep on all sides and for a few minutes I thought he might be dead but his horse managed to get a foothold and scrambled out'.

Their first journey together was to last for eighteen weeks, during which they covered over one thousand miles, exploring the area between Cape Town and the Karoo. They had with them an ox wagon laden with boxes and bags for collecting seeds and bulbs and a supply of paper and presses for dried plant specimens. They also took fire-arms for hunting and for defence, a quantity of shoe leather and the usual trinkets, mirrors, beads and tobacco with which to make friends with the natives of the country through which they were to pass. Masson also had an European servant and three Hottentots as drivers and general servants. Masson's diaries detail the plants they met in crossing the Veld on their way to the more arid lands of the great and little Karoo to the east of Cape Town. The Veld particularly excited Masson: 'the whole country affords a fine field for the botanist, being enamelled with the greatest number of flowers I ever saw of exquisite beauty and fragrance'. He collected over a hundred Cape Heaths, many Ixias, Lachenalias, Romuleas as well as more familiar Cape plants such as Gazanias, Mesembryanthemums (of which he found seventy) and the white Arum Lily (*Zantedeschia aethiopica*). In the drier areas he found some forty species of a group of plants on which he was soon to become the world authority, the Stapelias. These highly succulent plants have showy flowers in reds, purples, yellows and whites but unfortunately all have a foul smell of rotting meat to attract the flies on which they depend for pollination. Masson's book, *Stapeliae Novae* (New Stapelias), which he published between 1796 and 1797 is still a classic and important work on this plant group.

By the end of January 1774 the two botanists were back in Cape Town from which they made shorter excursions, sometimes together and sometimes independently. It was probably during this time that Masson found *Nerine sarniensis*, the Guernsey Lily. Despite its name (*sarniensis* means belonging to the Channel Islands) the plant had been thought to come from Japan as it first arrived in Britain on a Japanese ship which was wrecked in the Channel Islands. Only when Masson discovered its home on Table Mountain, just above Cape Town, was its true origin known. Presumably the Japanese ship had stopped at the Cape on its way to Britain.

In September of that year they were off together again on another voyage of discovery in a different area of the Karoo, again collecting several hundred new species. In March 1775 Masson returned to Britain and added around five hundred new species to Kew's collection of living plants. Masson's reputation was made, and a year later he set off on a second voyage, this time to the Canaries, Azores and West Indies.

It was ten years before Masson was back at the Cape. Unfortunately his second journey is very poorly recorded. In many ways the excitement of the first visit had gone: Masson lacked the enthusiasm he had during the former trip and even Banks, back at home, seems to have lost some of his interest in Cape plants. Masson established a small garden near Cape Town and made forays into the hills to collect new plants. He employed a gardener to look after these during his absences. His explorations were cut short by the uncertainties following the French Revolution when there was a possibility that the French, who had already overrun Holland, might also take over the Cape.

Back home he completed his *Stapeliae Novae* and then in September 1779 was again on the high seas, this time bound for Canada. On the way his ship was twice attacked by French pirates, the second attack resulting in the loss of the ship. Masson, together with some of the crew, finally reached New York in December after an appalling bad-weather journey on a German ship which had too little food for its extra passengers. Rather little is known of his explorations in Canada although Kew continued to receive the usual large quantities of excellent seeds. The marvellous woodland garden plant *Trillium grandiflorum* was probably the finest species he collected during this time. During 1805 Masson, then aged sixty-four, became ill, probably due to an exceptionally severe winter. He wrote to Banks asking to be recalled but, before permission to return arrived he was dead. In retrospect it does seem rather unkind that Masson, after a lifetime spent collecting in hot parts of the world, should have been sent to icy Canada at an age when most people would be looking forward to a comfortable retirement. Pensions, however, existed only in exceptional cases and Masson's salary was never enough to allow him to save for this eventuality.

Masson's life encapsulates all that is best in plant collectors. A dedication to duty in the face of extreme physical discomfort and prolonged solitude; a deep knowledge of the flora of the country in which he was working and a great enthusiasm for one particular group of plants (succulents in Masson's case) making his collections and writings on that group of the greatest importance. We will meet these characteristics again and again in other collectors from Scotland.

The tolerance of discomfort and solitude shows up particularly well in the work of Thomas Drummond. Twenty years after Masson's death Sir John Franklin's second Arctic Expedition arrived in Canada with Thomas Drummond, a nurseryman from Forfar as assistant naturalist. The expedition travelled from Hudson Bay westward as far as Cumberland House in Saskatchewan where the party split up. Drummond was sent to explore the Rockies and immediately set off to Edmonton House* in Alberta where he left most of his equipment, including his tent. He continued, sometimes on horseback and sometimes by canoe, passing Jasper House on 11 October. Eight days later, with the winter snows already deepening, he left his last European companion and set off accompanied only by an Indian hunter as a guide. He was hoping to reach the Hudson's Bay Company's staging post on Smokey River for the winter but problems with his guide and the severity of the weather forced him to halt at a wintering station at the Baptiste river. There his guide left him and Drummond, having no tent and few supplies, had to build himself a brushwood hut. He stayed here from the end of 1825 until the beginning of March the following year when his guide returned for him. He was dependent for food on what he could shoot. He had the expected encounters with grizzly bears and discovered that they could usually be scared off by rattling his collecting tin. Most remarkable

FIGURE 12
The woodland garden plant, Trillium grandiflorum, *collected in Canada by Francis Masson*

* These 'Houses' were Hudson's Bay Company's staging posts.

though, is that he accepted unquestioningly his two months of solitary confinement as part of his job as collector.

He had a successful year collecting plants and spent that winter in comparative comfort at Edmonton House in Alberta. On his way back east the following March he was forced to take a roundabout route to avoid hostile Indian tribes. He and his two guides had with them dog sleighs carrying his plant material and food to get them as far as Carlton House, the next staging post on their route. They lost their way and rapidly ran out of food. Unfortunately all three had bad snow blindness which prevented them from shooting game. Except for one lucky shot which killed a skunk and which provided them with a good (if not pleasantly flavoured) meal, they were forced to resort to eating meat scraped from the inside of Drummond's preserved deer-skins. Shortly before they reached Carlton House they had to take over the work of their exhausted dogs and carry the loads themselves.

Drummond's collections were mainly for scientific study and he is principally remembered by a number of garden plants which bear his name, especially a rather fine Dryas, *Dryas drummondii*. He serves as an introduction to one of the truly great collectors of garden plants in North America, David Douglas. On the 1 September he and Douglas set out in a boat from York Factory on the Hudson Bay to visit the ship from England which was anchored 5 miles offshore. They were accompanied by eight crew and three other passengers. On their return they ran into a violent storm which snapped the mast of their ship and gradually forced them further and further from shore. They baled vigorously all night and all through the following day only just keeping the boat afloat. It was not until their second evening that the storm dropped sufficiently for them to begin rowing back to the ship, by this time over 60 miles away. Drummond survived the ordeal well, but Douglas was seriously ill for most of the journey home.

David Douglas was born in 1799 at Scone near Perth. At school he was a poor pupil but once in full-time employment as a gardener his real worth showed. His first jobs were in private service both of the Earl of Mansfield and later at Sir Robert Preston's garden at Valleyfield near Culross. In 1820 he moved to Glasgow Botanic Garden where he gained a good grounding in botany by attending Dr W. Hooker's lectures (Hooker was later to become director of Kew Gardens). Three years later he was to be in the employ of the Horticultural Society (later the Royal Horticultural Society) and on his way to New York for the first of a series of well-known and extraordinarily successful expeditions.

This first trip was something of a reconnaissance and resulted in little other than a few fruit trees. His second trip (during which he met Drummond and had the adventure mentioned above) was an outstanding success. This time his approach to North America was via Cape Horn and the Galapagos Islands. He finally arrived at the mouth of the Columbia River on the western coast of North America in 1825. Almost immediately the Flowering Currant, *Ribes*

FIGURE 13
A fine dryas, Dryas drummondii, *brought from Canada by Thomas Drummond*

sanguineum, and a superb Bramble, *Rubus spectabilis*, were 'in the bag'. So was that excellent ground-cover plant *Gaultheria shallon* (though many gardeners on the west coast of Britain may regret the introduction of this plant which likes the climate so well that it is now a rampant weed in many places). The Californian Poppy, *Eschscholzia californica*, several Lupins, many Penstemons and Clarkias were added to his collections soon after as were *Cornus alba*, *Mahonia aquifolium* and the Monkey Flower, *Mimulus moschatus* which is now naturalised in so many parts of Britain that it is often thought to be a native British plant. He had a particular affection for conifers and collected seeds of many for the first time. He was aware of the large part conifer seed played in his consignments of plant material to Britain as he wrote to Hooker, 'you will begin to think that I manufacture Pines at my pleasure'. His most famous conifer is the tree which bears his name, the Douglas Fir.

On his return to Britain Drummond vanished into comparative obscurity but Douglas became the 'man of the year'. His collections amazed everyone, especially the Horticultural Society, who had great difficulty coping with the distribution of so large a quantity of seed. Though, at the beginning, Douglas loved the special treatment his fame gave him, he rapidly lost patience with the respectable dinner parties he was expected to attend and longed to be back at work in the field. Initially the Horticultural Society were unwilling to listen to his wishes to collect in California (then part of Mexico) but later they relented and at the end of October 1829 he was on his way back to North America. Warring Indians and the difficulty of obtaining a permit from the Mexican authority to travel in California delayed his explorations. Nevertheless his consignments of plants continued to reach Britain and a superb red Larkspur, *Delphinium cardinale*, the Poached Egg Plant, *Limanthes douglasii* and *Garrya elliptica*, a fine catkin-bearing shrub resulted from this period.

Douglas had the usual explorer's disasters. On his way down the Fraser River his canoe was smashed to pieces in a series of rapids and all his botanical notes, collections and journals were lost. Douglas miraculously emerged from this alive after an hour and forty minutes spinning in a whirlpool.

He visited Hawaii several times and the island on which Captain Cook had been killed was also to result in Douglas's gruesome death. Covered pits were dug all over the island as a way of trapping, for food, the cattle which had first been introduced by Captain Vancouver. Douglas, as far as is known, was standing on the side of one of these pits to examine a trapped animal when the bank gave way. Unable to escape he was gored and trampled to death by the enraged occupant. He was only 35 years old but during his short life had immeasurably enriched our gardens with a great many hardy plants.

North America provided hunting grounds for several other Scottish botanical explorers. John Fraser (1750-1811) collected extensively in the eastern half of the country, bringing back among other plants *Uvularia grandiflora* and it is to John Lyon (whose exact date of birth is unknown but was probably around 1770) that

FIGURE 15
The monkey flower, Mimulus moschatus, *collected in N. America by David Douglas*

FIGURE 16
One of the finest of all gentians, Gentiana sino-ornata, *collected in China by George Forrest*

we owe such plants as *Iris fulva, Dicentra eximia* and *Pieris floribunda*.

The New World contributed many more garden plants, and is still doing so, but the Himalayas, China and Japan have also between them given us many excellent hardy species. James Main (roughly a contemporary of Fraser and Lyon) shows some of the problems of collecting in China at the beginning of the nineteenth century. Main left Britain on board the *Triton* in autumn 1792 on his way to the first main stop at Cape Town. He was introduced to Francis Masson and saw his gardens and collections. He also collected plants where possible but many of these suffered from the delays when the *Triton* was commandeered to take part in the siege of a French settlement. When he finally arrived at Canton, his travels were severely curtailed by treaty agreements which prevented foreigners from leaving the coastal ports. His main way of collecting plants was by visiting nurseries and by buying plants already in cultivation. When the *Triton* sailed for home in March 1794 she had aboard many custom-built cases containing Camellias, Tree Peonies, *Spiraea crenata, Chaenomeles speciosa* and other fine plants.

Many of his collections suffered from the tropical heat as the boat travelled around the Malaysian peninsula. Those which survived had a hard time when the *Triton* met two prolonged gales near the Cape of Good Hope. Another blow came when, in sight of home and safely in the Channel, the *Triton* collided with a frigate and two of her masts collapsed on top of Main's precious cases. The final blow was to fall after the ship had docked; Main's employer, a Mr Gilbert Slater, had died while Main was away. Main had no formal agreement with Slater, and failed completely to get a penny of what was owing to him for his travels. This story of disasters may be exceptional but the incidents are often repeated in the stories of plant collectors before and after James Main.

As a result of the 1840 opium war, Britain gained the Island of Hong Kong and also more favourable trading conditions on the mainland of China. The greater, though still limited, freedom to travel resulted in the Horticultural Society sending the thirty-one year-old Robert Fortune to China in 1843.

Fortune had trained at the Royal Botanic Garden, Edinburgh and had a good knowledge of plants. His main job was to collect new varieties of Tea Plant to be grown in India. The increased freedom of travel allowed Fortune to move up to twenty miles from any of the treaty ports. Fortune was determined to get further into the interior than this and did his best to remain inconspicuous by wearing Chinese dress and even growing a pigtail and shaving the rest of his head. This was only a partial insurance and on several occasions he only escaped death by a hair's breadth. In one incident, although suffering badly from fever, he repelled, single handed, an attack from six pirate ships using his double-barrelled shotgun. His return to Britain with new plants such as Chrysanthemums, Azaleas, Camellias, the Winter Jasmine and Japanese Wind Flower created a similar stir to that of David Douglas' first major collection. Like Douglas he very rapidly returned to the field for three more trips, all to either the

FIGURE 17
Robert Fortune

Chinese mainland or Japan, and each resulted in a hundred to two hundred cases of new plants including *Lilium auratum, Clematis lanuginosa* and the fine Rhododendron which bears his name, *R. fortunei*.

Coming forward to this century and taking exploration deep into China we have to mention George Forrest who ranks (with two or three others) among the greatest plant collectors of all time. Though we still lack a detailed biography of George Forrest, much is known about his collections from his superb field-notes, detailed letters to family and colleagues at home, and a large collection of photographs taken by him in China between 1905 and 1932.

He was born at Falkirk and educated at Kilmarnock Academy before embarking on a series of adventures in Australia. He was over thirty-one years old when, though by this time an employee of the Royal Botanic Garden, Edinburgh, he was sent with private patronage to collect in the Yunnan province of China. Forrest had more than any explorer's fair share of adventure in his first year. He was staying at Tseku, a small village and mission post just south of the Tibetan border, with a party of seventeen helpers when the Tibetans launched a full scale attack from the north bent on slaughtering Chinese and European alike. Forrest's party, together with the missionaries and some sixty Chinese, headed south, but were rapidly overtaken. Out of the party of eighty or so, only fourteen lived to tell the tale and Forrest was the sole survivor from his own party. Forrest escaped by living on nothing but a few ears of barley for some eight days when hiding from his pursuers. In desperation from lack of food he decided to 'hold-up' a tiny village. Fortunately he found himself among friends. It took him over twenty days to reach the safety of the town of Tali Fu but unfortunately the news of his massacre had travelled ahead of him. Notification of his death had already been sent back to Edinburgh and his friends and family passed a miserable time before news of his remarkable escape finally reached them. Despite this incident and the low state of health in which it left him Forrest was to go on and make over forty thousand plant collections during the seventeen years (covering several expeditions) he was to spend in China.

It is impossible to do justice to Forrest's collections which contain literally hundreds of new Rhododendrons and Primulas and one of the finest of all Gentians, *Gentiana sino-ornata*. He also collected some fine Himalayan Blue Poppies, many Lilies and a huge collection of dwarf plants beloved of rock gardeners and alpine-plant enthusiasts. It is the genus Rhododendron, though, for which he will be remembered. His introduction varied from the dwarf species which bears his name, *Rhododendron forrestii*, which produces huge bell-like flowers of deep crimson at ground level to the tallest rhododendron of them all, *Rhododendron protistum* which grows to over 70 feet in height and has trusses of pinkish flowers the size of footballs. Among the three hundred and nine species of *Rhododendron* which were described as new, twelve received the First Class Certificate of the Royal Horticultural Society for excellence as horticultural plants and no fewer than 48 received their Award of Merit.

FIGURE 18
George Forrest and collector in Yunnan

In the past few pages we have concentrated very much on the nineteenth century with only Forrest representing the last eighty years. We have not, for example, found space to discuss the very important horticultural collections made in Tibet by Major George Sheriff, Frank Ludlow and Sir George Taylor (then Director of Kew Gardens). This gives a rather unbalanced view as plant collecting continues to the present day. Of course many of the spectacular species have been found long ago, but every year sees a trickle of plants from the few professional collectors sent out by national gardens such as those at Kew and Edinburgh, from the members of University expeditions, from the rare collector working for a nursery and from the ever-increasing band of amateur collectors bent on enriching their own gardens. Many of the objective dangers have now gone, transport of plants by air is usually efficient and plants can be happily growing in a British garden in less than a week from their collection on the other side of the world. Fortunately, because many attractive wild species would be rapidly exterminated by the combined efforts of innumerable collectors, most countries have lists of protected plants and some groups such as orchids and cacti are protected totally by international agreement. Nevertheless careful collecting of small quantities of seed, or the careful taking of cuttings, rarely does any lasting damage. We can still look forward to a steady influx of new plants to add to those imported in such outstanding numbers by the great collectors of the past.

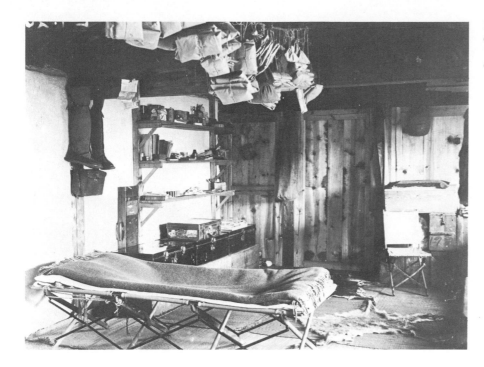

FIGURE 19
*George Forrest's bedroom,
Yunnan (photographed by
George Forrest)*

PLANTS IN SCOTTISH GARDENS

Alfred Evans

SCOTLAND'S WEATHER IS DIVERSE, AND IT INFLUENCES THE choice of plants that may be grown in her gardens. The variation in weather conditions manifests itself in the high rainfall on the western seaboard, resulting from the rain brought in on the west Atlantic winds, on the one hand, and on the other, the much drier conditions more normal on the east coast. Naturally this phenomenon has a bearing on plants cultivated in other parts of the British Isles, but its effects are very obvious here in Scotland. The steep graph which indicates the build-up in rain, from east to west, measures only one of the natural elements affecting our shores. The proximity of the land mass of Scandinavia to the east, where winter temperatures can plummet, also has an effect, and this is more noticeable on the east coast. Furthermore the west benefits from the much publicised warm current sweeping up from the Gulf of Mexico, a drift which is credited with giving the western beaches a banana belt-type climate. So Scotland's geographical position, set between an expansive ocean and a huge land mass, has been and still is exploited by those interested in the growing of plants.

Nowhere will one find garden owners more enthusiastic about their plants than in this country and in many ways Scotland's gardens, both large and small, have been trial grounds for the cultivation of much of the world's temperate and sub-arctic flora. Over the years and by trial and error, patterns of plant association have evolved and these are now accepted as being complementary and well balanced. The older, larger gardens, being planted during the hey-day of gardening, are the repositories for comprehensive groupings of the taller, woody plants, but in addition still include some of the more interesting herbaceous genera. The owners of smaller gardens, on the other hand, although maintaining a well balanced garden flora, concentrated more on cultivating plants for their interest. In some instances the accent of planting may have been towards assembling collections for study or growing what was new, but always there was someone who would accept the challenge of trying to grow plants which were difficult to cultivate elsewhere.

Many small garden owners also showed interest in design, and here they had to resist the temptation to include a wide variety of plant material for fear of spoiling the overall effect. True plantsmen, on the other hand, belong to that group of growers who welcome most plants into their gardens and, having accepted a particular specimen, invariably find the correct site to suit its needs.

FIGURE 20
One of the group of candelabra primulas, Primula pulverulenta

At the same time they appear to have the knack of associating it with plants requiring similar conditions.

Conifers play a very large part in a garden's plant complement. They are attractive at all times and are so suited to our west coast climate that they have been extensively used. Perhaps the most widely planted conifer in Scotland is *Picea sitchensis*, Sitka Spruce. It dominates and occupies vast areas of our hillsides, much to the chagrin of purists, but in such situations it is grown for timber; it is not a particularly handsome tree, aesthetically. Garden conifer populations are the result of much more selectivity. Many conifers were introduced from the north American continent; *Sequoiadendron giganteum,* Big Tree or Wellingtonia, although not the most common garden conifer, was planted as a feature tree on numerous large estates. Today many mature specimens, mostly over one hundred years old, dominate the skyline in many parts of western and central Scotland. Another is Douglas Fir, *Pseudotsuga menziesii,* rather a brittle tree but none the less handsome for that. Its bark is quite distinctive, being rough and fluted. It was introduced into Britain by David Douglas around 1827, and some of the originals are to be seen at Scone Palace gardens. One often encounters large specimens in quite modest plantations. Lawson Cypress, *Chamaecyparis lawsoniana,* named in honour of an Edinburgh nurseryman, not only has numerous growth forms but its foliage occurs in myriad tones. Like many conifers of this type it sports numerous aberrant forms. *Thuja occidentalis*, White Cedar, is yet another New World conifer and along with the species from the Far East, *Thuja orientalis,* Chinese Arbor-vitae, greatly influences our garden landscape. Most of these species are also noted for their range of retinispora, juvenile foliage forms.

The alien evergreen giants are not confined to the northern hemisphere, however, for Chile contributes the Monkey Puzzle or Chilean Pine, *Araucaria araucana,* introduced in 1844. This is not a plant which ever looks really comfortable here or just right, but it must have been popular at one time. Monkey Puzzles, Cryptomerias, *Abies,* Piceas, Pines and the deciduous Dawn Redwoods and Swamp Cypresses all feature widely in the larger gardens. Apart from the Dawn Redwood, *Metasequoia glyptostroboides,* introduced into cultivation as recently as 1948, many are now mature and give our gardens an established look.

Many other broad-leaved arboreal giant trees can also confront the garden visitor on his ramble round an old estate, and one need never be surprised at the variety. At one time there were numerous tree and shrub nurseries trading in estate and decorative trees. These are not the same thing, for the ultimate aim in estate planting was often a timber crop, although not infrequently specimens could be chosen for their beautifying impact on the landscape. The more intimate tree plantings were usually sited round the perimeter of a small woodland or copse, planted as individual specimens much closer to the residence or, as happened on some estates where the owners were especially conscious of the virtue of trees, in arboreta. Some trees — columnar, spreading or pendulous — were grown for their shape, while others, with coloured or variegated foliage, affected the general colour patterns directly. Leaves which were of differing shades of colour, as in the case of variegated Maples or even Copper Beeches, could be used most effectively among the ubiquitous greenery of mid-summer, but their effect could be lost entirely once the woodland took on its autumn tints. Many Chestnuts, for example, although spectacular and much admired when adorned with candle-like inflorescences, are also a source of pleasure towards the end of summer because of their bright, early autumn shades. Numerous species of *Acer,* too, provide this effect in the landscape.

By the very nature of their shedding leaves, deciduous trees can be enjoyed at all times. The beauty of the intricate tracery of the bare branches etched on a wintry sky is often the inspiration of photographers and artists. The bursting buds and the freshness of new foliage are harbingers of spring. Summer's dense canopy effectively displays the full splendour of trees over other vegetation and this, in time, is followed by the glorious flaming colour of some species before they shed their leaves.

The various effects displayed by all trees, be they large forest monarchs or much smaller decorative kinds to which *Amelanchier, Malus, Prunus, Pyrus* and the less vigorous Maples belong, may be increased by grouping them together. Not a few are ornamental because of features other than flowers. Foliage, fruit and bark play their part. In the last category the mahogany bark of the Tibetan Cherry, *Prunus serrula,* the white-powdered bole of the White Birch, *Betula pendula,* and the beautifully patterned Snake-bark Maple, *Acer rufinerve,* are examples which are often used to terminate short vistas.

While in the long term the permanent plants must be protected from more robust neighbours, the fillers, those woody plants which occupy large areas in a garden and carry interest over from season to season, are often the more colourful. As individual specimens they can have an impact on the display during a particular period but, when used collectively, as in a shrub border, they provide a fascination and interest extending throughout the year. Many shrubby plants are spring- or summer-blooming, although others can be at the height of their flowering season later. It is mostly to the early-flowering group that our gardens owe the wealth of autumn fruits which naturally follow a good flowering year.

The range of flowering shrubs in Scottish gardens is truly vast. Quite apart from the ever present Rose, examples of which are found in virtually every plot, the Rhododendron (Tree Rose) has been popular where large areas had to be planted. Plants belonging to this genus are to be found wild in every continent of the northern hemisphere. In addition they occur in a continuous line going south through the Malay Peninsula and the archipelago of Sumatra, Java, Borneo and New Guinea into Queensland in north Australia. Rhododendron mania is a harmless disease which affected many Scottish landowners, and still does,

FIGURE 21
The tracery of the bare branches of Weeping Ash (Fraxinus excelsior)

FIGURE 22
The colourful leaves of Sorbus torminalis *in autumn*

FIGURE 23
The mahogany bark of the Tibetan Cherry (Prunus serrula)

FIGURE 24
The white-powdered bole of the White Birch (Betula pendula)

as a much branched bush up to 20 feet, sometimes less, with rich crimson globes. *Embothrium coccineum* represented by a number of clones, is another from that country, here colloquially known as Chilean Fire Bush on account of its brilliant scarlet flowers. It is fast growing and in May individual specimens become pillars of fire. When planted in an avenue they are breath-taking. The *Eucryphia,* too, for later flowering, that is from August onwards, includes both beautiful and spectacular plants. There are five or six species and these develop into tall bushes, becoming smothered with large white flowers, the centres of which are filled with clusters of stamens. The handsome Magnolias, the brilliant, early flowering Camellias, the multi-flowered evergreen *Berberis* from South America and the reliable Diervillas from China and Japan are all represented and contribute towards the complete garden of flowers.

Apart from the woody species and cultivars which subscribe a great deal to the structure of a garden, there are the more numerous herbaceous and bulbous plants without which our gardens would be dull. These hardy perennials bring an extra dimension to the garden and are frequently introduced because of the value of their flowers. While many may appear commonplace and are often seen, quite a few are unique and are included because they are special.

Long herbaceous borders are seen less often these days. Relics of former times remain but, regrettably, lack of labour necessitates that most be much simpler. Staking, once looked upon as an aid to supporting wonderful plants, is now considered a chore and discouraged. Plants needing the minimum of support or advertised as requiring no staking at all are offered as though this factor were the main attraction. Fortunately Delphiniums, Heleniums, *Helianthus, Galega,* Sidalceas and other suitably-supported plants are still to be found. These provide a riot of colour and give borders and the garden an extended period of flowering. Plants in the herbaceous border usually begin to flower in June and, provided the selection of varieties is right, should continue to display patches of colour until the arrival of the first frosts. Hardy herbaceous perennials are a race of plants not to be despised. The half-hardy plants, those used to boost or augment colour late in the year often find a place in herbaceous borders. *Salvia patens,* Penstemons, Dimorphothecas, *Agastache mexicana, Lobelia fulgens* and others are used in this valuable rôle.

Not all herbaceous plants are suited to the open, sun-drenched border; many require quite a different type of environment if they are to succeed and flourish. Some are most attractive in flower while others may be included because of their foliage, and despite a shortage of time should receive additional attention. Two familiar examples are the Himalayan Blue Poppy, *Meconopsis betonicifolia* and Primulas, especially those belonging to the candelabra section. These are the Primulas which produce their flowers in tiers. Few gardeners must be ignorant of the virtues of *Meconopsis betonicifolia* although many may still be more familiar with its more commonly used epithet, *M. baileyi*. It is often stated that it performs less well in one garden than another and while sometimes this may

FIGURE 25
Rhododendron hodgsonii, *named in honour of Brian H. Hodgson of the East India Company*

FIGURE 26
Penstemon davidsonii *in the Cascade Mountains, Washington, USA*

appear to be true, the explanation could be that a poorer form was being cultivated. The species is quite variable. The outstanding hybrid often seen, *Meconopsis × sheldonii*, is supreme for garden effect and reliability. The same applies to Primulas. Although the growing of species may be both educational and instructive, to see a hybrid swarm of candelabra Primulas in full flower leaves little to be desired as a colourful floral feature. The group is usually a mixture of *Pp. beesiana, bulleyana, cockburniana, japonica* and *pulverulenta*. Primulas are often considered as plants for spring or early summer but *Primula florindae,* native to south-east Tibet and one of the more robust is planted generously in larger gardens and will scent the immediate vicinity with an aromatic-type pungence until the end of October. It flowers and produces seeds at the same time. Liliums, often considered capricious, are only to be met with occasionally but, when grown well, add a certain quality to a garden. They are plants for the enthusiast and some Scottish gardens are rich in the representation of Lilies, for the cooler conditions of the north seem to suit them. Astilbes, Spiraeas, Hostas and a multitude of others seem to have captured the gardener's interest for they, too, are much sought after. While it can be said that some plants perform well even in neglect, some respond better in chosen areas, in partial shade, in the proximity of shrubby plants and in association with others similar to themselves. So, quite apart from open areas where traditional-type herbaceous border plants flourish, the specialised gardens may also contain a woodland-type flora. These are often the bigger gardens where space is not restricted, but enthusiastic amateurs cultivating a few square yards can be knowledgeable about these very special kinds.

There is yet another facet of growing plants which must be mentioned. This is the one which owes its popularity to individual gardeners, most of them keen amateurs who cultivate dwarf plants not only for pleasure but often for the challenge. Few have large gardens but most of them manage plant collections as varied as those found in bigger establishments. Here plants of small stature are assembled. Some of these gardens are open for inspection or the plants they contain may be seen at specialist flower shows. The cultivators of these miniature plants are the alpine devotees. Some of the rarer dwarf species are difficult to manage while others thrive. The easy ones would include names like *Alyssum, Saxifraga, Sempervivum, Sedum, Helianthemum,* Alpine Primula, *Daphne, Geranium, Penstemon,* hardy *Cyclamen* and a host of other diminutive and bulbous kinds. They are the ones most likely to be seen on a garden visit. Many of the really difficult ones are from high mountain regions where conditions are extremely rigorous but here, at sea level, Scotland's cooler climate can compensate for a lack of snow cover in some instances. The beauty and value lie in the fact that a comprehensive range of different plants may be assembled in a relatively small space.

Although our gardens then are veritable storehouses of botanically and horticulturally interesting plant types, the skill of the amateur gardener still con-

FIGURE 27
Primula involucrata, *one of the easier grown and perennial species of primula*

FIGURE 28
Hosta crispula *(sometimes
known as* Funkia*),
showing its decorative
creamy-edged foliage*

tributes much to the overall plant content. Even today this is extremely rich and must compare favourably with the complements of earlier times. The number of large plants grown may not be so great but the quantity of species cultivated and the standard of excellence must still be considered as very high. It is this which makes garden visiting a most pleasurable hobby.

CHAPTER 4

THE FUTURE

Peter Bellchambers

Few people who visit the outstanding gardens featured in this book will be aware that they are indeed a privileged generation. They are witnessing, possibly for the last time, a beautiful and valuable part of the country's heritage which, through ignorance and misunderstanding, is being allowed to decay into near extinction. Put into their context in the twentieth century, the outstanding gardens — particularly the privately owned outstanding gardens — are following a steady trend of change and decay.

At the beginning of the century the country house and garden formed the hub of a society and social system which has all but disappeared. Based around large families and frequent resident guests, the garden was a centre for recreation which was maintained by a large team of poorly paid staff and gardeners. A team of eight gardeners was typical, rather than exceptional.

Virtually all estates and families suffered losses from World War I, and losses in staff were not replaced. Up until the beginning of World War II, the garden was changed and developed to meet such staff changes, but after World War II, with the inevitable further loss of members of families and staff, the development of outstanding gardens virtually ceased. The following thirty-five years have seen an acceleration in the decline and decay of outstanding gardens in Scotland. Those gardens which have survived have done so mainly thanks to the involvement and interest of the garden owners, who have in many instances become the main workforce within the garden.

The decline described here can be identified in its various stages through changes in the actual appearance and design of these outstanding gardens.

At the turn of the century, many gardens had large areas of ornamental flower beds in elaborate geometric shapes, designed for viewing from the house. This garden was usually surrounded by protective shelter woodland planting, incorporating specimen shrubs and trees. At a distance from the house the walled kitchen garden was fully stocked with vegetables and fruit to keep the large household supplied, and cut flowers from the greenhouses kept the house itself decorated.

Between the wars, fashions changed and the 'parterre' flower beds were replaced by lawns which in turn were used for active sports such as tennis and croquet. The garden itself could still be said to be in a period of positive change, rather then decline. Although labour-intensive features were gradually dis-

FIGURE 29
Birkhill Garden, not a neglected garden but one which is seriously undermanned

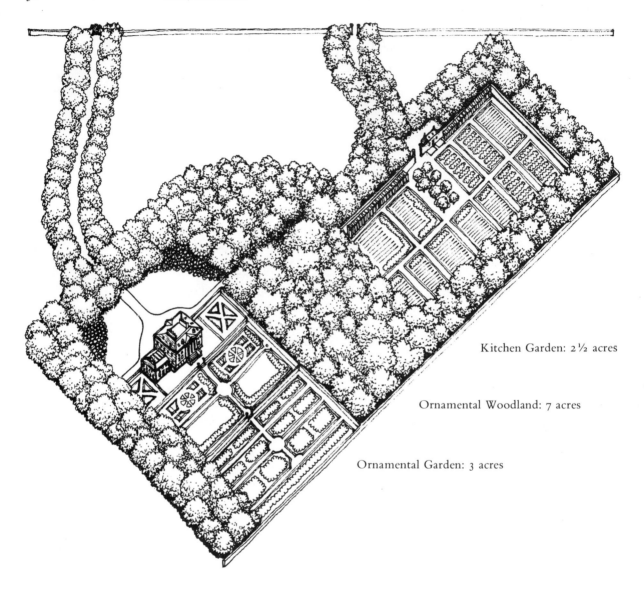

Kitchen Garden: 2 ½ acres

Ornamental Woodland: 7 acres

Ornamental Garden: 3 acres

FIGURES 30-34   HOUSEHOLD: 30   KEY:
Scot House: a hypothetical   Family and guests: 13
house and garden   Garden staff: 8   Trees
(size 12 ½ acres)   House staff: 9
Design changes from 1900   Shrubs
onwards
                                                         Flowers
FIGURE 30
Scot House in 1900   Scale: 1:2500   Fruit/Vegetables

appearing, visual planting interest was retained with new ornamental planting, particularly of shrubs in the garden and within the woodland. With the ever-decreasing household, there was less need for the whole kitchen garden, so this was reduced in size.

In general, World War II represents a watershed in the development of outstanding gardens in Scotland. Since 1945, most gardens have been reduced in size, content and interest, with new planting being severely cut back. Gardening became an exercise in maintaining the status quo as far as possible, rather than positively continuing the development of these outstanding gardens.

Since World War II, there has been a steady decline in the quality and number of outstanding gardens in Scotland, and this trend is likely to accelerate rather than diminish for reasons which are outlined below. Having recognised that there is a problem facing these outstanding gardens, it must be questioned whether it is acceptable to let the decline continue. Should these houses and gardens, which were built in an age of extreme privilege, be conserved at all in the last quarter of the twentieth century?

I believe that the outstanding houses and gardens should be conserved, because they represent a very important aspect of the nation's cultural heritage, and for a nation to lose its heritage is akin to a man losing his memory. But a man's memory is selective, and only the outstanding events are clearly recalled, and the same can be said for the conservation of these gardens. The outstanding houses and gardens should be retained, whilst others, being less outstanding, should fade away and change.

The government states that it accepts these principles, but still the quality and number of important gardens declines. The costs and problems of garden conservation have only recently been accurately defined, and without this information the government machinery for helping to conserve these gardens could not be guided along the correct lines. The resulting confusion has led to crippling anomalies which have left outstanding gardens and landscapes unprotected, unaided and over-burdened by taxation.

The Costs of Running an Outstanding Garden

As all garden lovers know, to maintain a beautiful garden requires a large amount of time and labour. It is rarely appreciated, however, just how much time and labour is expended on a garden to retain it in an outstanding condition. When the time and labour is translated into financial terms such as man hours and actual salaries, then the large cost of those gardens becomes more immediately appreciable.

Outlined here are two sets of expenses which have been drawn up for very similar gardens; each set represents a different standard of quality in the maintainance of the garden. (The figures quoted here are based on actual expenses incurred during the financial year 1977/78, updated at an annual inflation rate of 15%, with December 1980 wage levels.)

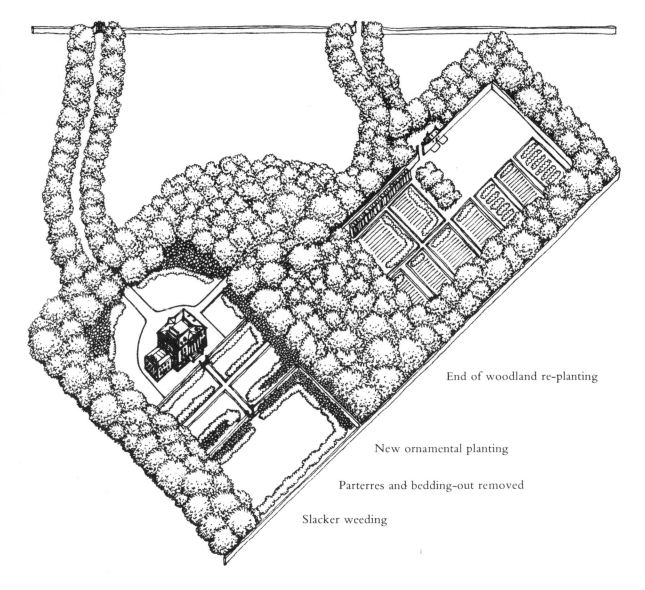

End of woodland re-planting

New ornamental planting

Parterres and bedding-out removed

Slacker weeding

FIGURE 31
Scot House in 1939

HOUSEHOLD: 18
Family and guests: 7
Garden staff: 6
House staff: 5

Scale: 1:2500

KEY:

Trees

Shrubs

Flowers

Fruit/Vegetables

Expenses. Garden Type One. 1980/81

(Both owners work 10 hours per week in the garden)

Head gardener	£4,100
Under gardener	£3,700
Part-time gardener	£1,850
Part-time handyman	£1,850

TOTAL WAGES	£11,500	
Perquisites	£1,100	
TOTAL LABOUR	£12,600	(75%)
Greenhouse, heating, etc.	£1,000	(6%)
Machinery, weedkillers, etc.	£2,500	(15%)
Plants, bulbs, seeds	£700	(4%)
TOTAL	£16,800	

These costs are typical for a garden which, through good management and a large household income, has postponed the later stages of the typical decline as outlined previously, and thus a standard more typical of the early 1960s has been retained.

One of the main points to note is that labour costs account for three-quarters of the total expenses, despite the fact that head gardeners are seriously underpaid. Greenhouse heating costs have risen dramatically, and can rise to over 10% of total garden expenses if any form of hothouse is still kept. Investment in the future of the garden, through the purchase of new plant material, is sadly very low at only 4% of total garden costs.

Expenses. Garden Type Two. 1980/81

(Both owners work 20 hours per week in the garden)

Gardener	£3,800
Part-time gardener	£1,850

TOTAL WAGES	£5,650	
Perquisites	£750	
TOTAL LABOUR	£6,400	(80%)
Machinery, weedkillers, etc.	£1,300	(16%)
Plants, bulbs, seeds	£300	(4%)
TOTAL	£8,000	

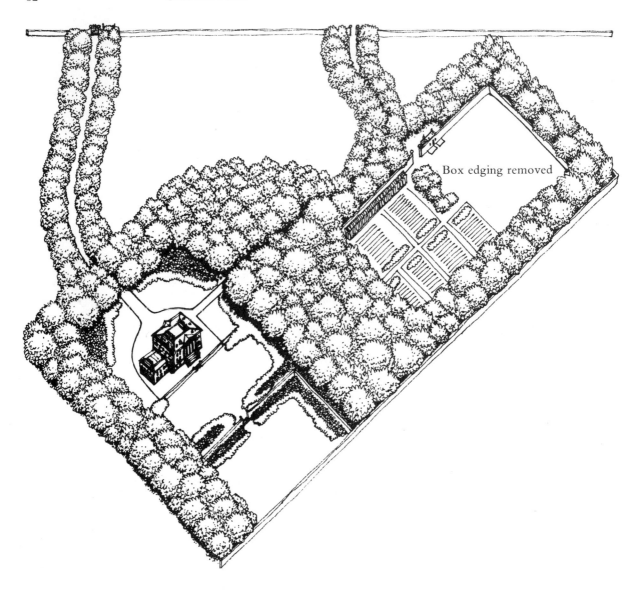

Box edging removed

FIGURE 32
Scot House in 1945

HOUSEHOLD: 14
Family and guests: 6
Garden staff: 5
House staff: 3

Scale: 1:2500

KEY:

Trees

Shrubs

Flowers

Fruit/Vegetables

The above expenses are for a garden which only fifteen years ago was run on similar lines to the preceding garden (Garden Type One). The standards of appearance and maintenance are much lower, but the costs of such a garden are nevertheless still high. The owners themselves, as much from a feeling of responsibility as from self-interest, now constitute a major workforce in the garden. As with Garden Type One, investment in plants is minimal at around 4% of total costs, and this poor investment in the future is a certain indicator that the decline of the garden will continue.

These figures are typical of the expenses for a high proportion of the gardens mentioned in this book, but there still remains a substantial (yet unknown) number of outstanding gardens which are not maintained even to the standard of Garden Type Two. These gardens are in perilous danger of being lost as outstanding gardens altogether.

Outstanding Garden Ownership

Just over half of the outstanding gardens in Scotland are owned privately, and therefore their maintenance is paid for out of privately earned, and therefore taxed, income. Around a quarter are maintained or run by some form of commercial enterprise — such as nurseries, hotels or holiday homes — and for taxation purposes their garden expenses can be offset against the profits gained from that commercial enterprise. Only about an eighth of Scotland's outstanding gardens are owned by Trusts — including charitable Trusts and the National Trust for Scotland.

It is perhaps not surprising that the gardens which are best maintained — and therefore most attractive to the public — are mainly found in the last two groups, namely the commercial enterprise gardens and the Trust gardens. Only very rarely can a private individual afford the £16,800 a year needed to run his or her garden out of taxed income. The future of the privately owned outstanding garden is indeed bleak, and if society cares about losing over half of its outstanding gardens, some form of financial help is needed in this area.

Staffing

As outlined above, the major cost of running an outstanding garden is in staff wages and their normal perquisites, such as free housing and vegetables. In nearly all cases, the gardeners' wages are low, being kept parallel to agricultural workers' wages. The normal wage is around one grade above the minimum agricultural wage, which means in 1980/1981 a weekly rate of about £73.00 a week rising to about £78.00 a week for a head gardener. In terms of annual salary this means £3,700 to £4,100. Wages will inevitably continue to rise with the rate of inflation, and consequently a growing number of owners will not be able to afford to pay their gardening staff, and yet more gardens will disappear.

Garden staff came traditionally from the local area or from the estate itself, but as the rural population and the number of estate staff have decreased, so it has

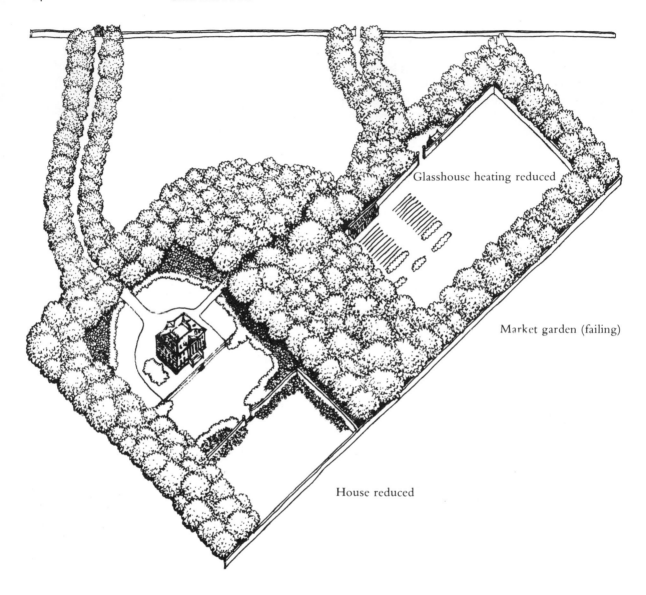

Glasshouse heating reduced

Market garden (failing)

House reduced

FIGURE 33
Scot House in 1960

HOUSEHOLD: 8
Family and guests: 4
Garden staff: 3
(including one of family)
House staff: 1

Scale: 1:2500

KEY:

Trees

Shrubs

Flowers

Fruit/Vegetables

become far more important to look further afield for staff. Conditions of work must therefore be provided to lure outsiders and city dwellers away from the rival municipal parks departments, or the number of staff in private gardens will continue to fall.

Training as a gardener has also changed from the estate system of apprenticeship to the granting of formal qualifications by colleges, and thus the concept of a career structure in gardening has been introduced. This change has financially benefited those gardeners not working in the privately owned outstanding gardens, and the higher wages offered by corporation parks departments are luring experienced gardeners away from the private sector. Private gardens are not only failing to offer competitive wages, but are also unable to afford to train gardening staff within the new career and qualifications structure.

The main reason for this is the actual physical distance between the majority of the private gardens and the training centres, which are primarily situated within the Central Belt of Scotland. In an attempt to alleviate these difficulties, some of these colleges offer a system of training by block release, whereby the trainee gardener is sent for a longer session of two weeks out of every five or six weeks. In practice, however, it seems that only the largest gardens, with four garden staff and over, can afford the time and money to train their staff externally. As if these losses aren't crippling enough, there is the very real likelihood that once trained, the gardener will then move on to the financially and professionally more rewarding world of local authority parks and gardens.

Through the lack of competitive wages, gardening as a service for private and Trust gardens is dying out, and the situation is likely to worsen under the present taxation system, where gardeners' wages have to be afforded out of the private garden owner's taxed income. Compounding this bleak future is the fact that the number of recruits entering gardening as a career is continually decreasing, and of these new recruits, the most skilled and gifted are the ones least likely to be attracted by the outstanding private garden's low wages and lack of promotion prospects. There is a bleak future under the present conditions for the outstanding garden in Scotland, and as many of these conditions are caused by government policies, it is to the government that these gardens must look for help.

Government Help

Gardens are undeniably loved by the majority of the British public, and the hitherto unappreciated decline and disappearance of many of our outstanding gardens must surely be considered unacceptable.

The government has made various statements of intent to the effect that outstanding properties — including gardens — should be preserved for the heritage of the nation, and has evolved some legislation which punishes offenders. As a gesture of help, there are indeed some tax concessions which are available to owners of outstanding gardens — for instance, when opening the

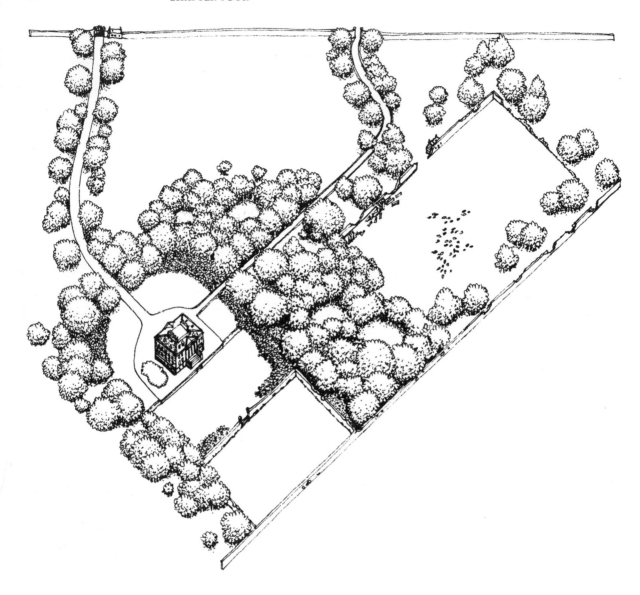

FIGURE 34
Scot House in 1981

HOUSEHOLD: 5 ½
Family: 3
Garden staff: 1 ½
(one member of family full-time,
one half-time)
House staff: 1

Scale: 1:2500

KEY:

Trees

Shrubs

Flowers

Fruit/Vegetables

garden as a profitable commercial enterprise — but in general these concessions have been of little relevance to the majority of outstanding gardens, and because they have been unwilling to accept many of the strings attached, few owners have benefited from government policy.

Similarly, very little advantage has been taken of the grants available to these gardens, mainly because they fail to cover labour costs, which are, as previously illustrated, easily the most expensive maintenance items in all these gardens. It is recognised that the most economic, as well as the most attractive way of making this heritage available to the general public is to encourage the owners to stay on and open their houses and gardens to the public.

Government policy for preserving houses, collections and gardens is that the remaining private owners should organise that preservation and make their property available and accessible to the public upon a reasonable basis.

Statutory Listing of Gardens and Landscapes

Unlike the comparable situation as regards architecture and buildings, nobody actually knows the number of existing outstanding gardens and landscapes in this country, so the government has no real idea of the size of the problem. A major hurdle in practical terms, which is hindering the implementation of any form of government aid, lies in determining which gardens and landscapes should be eligible for this aid. Therefore it is essential that all outstanding gardens and historic landscapes should be surveyed, and a listing system agreed and a list compiled.

Several attempts at surveying and listing gardens and landscapes have been made, but across the United Kingdom these attempts have been extremely uneven and unco-ordinated. Owing initially to a lack of understanding, and more recently a lack of finance, little or no listing work is in progress in Scotland. A successful listing system is of paramount importance to help the survival of the outstanding gardens and landscapes of Scotland. To ensure their survival for future generations, these gardens must be managed on a better basis than has generally been the case since the last war.

Management Plans

Having determined, through the system of listing, which gardens are of an outstanding nature, some form of financial help should be given by the government, either in the form of tax concessions or grant aid. This money must be channelled towards better long-term management of these gardens. Avenues, specimen trees and shelter belts have long been neglected, and no replacement trees planted. Former open areas have become densely overgrown, and historic vistas screened off.

Each government-aided garden should draw up a management plan outlining planting and maintenance objectives, and, where necessary, professional advice should be sought, to ensure the necessary priorities and standard of quality. Also within any proposed management plan should come arrangements for opening the garden to the public.

Although government aid and professional advice may sound like an over-dose of state intervention, this is far from the intention. It is indeed the government's policy to ensure the continuance of the private ownership of outstanding houses or gardens and it is accepted that such owners are the most economic and diligent custodians of this part of Scotland's heritage. It has been tragically shown that the private owner has recently been unable to perform this rôle of custodian, and therefore desperately needs help from the government.

Public Access

The political justification for expenditure of public money on private gardens has always been the granting of some form of access to these gardens for the general public. There has long been a presumption that because the public enjoy visiting a garden, the more that garden is open, the more the public will enjoy it; but this presumption is sadly mistaken, because it has been found that garden visitors appreciate quality above all else.

The amount a garden can open to the public is dependent, not on its size, but on the amount of labour employed in that garden, and hence on the quality of the experience of that visit. Even this yardstick could be misleading, as some forms of garden can absorb visitors far more readily than others. For example, a garden's outstanding quality may be its feeling of intimate privacy, and this very character could be ruined by indiscriminate opening to the general public. This sort of problem should be overcome by determining at the outset the necessary form of government aid, and the appropriate form of management for each garden, including an amount of public access which is both reasonable to the general public and reasonable for the garden itself.

Conclusion

Of the various ways of financing these gardens at present, none is effectively ensuring their conservation, and therefore the present administrative machinery and legislation must be adjusted to solve the real, rather than the supposed, problems of retaining these gardens. Without such changes, the present decline in the number of outstanding gardens in Scotland will continue. These changes must be aimed at conserving the outstanding gardens in the hands of their private owners, but with appropriate management and public access to allow people to see at first hand what must surely be one of the most loved and beautiful parts of Scotland's historical heritage.

THE GARDENS

BOOK ON SCOTLAND'S GARDENS HAS TO RECOGNISE THAT our finest plants have been introduced from abroad, often by our own plant collectors. In the seventeenth century Scotland was a barren country, a fact corroborated by early visitors like Sir Anthony Weldon, a member of the entourage of James I of England, VI of Scotland, on his long-promised return to his native land in 1617. 'There were few trees', Weldon commented, 'also little grass but in their pottage; the thistle is not given of nought, for it is the fairest flower in their gardens.'

It is probable that some of our most celebrated gardens reached their apogee in the palmy days of Edward VII, and in 1908, a year when Income Tax rose to 1/– (5 New Pence) in the £, the Rt. Hon. Sir Herbert Maxwell launched his book entitled 'Scottish Gardens', a description of those that embellished large mansions like The Hirsel, Culzean Castle, and Balcaskie.

The differences between Edwardian times and our own do not need to be enlarged upon here, but of one fact we can be certain: before the establishment of such worthy institutions as Scotland's Gardens Scheme and the National Trust for Scotland the public did not have the same insight into the delights of large privately-owned gardens which they do today.

What follows is in no way an exhaustive catalogue of Scotland's best gardens. I have, however, endeavoured to make the account as representative as space will allow of the varied types of gardens to be seen in Scotland today: the formal and the informal; gardens by the seashore, on steep mountainsides, or bleak moorland; gardens at the hearts of busy cities; gardens in lonely, far-flung places, crying out to be visited.

In the course of my travels through Scotland, collecting material for this book, someone — to encourage me on my way — expressed his belief that gardeners in general are congenial, kindly folk. Looking back on our completed task, I would endorse this theory wholeheartedly, and offer once more, to all who helped us, our sincere thanks.

Note: In the list which follows, opening dates and times are not usually given, since they vary from year to year. Up-to-date details of these, and many other fine gardens which we had no space to include, will be found in the *Scotland's Gardens* handbook, available from the Scotland's Gardens Scheme, 26 Castle Terrace, Edinburgh EH1 2EL.

May, 1981.   G. Allan Little

FIGURE 35
Netherbyres — the walled garden

MAP OF LOCATIONS:

1 *Abbey St Bathans*
2 *Abbotsford*
3 *Addistoun House*
4 *Belhaven*
5 *Bemersyde*
6 *Biel*
7 *Bowhill*
8 *Bridgelands*
9 *Broughton Place*
10 *Bughtrig*
11 *Chiefswood*
12 *Cleuchhead House*
13 *Crailing Hall*
14 *Dawyck*
15 *Easter Weens*
16 *Eden House*
17 *Elvingston*
18 *Floors Castle*
19 *Glenburn Hall*
20 *Hawthornden Castle*
21 *Haystoun*
22 *The Hirsel*
23 *The Holmes*
24 *Hopetoun Gardens*
25 *Hopetoun House*
26 *Houndwood House*
27 *Inveresk Lodge*
28 *Kailzie*
29 *Kirklands*
30 *Lambden*
31 *Lochside*
32 *Luffness*
33 *Mainhouse*
34 *Malleny House*
35 *Manderston*
36 *Marchmont*
37 *Mellerstain*
38 *Mertoun*
39 *Netherbyres*
40 *Royal Botanic Garden*
41 *St Mary's Pleasance*
42 *Stevenson House*
43 *Tyninghame*
44 *Whitchester*
45 *Winton House*

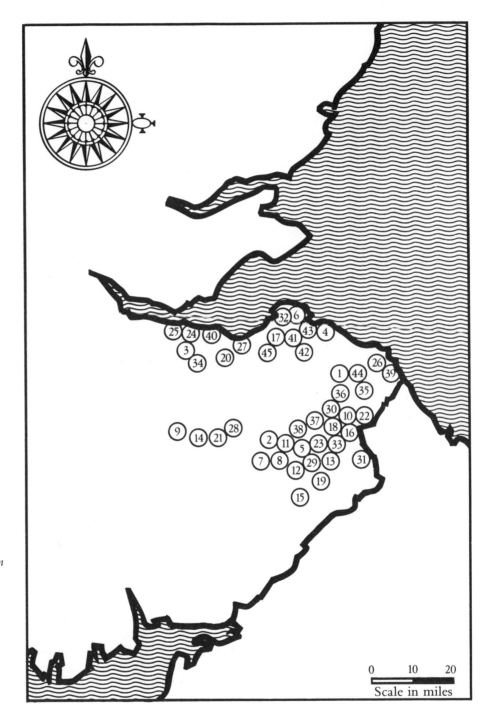

Scale in miles

THE SOUTH EAST

The village of Abbey St Bathans took its name partly from a Cistercian nunnery, partly from Baithene, St Columba's cousin and successor at Iona. The house of the same name is a late eighteenth-century cottage, built in the Bavarian style with gables and turrets. It was enlarged in 1866 and again in the 1880s, with stables close by.

The garden was landscaped by John Turnbull at the end of the nineteenth century. The house is situated on a bank covered with old hybrid Rhododendrons and massed Azaleas. There is a small walled garden, complete with herbaceous border, Rose beds, and vegetable patch, all quite informal. A coppice of Scots Pines crowns the hill behind. On the opposite side of the river there is a woodland of Oak, Copper Beech and Cypresses, designed to provide good autumn colour.

1 ABBEY ST BATHANS
Duns
7 miles north of Duns,
5 miles west of
Grantshouse.
(MR W. S. J. DOBIE)

Sir Walter Scott is said to have planted nearly every tree on the Abbotsford estate, and his part in the planning and making of the gardens was no less active.

Abbotsford was erected between 1817 and 1821 on a terrace above the right bank of the Tweed. The entrance is down a drive through the natural garden, planted with ample bushes of Viburnums, Dogwoods, fragrant old shrub Roses, Azaleas and Rhododendrons, and Potentillas, all interspersed with bosky Yews and other conifers, Silver Birch, and Rowans, much used in old Scots gardens to ward off evil spirits.

The South Court garden is severely formal. The Yew hedge, close against the south wall, was planted by Mr Hope-Scott in the 1860s, and spaces have been cut to show five medallions from the old Edinburgh Mercat Cross and the alternating rectangular stones from the Roman Camp at Old Penrith (Mercury, Jupiter, Venus, Apollo and Mars), and part of a legionary inscription of the 22nd Legion.

At the centre there is a fountain, the bowl of which once formed part of the same Mercat Cross in the Edinburgh High Street. Along the east side is a stone pergola, sculptured with a leaf design. Guardian Yews stand at each corner of the lawn. Beyond, in the East Court, is Sir Walter's sun-dial; here also is the suppliant statue of Morris, the exciseman in *Rob Roy*, pleading for mercy from Helen Macgregor. There is a fine screen of two intertwining Ivies, one plain and the other variegated. A Clematis and an old Apple tree, forming an indissoluble partnership, overhang the gate into the walled garden, typical of its kind, with Strawberry beds, Raspberry canes, cordoned fruit trees, and herbaceous borders full of 'bonny flouers'. There is also a fernhouse of an early nineteenth-century

2 ABBOTSFORD
Melrose
2½ miles west of Melrose.
(MRS MAXWELL-SCOTT, OBE)

design, full of potted pink and red and white Geraniums — some Ivy-leafed — Begonias, Indian Azaleas, Orchids, and Asparagus and Maiden-Hair Ferns.

Thousands of visitors come to Abbotsford each year. Yet this remains a charming old garden which still recaptures the romantic spirit of its founder.

The present Addistoun House is modern, built in 1938 by Charles Soutar, a Dundee architect. The site was formerly occupied by the dower house of Dalmahoy Estate, and the dower-house garden.

The Misses Smith acquired the demolished house and land in 1937. It was in a derelict condition, but they remade the garden, partly to a plan drawn by Mrs Stebbing, a garden designer, and repaired the walls and terrace, in all of which they were ably assisted by their gardener, Peter Campbell.

The house site, curiously enough, is within the original walled garden, and there are about 3 acres of garden and orchard, all on flat ground, and a further 5 acres of woodland extending to the glen of the Gogar Burn. The climate is good, and the soil in the garden is a light, non-acid loam.

The eighteenth-century walls and the even older stone archway confer an antique grace. Another interesting feature is the dower-house well, described in the New Statistical Account of the early nineteenth century. The style of the garden is formal, with herbaceous and shrub borders, Lilacs and Apple and Cherry trees, old Yews and Hollies.

3 ADDISTOUN HOUSE
Ratho
On A71, 1 mile east of Dalmahoy.
(MISSES A. & J. M. SMITH)

East Lothian is one of Scotland's most fertile districts, and the climate is generally dry above the national average, but not particularly mild. Sir George Taylor's garden at Belhaven, however, is a botanist's garden containing several specimens which are usually regarded as suitable only for warmer climes.

Mimosa (*Acacia decurrens var. dealbata*), for example, with its bright yellow flowers in ball-like clusters and heady fragrance, is at home by the shores of the Mediterranean, yet it blooms here, sheltered from the winds off the North Sea. *Pittosporum tenuifolium*, a New Zealand evergreen, and *Colquhounia coccinea*, a tender Himalayan shrub bearing bright orange-red flowers, also flourish here.

Another of Sir George's successes is the beautiful *Olearia semidentata*, native of the Chatham Islands off the east coast of New Zealand. The flowers, about two inches in diameter, have deep violet discs surrounded by numerous mauve ray-florets, and appear in July. There are several rare species of *Olearia* at Belhaven.

The *Abelia triflora*, a very fine specimen, is the pride of the garden. It is one of the hardiest of these graceful north-west Himalayan shrubs, and the flowers grow in clusters of fragrant white. Another tree to admire and wonder at is the Killarney Strawberry Tree (*Arbutus unedo*); the flowers are creamy-white, followed by strawberry fruits in autumn. Yet another is the *Davidia involucrata*, variously called the Pocket-Handkerchief Tree, the Dove Tree, or the Ghost Tree, for reasons that become apparent when it is tossed by the wind and the

4 BELHAVEN
Dunbar
On A1087, just west of Dunbar.
(STANLEY SMITH HORTICULTURAL TRUST)

FIGURE 37
Nerine bowdenii *and* Hydrangea macrophylla *at Belhaven*

white flowers are more conspicuous. The fruit ripens in the autumn.

In the Woodland Garden, one comes upon the most beautiful of the Eucryphias, *Eucryphia* × *nymansensis* 'Nymansay', like a dark evergreen pillar, carrying pure white, yellow-stamened flowers. It is a hybrid of the Chilean species *Eucryphia* by *cordifolia* × *glutinosa*, both of which also grow in Belhaven.

5 BEMERSYDE
St Boswells
Off the B6356 St Boswells-Earlston road, between Scott's View and Dryburgh Abbey.
(THE EARL HAIG)

Once a Roman outpost, Bemersyde estate has been held by the Haigs, originally the De Hagas, a Norman family, since 1162, in an almost unbroken line of descent, thus fulfilling the prophecy of True Thomas of Ercildoun (Thomas the Rhymer) when he said:

> 'Tyde what may, whate'er betyde,
> Haig shall be Haig of Bemersyde.'

The core of the mansion is the ancient peel tower. It was built in conformity with an Act of Scottish Parliament of 1535 'for bigging of strengthis on the Bordouris', but English raiders greatly damaged it a decade later. The restorers took stones from Dryburgh Abbey. A top storey was added in 1690, and the dimensions of the peel were extended laterally in 1790 and 1862.

Towards the end of the nineteenth century, Bemersyde became the property of the Clackmannanshire branch of the Haigs. In 1921, however, it was purchased by national subscription and presented to Field Marshal Earl Haig, father of the present owner, who spent the last seven years of his life planning and executing personally his own designs for the Bemersyde garden.

Today, by reason of the labour shortage and high costs, the ten acres of Border hillside are mainly park land and woodland, except for the sunken garden, which the Field Marshal designed, taking for his model a knot garden at Hampton Court. He also erected the rose trellises in the same vicinity, and placed more against the red brick wall of the eighteenth-century stables. A sundial, bearing the date 1690, and an ancient well head, mounted over the peel's well, accord with the character of the sixteenth-century tower.

Many of the trees in the woodland garden were received as gifts. They are surpassed by two Spanish Chestnuts, the larger of which is estimated to be eight hundred years old. For centuries it has been the trysting tree of the Haigs. From the lookout of the peel one commands magnificent views of the country around — all Lauderdale, the meanderings of the Tweed, and the triple peaks of the Eildon Hills.

FIGURE 38
Ancient Spanish Chestnut at Bemersyde

The Bemersyde garden possesses charm throughout the entire year, even in the nakedness of winter-time; but it reaches its peak in spring, when Daffodils grace the lawns. and all the Cherry trees are hung with blossom.

Little wonder that Sir Walter Scott was a frequent visitor here.

6 BIEL
Dunbar

Biel is an early tower house, extended between 1800 and 1840, and reduced to its present form in 1951. It was the home of John, 2nd Lord Belhaven and Stenton, who was imprisoned in the Tower of London for strongly opposing the Union

of 1707. He died the following year, so he had little chance to enjoy his beautiful garden.

BIEL (contd.)
On A1 between East Linton and Dunbar. Lodge at end of drive.
(MR & MRS C. G. SPENCE)

The large garden lies in the valley of the Biel Burn and is rich in alluvium. It is notable for its three south-facing terraces with their buttressed retaining walls, half of which were constructed in the mid seventeenth century by the 1st Lord Belhaven, and the remainder in the early nineteenth century. Central steps lead from the terraces to a sweep of lawn, flanked by the Biel Burn and planted with numerous specimen trees. These include several *Sequoiadendron giganteum* up to 43 metres in height, *Sequoia sempervirens*, and a *Metasequoia*. There is also a rather rare fastigiate *Ginkgo biloba* and a *Araucaria araucana* (Monkey-Puzzle Tree), much loved by Victorian gardeners. An ancient Copper Beech (*Fagus sylvatica* 'Purpurea') has drooping branches which have themselves taken root in the soil, forming a thicket.

On the terraces and throughout the garden one comes upon rare and very beautiful shrubs and ornamental trees. One which is sure to attract attention is the Chilean Potato Tree (*Solanum crispum* 'Glasnevin'), whose potato-like flowers provide colour throughout the summer. Another, also from Chile, is *Aloysia citriodora* (syn. *Lippia citriodora*); its pale purple flowers are not conspicuous, but the leaves have a strong lemon fragrance — hence the common name Lemon Verbena.

The old twin staircase is draped in summer with blue-purple Wisteria, and the sunny East Lothian climate has induced a Hibiscus to put forth blossom on more than one occasion. Another prize exhibit is the Peregrine Peach in the kitchen garden; it produces its large, brilliant crimson fruits with regularity and they are said to be 'melting and excellent'.

Bowhill has been the Border home of the Dukes of Buccleuch since about 1800 when the architects involved, notably William Atkinson (1773-1839), William Burn (1789-1870) and David Bryce (1803-76), added to the original building of 1756.

7 BOWHILL
Selkirk
Just off A708 Selkirk-Moffat road.
(THE DUKE OF BUCCLEUCH AND QUEENSBERRY, KT)

There are 7 acres of garden, much of it in process of renewal or restoration, including terraced lawns, shrub borders, a new rose garden, a rock garden under construction, a formal flower garden with herbaceous borders, and a kitchen garden containing fruit and vegetables.

The policies are 580 feet above sea level, with 30 inches of rainfall. The soil is a lime-free light loam, very suitable for the predominant conifers, Rhododendrons, Azaleas and other ericaceous plants, many of which are in flower during April, May and June, the best season for this garden.

While the new garden becomes established, Bowhill's main attractions lie in its magnificent setting, in Border scenery of rolling hills, woods and the darkly gliding Yarrow and Ettrick Waters — so rightly named 'sweet Bowhill' by Scott.

FIGURE 39
Bowhill, seen across the Tweed

8 BRIDGELANDS
Selkirk

1½ miles north-east of the town of Selkirk.
(MAJOR M. I. & MRS C. LESLIE MELVILLE)

This is a farmhouse, built about 1720 and improved and slightly enlarged in 1900. Situated in beautiful Border lands, it looks out upon gentle hill scenery. The policies contain two small walled gardens, a rock garden, plantings of shrubs, an orchard and an arboretum. The slightly acid loam favours a high standard of fertility, maintained by additions of peat and garden compost as required. The climate is described as 'reasonable', with an annual rainfall of 35 inches. Spring frosts occasionally cause harm to the fruit blossom and tender plants. Hedges, walls, and tree plantations give good shelter from the wind.

The variety of plants, shrubs and trees planted is remarkable. The lawn is golden in early May with masses of Daffodils. Early June is the time for the Rhododendrons and Azaleas, their gorgeous colours offset by a background of fine and varied trees, both broadleaved and coniferous. The shrub Roses and Peonies follow in July.

The rich autumn colours smoulder on through October into November, and this is a garden that never looks drab, no matter the time of year.

9 BROUGHTON PLACE
Broughton

Just north of Broughton Village, on the A701 Edinburgh-Moffat road.
(BRIGADIER A. I. BUCHANAN-DUNLOP *and others*)

Broughton Place was designed by Sir Basil Spence in the style of a Scottish tower house, and completed in 1938. The garden was laid out by Mrs T. E. Elliott in the same year. It is almost 900 feet above sea level, commanding extensive views of Tweeddale and the Peeblesshire hills, and is sheltered from the west by Beeches, though otherwise exposed.

The 2 acre walled garden occupies a hillside and is formal in character. There is a knot garden, 'water steps', and a dovecote, also by Spence. The soil is shallow loam, quick-draining, and in the cold climate plants and shrubs are slow to become established. There is a wide variety of spring and summer bulbs, also several unusual herbaceous plants and modern as well as old Roses.

10 BUGHTRIG
near Leitholm, Coldstream

¼ mile north-west of Leitholm village, on B6461 Eccles-Swinton road.
(COLONEL & THE HON MRS CHARLES RAMSAY)

Bughtrig House is a Georgian building, dating from 1790, with a new porch, balustrades and other features added after 1875. The owner between these years was a lover of conifers, and many of his plantings survive on either side of the avenue leading up to the house and on the fringes of the wide front lawn. The mother of the present owner, Lady Ramsay, widow of Admiral Sir Bertram Ramsay, designed the present gardens in 1930.

The garden lies in the Berwickshire Merse, a highly productive agricultural area, and the soil is heavy. Yew hedges divide and shelter and there is an inner orchard with a Bramley Seedling Apple Tree, judged to be a hundred and fifty years old, besides Conference and Jargonelle Pears.

The greenhouses grow Peaches, Nectarines and Grapes, and the fernhouse supplies a good selection of 'stove plants' — Cape Primroses (*Streptocarpus*), sweetly scented Carnations, Abutilon, and 'rose-scented' Geraniums.

There are hedges of *Rosa moyesii* 'Geranium', covered with deep red single flowers in summer, followed by autumnal orange-scarlet Hips; and many fine herbaceous plants, in particular an uncommon pale-blue Astilbe, *Lobelia fulgens*

'The Huntsman' with purple foliage and brilliant scarlet flowers, *Phytolacca* or Poke Weed for autumn foliage and berries, and Snake's Head Fritillarias.

The *Betula costata* on the verge of the drive is most attractive. This lovely Birch from north-eastern Asia has creamy-white bark peeling in large flakes, and its perfection is a joy to behold.

Sir Walter Scott built Chiefswood for his daughter when she became the wife of J. G. Lockhart in 1820. The Lockharts used it as a country cottage; it contains many mementoes of Scott, was painted by Turner, and stayed in by Disraeli who described it as 'a cottage *orné* in the most romantic part of the country'.

11 CHIEFSWOOD
Melrose
½ *mile west-south-west of Melrose.*
(LORD & LADY DACRE OF GLANTON, *formerly* TREVOR-ROPER)

The situation is beautiful, close to the Eildon Hills. The garden in its present form was improved by Lady Alexandra Dacre and contains a rosarium, carefully colour-schemed herbaceous borders, a shrub and a bog garden, and a glen with ferns through which flows the Huntly Burn.

The soil is acid and frost pockets are inclined to form in low-lying areas. Roses, Potentillas, Fuchsias, Astilbes all flourish; also ferns, including the Royal Fern (*Osmunda regalis*), but among the Hydrangeas only *H. paniculata* 'Grandiflora' can tolerate the severe winters.

Cleuchhead House, home of the Earl and Countess of Minto, was built for the factor of the Minto estates before 'Gibbie' Elliot (1651-1718) was elevated to the bench in 1705 as the first Lord Minto; and there is a marriage lintel let into the west gable which is carved 'E.C. and W.T.H.T. 1692'.

12 CLEUCHHEAD HOUSE
Minto
1 *mile north-east of Minto village, along a farm road.*
(THE EARL & COUNTESS OF MINTO)

The house and garden occupy a sandy gully, 400 feet above the Teviot valley, with fields at the back, strewn with rocks cast down from the Minto Crags. Despite this lofty site, the situation is damp; even during summer droughts one may still hear underground streams coursing down hidden channels beneath the garden soil.

The mixed woods of Minto Glen, containing gigantic Larches, Douglas Firs, and Redwoods as well as Beeches, Sycamores and Spanish Chestnuts, halt their rise out of the valley by the road to Cleuchhead. The Minto Hills lie to the west, and to the south is Ruberslaw (1392 feet), notable historically as the venue for hill-meetings in the time of the Covenanters' persecution.

Because of the good drainage, Roses flourish in the clay soil. Some, growing against the house wall, were planted by Lady Ruby Florence Mary Elliot, whose father, the fourth Earl, was Governor-General of Canada and thereafter Viceroy of India 1898-1910. The present Earl planted the 'Rose Wall' in the front garden of Cleuchhead, when he restyled the entrance and changed the position of the front door.

A cobbled path leads through buttressing archways to the coach-house and back courtyard, then turns into the 1½-acre garden, mostly lawn and side borders of Victorian and turn-of-the-century Rhododendrons and Roses. There is also a long herbaceous border, containing favourite cottage garden flowers;

and a Birch tree, gnarled with age, but still standing firm against the winds.

Primulas grow in abundance along the road verges, blooming with the many Daffodils in April and May, when the sound of the ewes calling their lambs on the hill fills the spring air.

On ideas supplied to him, Mr Laurie of Ninewells Nursery drew up a comprehensive plan of the Crailing Hall garden to be, including a new terrace for a formal Rose garden.

The situation lies in wooded, undulating Border country, 350 feet above mean sea level, with an annual rainfall of only 25 inches. Some shelter is provided by a belt of trees on the north side. The soil is light/medium, stone-free loam. Much consideration has been given to a labour-saving layout of the garden, which is formal in style with long narrow Rose beds and herbaceous borders, easily workable from the sides, with grass paths between, and all on the level 'so that a gardener can wheel a barrow from end to end without too much exertion'.

The low rainfall means that shallow-rooting shrubs such as Rhododendrons and Azaleas do not do very well, as they can succumb to a prolonged drought. Nevertheless, the garden contains many other rare and unusual trees and shrubs and Roses, all looking thoroughly well-rooted, despite the fact that the garden was only made in the mid-1960s. Some of these were brought from the Baleans' previous gardens, in Derbyshire and at Tournaig in Ross-shire, close to The National Trust for Scotland's gardens at Inverewe. The Crailing Hall garden is at its best in April when its wide collection of named Daffodils are flowering.

The front windows of the farmhouse look out on the garden. Urns of a classical design add a pleasingly formal effect at a junction of the paths, and the view of the hills beyond is framed by two stone obelisks, made to the Squadron Leader's own design.

13 CRAILING HALL
Jedburgh
2½ miles east of Jedburgh.
(SQUADRON LEADER & MRS PETER BALEAN)

The earliest recorded lairds of Dawyck were the Veitch family, holders from the thirteenth to the late seventeenth century. Little is known about them, except that they were hosts to James IV, when Dawyck's herons provided quarry for the King's falcons; and that the cold blasts about their domain persuaded them to ring it round with plantations of trees.

In 1691 ownership passed to James Naesmyth, a lawyer of doubtful repute, called 'the Deil o' Dawick'. His grandson and namesake, having been a pupil of the Swedish botanist Carl Linnaeus, improved the policies by planting an avenue of European Silver Firs (*Abies alba*). He communicated his zeal to his successors, and between 1800 and 1897 all of them gave support to plant hunters' expeditions abroad, from which originated many specimens in the Dawyck arboretum.

Dawyck's world-famous tree is the Fastigiate Beech (*Fagus sylvatica*

14 DAWYCK
Stobo
1 mile from Stobo, 8 miles south-west of Peebles.
(DEPARTMENT OF AGRICULTURE AND FISHERIES FOR SCOTLAND. *Annexe of Royal Botanic Garden, Edinburgh*)

FIGURE 40
Azaleas at Dawyck

'Dawyck'). It was discovered by Sir James Naesmyth growing among the ordinary Beeches and removed to the south side of the house, where it still stands, some 70 feet in height.

The Balfours, who took over the estates in 1897, were likewise assiduous planters. F. R. S. Balfour, creator of the garden in its present form, brought back many plants and seeds from his travels through North-West America. He was an enthusiastic collector of Rhododendrons, and although many of his trophies succumbed in Dawyck's severe frosts and tearing winds, about one hundred and twenty species Rhododendrons continue to flourish where he established them, in the garden's moist leaf mould. While in South Oregon in 1908, he found Brewer's Weeping Spruce (*Picea brewerana*), and was later able to import seed from this source. The previous year, the Wilson expedition to China returned with seed of the beautiful *Prunus × dawyckensis*. Another prize from West China was the tender Holly, *Ilex fargesii*, still burgeoning by the nineteenth-century Dutch Bridge over the Scrape Burn.

In springtime a tide of Daffodils sweeps across the gardens, and there are Trilliums and Himalayan Poppies flowering in the woodland clearings. The stream garden glows with Azaleas, Skunk Lilies (*Lysichiton americanum*), and Sorrel Rhubarb (*Rheum palmatum*). All the trees in the long Lime avenue are freshly, delicately green.

A striking feature of the gardens is the elaborate terracing, made in 1830 when the present house was built. There is a also a charming walled garden with its Italian well head, and the auld kirk of Dawyck which serves now as the lairds' mausoleum.

The arboretum was donated to the Secretary of State for Scotland in 1978, and is managed as an institution of the Royal Botanic Garden, Edinburgh.

15 EASTER WEENS
Bonchester Bridge
¾ mile out of Bonchester Bridge, on the B6357 Bonchester Bridge-Jedburgh road.
(MR & MRS J. R. CURTIS)

Bonchester Hill (1059 feet) has on it the remains of ancient fortifications, and may have been occupied by the Romans, since the name *Bona Castra* means 'a good camp'. The situation of Easter Weens, on the outskirts of the village, is also an enviable one. The fabric was originally part of the farm steading, converted to stables in 1780, and then into a dwelling-house in 1958.

The well-known landscape architect, the late Percy Cane, was commissioned to draw up plans for the garden, which received a Civic Trust award in 1962.

The garden, 500 feet above sea level and east-facing, is vulnerable to spring frosts and bitterly cold winds. Part of it is a flat courtyard, part a side of the Rule Water valley, overlooking grass parks with some fine specimen trees and a lake, formed by Mr and Mrs Curtis in 1980. Despite the very exposed situation, this is mainly a Rhododendron and Azalea garden, at its best in May and June, when the plants in the rock garden and on the rock wall are also mainly in flower. The policies include a pear-shaped walled garden, made in 1784, with a mill stream winding through it. This awaits re-development. The gateway and sundial have been incorporated into the formality of the flat courtyard.

In a charter, penned within Coldingham Priory, Thor informed his feudal lord, the good Earl David, brother of King William the Lion, that King Edgar (1097-1107) had bestowed on him the Ednaham waste; and that he had peopled it, and built from the foundation and endowed with a ploughgate of land a church in honour of St Cuthbert, referred to in a subsequent document as 'the mother church of Hedenham'.

The twelfth-century name, Ednaham, meant 'the village on the river', and although it was destroyed on at least one occasion by English raiders Ednam rose again and remains today a village of charming antiquity, built beside the Eden river, flowing East to join the Tweed, and 200 feet above sea level. The Scottish poet James Thomson (1700-48), author of 'The Seasons', was born in Ednam church manse.

Eden House was built in 1772 and had ties with a local brewery, which explains its situation close to the river; a high, long, narrow house facing south towards the Cheviots. This, and a north wall, provide the garden with shelter, though the prevailing winds are south-westerly. It is indeed a fine, sunny situation and the soil is rich with alluvium brought down by the Eden.

There had been a garden between the house and the river for many generations, but the present one was only started in 1958. It is part formal, part natural, and narrow in shape, constricted by the line of the house and the river running by.

The contents are varied: Roses both old and modern mingled together, many herbaceous plants, all in good heart; and a varied collection of flowering shrubs including Acers, Berberis, Azaleas, Buddleias, Ceanothus, Chimonanthus, Cistuses, Rock Roses and herbs. Trained against the stone wall are *Actinidia kolomikta, Ceratostigma,* the blue Plumbago and different species of Clematis.

The site of the small summerhouse, facing south across the river, could not be bettered. Banks of old Shrub Roses border the river which is stalked by herons, probing the mud for eels. Beyond the north wall, another garden, shaded by old trees, and reaching down to a triangular paddock, is the jealously guarded preserve of a family of white ducks, ranging happily in the river mud. The herb garden flourishes fragrantly by the garden gate.

One of East Lothian's loveliest sights in springtime are the twenty-two acres of Plum orchard around Elvingston Farm. Most of the trees are underplanted with Daffodils and the flowering times of both synchronise, the near-naked boughs hung with pure white blossom and the ground beneath carpeted with pale yellow blooms nodding in the April wind. There is also the 300-yard wild Hyacinth Walk, arched over by blossoming Plum trees.

Sir David Lowe (who died in the autumn of 1980) bought the farm and its handsome early Victorian mansion in 1944 and began breeding Narcissi. Some of his stock he acquired from the Brodie of Brodie, then regarded as one of the best suppliers of rare Daffodils, and concentrated his efforts on the production

16 EDEN HOUSE
Ednam, Kelso
2½ miles from Kelso, off the B6461 Kelso-Berwick-on-Tweed road.
(MR & MRS DAVID LYELL)

17 ELVINGSTON
Gladsmuir
½ mile east of Gladsmuir, on north side of A1.
(LADY LOWE)

and hybridisation of pale yellow varieties. These thrived in the good soil and kindly East Lothian climate, and there are now 12 acres of land under bulbs. Sir David never marketed his Daffodils as bulbs, though he gave a great many away.

The Plums are mostly Victorias, with some Washington Gage (also known as Washington Drooper) planted as a good windbreak. There is a large, high-walled kitchen garden planted with a variety of fruit trees — Peaches, Plums, Apples and Pears.

The farmhouse, substantially built of Craigleith stone, has it own doocot in the steading, a listed building of much greater antiquity. Farmers today regard pigeons as parasites on their lands; but a 'doo fancier' might consider all these eight hundred and sixty empty nests ranged round the inside walls with some gloom.

18 FLOORS CASTLE
Kelso

Entered from Roxburgh Street, Kelso, or by the back entrance off the B6397.
(THE DUKE OF ROXBURGHE)

Floors Castle is said to be the largest inhabited mansion in Scotland, and 'so situated as to combine the ideas of ancient baronial grandeur with those of modern taste'.

It was built for the 1st Duke of Roxburghe, by William Adam in 1721, and extended and remodelled by William Henry Playfair in 1838-49.

The castle faces south, with grass terraces shelving down to the Tweed and an area of garden and a swimming pool on the west side. Part of the great encircling walls of the park were built by French prisoners of war. The garden was made in 1858, in a style that harmonised with that of the castle, and the main entrance gates of wrought iron overlaid with gold leaf were erected in 1929 along with the handsome lodges.

The walled garden (accessible from the B6397) was turned into a Garden Centre in 1978, where many outdoor and indoor plants are on sale.

Today, however, only a small part of the policies are given over to gardens, and it is the wide parkland and wealth of growing timber for which Floors is to be admired. Many of the trees have reached a ripe age, and an old Holly tree is said to mark the spot where James II was killed in 1460 by a bursting cannon during the siege of Roxburgh.

19 GLENBURN HALL
Jedburgh

Half a mile out of Jedburgh, on the road to Hawick.
(MRS A. C. GIBSON)

This handsome modestly-proportioned Georgian mansion occupies a lofty site, 500 feet above mean sea level, isolated and exposed to the prevailing westerly winds.

Turning off the hilly road to Hawick, the entrance carriageway plunges through the shade of a beautiful tunnel of pleached Beeches, sinewy with years, finally emerging on the brow of the hill on which stands Glenburn Hall. There is little in the way of a garden in its immediate surroundings, and the front looks south-east across plain lawns, high above the Jed valley. To the back there is a walled garden, built at the same time as the house, in 1815. It was re-designed in 1968, with the help of Miss Hawkins, Lynedoch Place, Edinburgh, and the wall bricks are a cheerful reddish colour. The soil within the garden is mostly heavy clay, and alkaline.

This is an unpretentious garden, full of good things. The long border, backed by the east wall, flowers variously and cheerfully for six months of the year. Nearby rows of vegetables, haphazardly planted in what is said to be 'the French Style', make easy neighbours; there are Rambler Roses and Clematis intertwined on wire pergolas; row upon row of leeks and onions, thriving in the shade of the overhanging hardwood trees; cordoned Apple trees that fruit ponderously without fail; and a Grape-Vine, graceful and decorative, that bears no fruit, and, at this elevation, never will!

The castle is perched amongst hanging woods, on the right bank of the North Esk, and high above a steep-sided ravine. The oldest part dates from around 1150, while the remainder is seventeenth-century, with the towers and turrets and gables characteristic of that period. It was built by the Scottish poet Sir William Drummond, who was of such repute in his time that Ben Jonson walked all the way from London just to meet him.

Directly beneath the castle are Hawthornden's famous caves, where Robert Bruce hid from his enemies during the Wars of Independence. It is thought they may have been an underground Pictish fort, linked by passages cut in the soft stone. A flat rock overlooking the gorge was used by John Knox as a pulpit from which to address the crowd gathered on the opposite bank.

There are in all some 120 acres of grounds, the original gardens and glen and river banks all so fused as to be indistinguishable. Nevertheless, the main layout is believed to have been made in 1650, when many of the ancient noble trees were first planted, including the huge Cedars and the Yew tree avenue.

Thirty years ago, Lady Drummond of Hawthornden attempted to discipline the wild garden. She planted many of the Rhododendrons and the spring bulbs. It is, in fact, an early spring to early summer garden, its joyous period commencing with Snowdrops in early February, followed by all the Daffodils and Narcissi, the Dog's Tooth Violets (*Erythronium dens-canis*), Primroses and Cowslips, reaching its climax with the blossoming of the Rhododendrons in June.

20 HAWTHORNDEN CASTLE
Lasswade
Rosewell Road, Lasswade.
(MISS DIANA M. B. ADAMSON)

Colonel Sprot's maternal ancestors, the Hays, acquired the estate in the course of the sixteenth and seventeenth centuries. The approach is by way of an avenue of fine Beech trees; the tower, now part of the house, was built at the end of the sixteenth century and occupies a knoll overhanging the right bank of the Glensax Burn.

In the eighteenth century it became a farmhouse, but was converted into a mansion house by the present owner's uncle, Sir Duncan Hay of Haystoun, Bart., using the original dwelling and the attached farm buildings. Together these form three sides of a quadrangle, with a courtyard in the middle. There are

21 HAYSTOUN
Peebles
1 mile south of Peebles. At south end of Tweed Bridge, take road to left front (NOT the road to Traquair, which is first left). Gates on right, at end of tarmacadam.
(LT.-COL. A. M. SPROT)

two seventeenth-century marriage stones over the doorways in the courtyard, carved with the armorial bearings of the Hays. A romantic loggia on the
far side of the mansion overlooks the gardens — a walled garden, made in 1729,
and a wild garden, at the foot of a dene, with a burn flowing through it.

Standing high, the mansion commands views of the surrounding countryside
— from the Glensax Hill to the Pentland Hills.

Wild flowers grow in profusion on the banks of the dene, also Daffodils in
springtime, and there are many Rhododendrons and herbaceous plants. A Yew
tree of great antiquity dominates the walled garden.

22 THE HIRSEL
☙ Coldstream
*1 mile north-west of
Coldstream.*
(DOUGLAS & ANGUS ESTATES —
LORD HOME OF THE HIRSEL, KT)

Hirsel can mean various things: a flock of sheep or the stock of sheep on a farm;
the feeding place of a flock of sheep or — and this is the Home interpretation —
the area in the charge of one shepherd.

The long, narrow mansion occupies a slight rise. There had been a land-
holding here since the twelfth century; part of the foundation charter of the
Cistercian Priory of Coldstream included a gift of land and the Church of
'Herishille'. The 1st Earl of Home is known to have lived at Hirsel in 1619, and
in 1621 a Charter of the Barony of Hirsel was served on the 2nd Earl.

The 3000-acre estate covers some of the best of the Berwickshire Merse,
yielding abundant crops of barley, wheat and potatoes and providing good
grazing for its flocks of sheep and cattle. There are also included 600 acres of
woodlands, and garden and grounds of some 12 acres. At 100 feet, with an
annual rainfall of 23 inches, and prevailing westerly winds, most plants thrive in
the good loamy soil over sand and clay.

But in Dundock, the Rhododendron and Azalea Wood, the soil is quite
substantially peaty. Why this should be remained for long a mystery. Then the
grand-daughter of a Hirsel carter remembered how, some seventy years before,
after a wood was felled by a storm in the 1890s, it was decided to replant with
Rhododendrons and Azaleas. But calcifuges would not thrive in the natural soil,
so hundreds of tons of peat were carted from the Bonkyl estate, then Home land,
some 16 miles to the north, a round trip for the men and their horses lasting
twenty-four hours. Many of these Rhododendrons have reverted in time to the
wild purple *R. ponticum*, an invasive nuisance, but these are being replaced with
hybrid plants.

Some beautiful softwood trees have grown up in the sheltering bushes — the
Scots Pine (*Pinus sylvestris*); Western Hemlock (*Tsuga heterophylla*); Silver Fir
(*Abies species*); the Norway Spruce (*Picea abies*); and with them specimens of the
deciduous hardwood *Cercidiphyllum japonicum*, selected for autumn colour,
whereas the others are at their best in late May and early June.

The Hirsel contains a lake, and because of the diversity of the terrain, and the
owners' friendly attitude to them, the estate has over many years become the
haunt of breeding and migrant birds; the Rhododendron and Azalea Wood of
Dundock, in particular, is alleged to contain a greater variety of birds than any

other wood of its size in Britain. Lord Home's late brother, Henry Douglas-Home, widely known as 'The Bird Man', frequently broadcast recordings of bird song from these woods.

This conservant policy applies also to wild flowers and animals and trees. A Sycamore (*Acer pseudoplatanus*) has weathered the seasons for four hundred years outside the walled garden, though its limbs are now held together with wire ropes. Its neighbour, a Tulip Tree (*Liriodendron tulipifera*), was planted in the walled garden in 1742, and its trunk is now hollow, yet it still puts forth blossom each summer. On the banks of the Leet, the remains of a Spanish Chestnut, estimated to be four hundred years old, continue to draw sap into its gnarled trunk.

Lord Home has been planting Daffodils, Roses and new shrubs in areas around the mansion since 1959. One border contains the Rhododendrons 'Elizabeth', *R. pseudochrysanthum,* and *R. yedoense*, growing happily with peat added and underplantings of Meconopses (the Tibetan Poppy), Primulas, and dwarf conifers, as well as a graceful Witch Hazel (*Hamamelis mollis*) whose winter blossoms and autumn leaves are a similar golden yellow. The Spotted Dead Nettle (*Lamium galaeobdolon*), having heart-shaped leaves blotched with silver and yellow flowers, is used effectively for ground cover among beds of herbaceous plants and Roses. One island bed is planted exclusively with *Scabiosa caucasica* 'Clive Greaves'. The large flowers are a beautiful shade of lavender blue. Where the hill shelves down to the river Leet, there is a copse of Cherry trees, underplanted in a formal style with Box, the best of our native evergreens.

23 THE HOLMES
St Boswells
Between St Boswells and Newtown St Boswells, on east side of the A68.
(Mr & Mrs William P. Dale)

In 1895, Norman Ritchie demolished the eighteenth-century house and erected on the foundations the present one of The Holmes. It retains many of the distinguishing features of a Victorian country house, with bathrooms and cloakrooms and fireplaces in the style of that period, and bell-pulls for calling the servants from the kitchen quarters.

The stable block, built in 1904, is still preserved. Bridges cross the wild garden ravine to the walled garden, made the same year and retaining its original formality, prolific old fruit trees, and a 'Mackenzie and Moncur' greenhouse containing a Grape-Vine.

The land hereabouts was once in the ownership of the Earl of Buchan, including Dryburgh Abbey across the Tweed, which then stood in the midst of his orchards, on a low green haugh by 'chiming Tweed'. The situation is a most desirable one, with views from the lawns of the river winding grandly, and the brown sandstone Abbey ruins shrouded in summer foliage.

The policies of The Holmes include more than 2½ acres of garden around the house (not counting the acre of walled garden), a derelict Japanese garden, woods of fine trees, parks and ¾ mile of the River Tweed. The soil is not easily cultivable — a mix of silt, clay, and rubble — but with the advantages of a mild,

reasonably dry climate and sheltered locality, a renewal of the garden is planned, to extend its appeal throughout the four seasons with many more plants and flowering shrubs and specimen trees. At present, it is at its best in mid April, the time of the Daffodils flowering across the lawns and parks, and Wild Garlic and Bluebells in the ravine.

These are the 4 acres of walled garden belonging to Hopetoun House (q.v.), the splendid ancestral home of the Marquess of Linlithgow. They are located unobtrusively within the magnificent landscaped policies and were designed to fulfil the customary 'kitchen' and 'picking garden' functions.

Throughout the years, ever since the great mansion was constructed by Sir William Bruce and the Adam father and sons in the eighteenth century, the gardens have been cultivated to meet the changing needs and desires of successive generations of the Hope family. Since 1979, however, they have been replanted and landscaped to complement the estate's Garden Centre at Hopetoun Gardens, whose function is to stimulate ideas, and to demonstrate to visitors plants grown on a commercial basis.

The walled garden has a central running stream, with a formal garden on one side and an informal woodland garden on the other, the whole being subdivided into an all-seasons mixed border and rock garden; a north-facing courtyard and water garden; a Rose garden; a woodland garden with a lake; a flower-arranger's garden; and a herb and vegetable garden.

The gardens are situated at sea level and are partially protected from the winds blowing up the Forth valley by woodland and high south-facing walls. Winters seldom bring much long-lying snow, and the proximity of the site to the Firth means that there is little danger from frost pockets.

Hopetoun House, ancestral home of the Marquess of Linlithgow, has been called a palace by virtue of its grand style and dimensions. The 1st Earl of Hopetoun employed an architect of palaces, Sir William Bruce, to design his new mansion, and building began in 1699. Later extensions were added during the period 1721-54 by William Adam and his sons John and Robert. They completed the magnificent central structure of a four-storied block, with curved arcaded wings and two-storied end pavilions, surmounted by cupolas.

The house, on its terrace site above the Forth, commands fine prospects as far west as Ben Lomond and east to the Isle of May, and the policies of 100 acres include a deer park with fallow and red deer and St Kilda sheep, and wide lawns limited by ha-has where the smooth grass merges into the rough.

The 12 acres of garden were originally laid out in the style of Versailles, and although the formal parterres have long since disappeared, their patterns can still be seen on the lawns after a hard frost or heavy summer dew. The Spring Garden, with a burn running through it, is generously planted with flowering shrubs and bulbs. Rhododendrons and Azaleas, under mature specimen trees,

24 HOPETOUN
GARDENS
South Queensferry
2 miles west of South
Queensferry, route A90 or
M9.
(MR DOUGAL PHILIP, tenant)

25 HOPETOUN HOUSE
South Queensferry
2 miles west of South
Queensferry, route A90 or
M9.
(HOPETOUN HOUSE
PRESERVATION TRUST)

FIGURE 41
Meconopsis × sheldonii,
*a wonderful garden-raised
hybrid which occurred
spontaneously at East
Grinstead, W. Sussex*

FIGURE 42
*The blossom of the Japanese
Flowering Cherry,* Prunus
yedoensis

bring pools of rich colour to the woods, and contrast with the dark foliage of Hollies and Yews.

26 HOUNDWOOD
   HOUSE
🐾 *Reston*
2 miles north of Reston on A1.
(MR W. W. QUARRY)

Standing on a hillside above the valley of the Eye, Houndwood House was built in 1140 as a hunting lodge for the Priors of Coldingham. It has the character of a Border keep, with massive walls, pierced with loops and tiny iron-barred windows. An interior stone byre was used for keeping cattle safe from border raiders. Mary, Queen of Scots, spent a night here, on her way to Craigmillar Castle after visiting her uncle, the Prior of Coldingham.

The policies amount to 10 acres, and 10 more are currently being landscaped. The garden consists of natural woodland, with extensive lawns, all well sheltered and gently undulating. The soil is dry loam and the average rainfall low — a mere 28 inches per annum. There is a Japanese garden, and a walled garden used for vegetables, as well as a greenhouse and vinery.

E. Waller Cameron, writing in the *Scottish Field* of June 1918, went into ecstasies over the Rhododendrons in the Houndwood House gardens: 'myriad hued, and when their riot of colour has subsided, the saffron tints of climbing Honeysuckle sprays take their place, and the warm insistent perfume hangs on the breeze and becomes an integral part of the drowsy midsummer day'.

Without the stone-rimmed water lily pond, the beauty of the garden would be incomplete.

27 INVERESK LODGE
🐾 *Inveresk,*
   Musselburgh
7 miles from Edinburgh on A1, then A614
(NATIONAL TRUST FOR SCOTLAND)

The village of Inveresk is in itself a place of considerable interest and charm. Full of contrasts, with its large mansion houses and small cottages, it has tremendous strength of personality, if anything emphasised by the unusual ochre colour of some of the buildings.

When Mrs Helen Brunton presented Inveresk Lodge to the National Trust for Scotland in 1959, it was seen as an opportunity to secure a foothold in an area of great historic and architectural importance, albeit well and conscientiously protected by a very active preservation society. The Lodge is situated on the south side of the main road which passes through the village, and at the extreme east end. Extending east from the house there is a section of about 3 acres above the retaining wall, which divides this, the garden area, from the remaining 6 acres or so of paddock and shelter woodland. From the higher level the view to the west is long and magnificent, even to the outskirts of the City of Edinburgh 7 miles distant.

Mrs Brunton was a keen gardener, but sadly a serious illness deprived her of the pleasure of enjoying her garden. Such was its state of disrepair that the Trust had to re-make the greater part of it. It was decided to design something small and easily maintained, in which could be illustrated a range of plants that are readily obtained. It was only later that a survey of 1851 came to light showing that, by pure chance, the same basic pattern had been followed.

The design is fairly simple. A cross axis through the centre of the garden allows beds to be gathered around the axis and borders along the perimeter of the garden, which provide a varying interest as well as an effective screen to ensure the garden will not be too obvious from any one point. There are several small to medium-sized trees, those such as Rowan and Cherry being prominent, carefully integrated groups of shrubs and herbaceous plants and a mixture of alpines in the paving by the house.

Graham Thomas designed the Shrub Rose border, and to complement this are displayed a selection of Climbing Roses on the wall behind. In the easternmost part a raised bed in front of a wall was covered with gravel, to keep it relatively weed free, and used to exhibit a range of small growing plants.

A very handsome glasshouse was acquired with the garden, and was subsequently restored by a Manpower Services Commission team. A fine sundial which was originally at Pitreavie now makes an excellent centrepiece for the garden at Inveresk.

The garden at Inveresk may not be outstanding, but it is certainly pleasant, and one which will most certainly appeal to those who own small gardens. It is here they can glean many ideas and find great enjoyment in their visit.

The gardens are open all year — Monday, Wednesday and Friday 10.00 a.m.-4.30 p.m. Also Sunday 2.00-5.00 p.m. when the house is occupied.

Kailzie House, a plain two-storied mansion of the early part of the nineteenth century, has been demolished and its place taken by a modern house, built on the old farm. The gardens extend to 17 acres, including the woodland and burnside walks.

28 KAILZIE
By Peebles
2 miles east of Peebles, on B7062.
(MRS M. A. RICHARD)

Gardening conditions in Peeblesshire are not generally easy, and although Kailzie's soil is a rich loam, the situation is exposed — at 650 feet above sea level — and subject to severe wintry weather. However, the walls of the formal garden are 15 feet high and it is surrounded by sheltering woods, among which is a Larch, said to have been planted in 1725, and an old Copper Beech which is split, and cured by iron braces.

The garden was laid out in the eighteenth century, but has been re-created by the present owner within the last fifteen years. It contains many beautiful hardy shrubs and a collection of Shrub Roses. The old conservatory, in the Regency style, has been extended and houses a very fine assemblage of exotic 'stove' plants, Camellias, Orchids, and Pelargoniums. A stream garden, planted with many different Primulas, Meconopses, Astilbes, Azaleas and bog plants, runs by a woodland walk, leading out to an aviary stocked with rare and beautiful birds.

Two miles east of Peebles, in the Tweed valley, Kailzie is becoming an attractive visitors' centre, with its aviary, art exhibitions in the old stables, a tea room, and the gardens where there is something of seasonal interest from March's early bulbs right through to October's brilliant autumn foliage.

This handsome Tudor-style mansion was designed by Blore of London and completed about the year 1830. The magnificent site, a wooded height over-hanging Ale Water, is said to have been chosen by Sir Walter Scott for his friend, Mr Richardson; and, indeed, there is a way through the garden called Sir Walter Scott's Walk. The house was enlarged to designs by Sir Robert Lorimer, and from the terrace one can hear the rush of Ale Water over the rocks below.

Apart from the kitchen garden, discreetly located a short distance off, there is little space given to horticulture, though several choice and beautiful plants flourish in borders against the house.

Worthy of particular mention is *Clematis orientalis,* called the 'Orange Peel' Clematis because of its deep orange-yellow flowers with petals thick as orange peel. It comes from the mountains of India and North Asia, and the clusters of silky white tails that are attached to the seed heads remain for much of the winter.

A fine *Magnolia soulangiana*, which has white chalice-shaped flowers flushed with purple, grows strongly by the front door; and a tender young plant of *Carpentaria californica*, carrying large clusters of fragrant white flowers, may soon cover much of the gable. A small shrubbery contains the Chinese woody-stemmed *Paeonia lutea*, also the semi-evergreen *Viburnum × burkwoodii* which has richly scented flowers, pink in the bud, in spring; several ornamental Cherries; and the bright yellow-fruited Malus or Flowering Crab, *Malus* 'Golden Hornet'. There was at one time a Rose garden, which was destroyed by roe deer which came down to the parkland from the wild country in search of winter feed.

29 KIRKLANDS

Ancrum, Roxburghshire

Less than a mile west-north-west of Ancrum village.
(LIEUTENANT-COLONEL & MRS MONTAGUE DOUGLAS SCOTT)

The present farmhouse of Lambden was built in 1840 by Robert Nisbet, in the distinctive Adam style. He had previously lived in a house by the farm steading, one field to the south, and, having contemplated the change for some time, made the walled garden in 1832 and established the other garden areas well in advance of moving his chattels into his new home. It stands on level, wooded ground, overlooking the Tweed valley and in sight of the Cheviot Hills.

Besides the walled garden, which is formal in layout, there are 3 acres of lawns, woodland and shrub borders, a rock garden made in 1920, and ½ acre of orchard and kitchen garden. The soil is heavy clay, with a high lime content. Lime-loving and lime-tolerant plants thrive here, as do Meconopses and Primulas, if given plenty of leaf mould.

The farm keeps racehorses, so there is always plenty of stable manure, and this to some extent accounts for the garden's beautiful Roses. There are over two hundred and fifty varieties of them — Species Roses, hybrid Teas, Floribundas, modern and old-fashioned Shrub Roses, and Climbers. Close to the house, a *Rosa filipes* 'Kiftsgate' and the Musk Rose, *Rosa moschata* floribunda, have clambered 40 feet into a large conifer, wreathing its sinewy limbs with creamy-white flowers. The giant Himalayan Lily (*Cardiocrinum giganteum*) has established itself

30 LAMBDEN

Greenlaw, Duns

8 miles north of Coldstream, 3 miles south of Greenlaw, 1 mile west of A697.
(MR D. M. THOMSON. *The garden is managed by* MISS JEAN THOMSON, *the owner's sister*)

FIGURE 43
Kailzie – the walled garden

in a bed of Musk Roses, its tall stems bearing glistening white trumpets in mid summer. A notable feature is a hedge of *Fuchsia* 'riccartonii', over seventy summers old, and a tribute to the climate and the sheltering trees on the north, west, and east. The garden also possesses a wealth of herbaceous plants.

31 LOCHSIDE
Yetholm

Off B6352 Kelso-Yetholm road, signposted 'Lochside'.
(MR & MRS J. HURST)

Mr Hurst, a dairy farmer, settled at Lochside twelve years ago, but his wife's kinsfolk, the Olivers, have resided there since 1778. In 1965 a Norway Maple (*Acer platanoides*) was planted in the parkland above Yetholm loch to commemorate the one hundredth birthday of Admiral of the Fleet Sir Henry Oliver, Mrs Hurst's great-uncle. The tree was a happy choice, being one of the few Maples carrying attractive yellow flowers, hanging in bunches from the twigs before the leaves open in the late spring. In autumn, the foliage turns a brilliant red or yellow.

The garden has recently been re-made by Mr Hurst and his wife. It occupies a dene, partially shaded by mature, overhanging trees, and had lain somewhat neglected ever since the 1914-18 war. Until they took it in hand, much of the flat area was a tangle of old Yew trees, planted in Victorian times as hedging or for ornamental effect.

Another obstacle was a small gas-works, installed by the enterprising Olivers in 1858, to provide domestic lighting and heating. Having removed the gasometer and an accumulation of tarry clinker and coal dross, Mr Hurst used the stone wall that had encircled the gas tank to make a garden pool. The garden is full of the sound of running water; a burn swirls through the centre, and water still flows down from the old mill lade, disappearing underground. Water in sunlight, water in shade enhance the garden's tranquil beauty, and increase the plantsman's scope. The growing area has been extended by bull-dozing the steep sides of the dene into terraces, retained by stones from the demolished walls of the water mill. This undertaking brought to the surface sub-soil, buried under loads of good loam, imported from the fields.

The garden's year begins with the Snowdrops, followed by many other spring bulbs. There follow the Primulas and Meconopses, rejoicing in damp soil and dappled shade. Herbaceous plants and an orchard occupy the high levels, and the garden reaches its zenith in June and July. To prolong the rich tapestry of colour, any gaps are filled with bedding plants.

Lochside's less well known plants include eight different varieties of Codonopsis, these delicate bell-shaped flowers on slender curving stems. If bruised they emit a foxy odour, and they depend on wasps for pollination. *Calamintha nepetoides*, having Nepeta-like foliage and aromatic lavender and white flowers, prefers partial shade. The Himalayan Whorlflower, *Morina longifolia,* has thistly leaves; its flowers turn from white to pink to crimson.

Gardens of this size can accommodate old Shrub Roses. Here you find the pink, semi-double sprawler *R.* × *macrantha* 'Raubritter' diffusing a slight fragrance.

Grey walls of the farm steading are smothered beneath flowering creepers, Clematis of different kinds, including *C. rehderana,* resembling a Hop with its delicate leaves and nodding clusters of small fragrant yellow-green flowers.

By September, the sun visits the garden less and less, until a dowdiness comes over it. Mr Hurst intends to correct this by planting the far bank of the dene with shrubs that will provide brilliant autumn foliage. Mrs Hurst's main interest is the greenhouse; one glass wall is hung with intertwining tendrils of *Passiflora caerulea,* the Passion Flower, dwarfed by the exotic *Tibouchina semidecandra,* whose flowers are a rich purple with a satin sheen.

Gospatrick, 6th Earl of March and Dunbar, was on his way to join the seventh Crusade when he fell gravely ill. As he lay dying, he besought a Carmelite friar to have his body embalmed and taken back for burial to his native land. The friar kept faith and, for his reward from Gospatrick's kinsfolk, received 6 acres of land nearby on which to build a monastery and pray for the soul of the earl.

32 LUFFNESS
Aberlady
1 mile east of Aberlady, off the A198 Musselburgh-Gullane road.
(COLONEL & MRS A. J. G. HOPE)

The ruins of the Carmelite church still remain, standing in the woods of the Friarsward, from whence a path leads to the thirteenth-century tower-house where Gospatrick lived, now part of a much ampler sixteenth-century dwelling, Luffness House, erected by the Hepburns, and acquired by Charles Hope, 1st Earl of Hopetoun, in 1715.

Perhaps the most illustrious of the Hopes, who are still the lairds of Luffness, was Sir Alexander Hope. He covered himself with glory at the battle of Corunna during the Peninsular War, became Governor of Edinburgh Castle, founded Sandhurst Royal Military College and was Governor of Chelsea Royal Hospital. In his time, French prisoners of war were put to work on the Luffness estate and erected the walled gardens in the style of a French *jardin clos*, that is with one walled garden inside another. The design is such that the gardens receive the maximum possible sun, and the walls have a coping of red pantiles.

The first Apricots to be grown in Scotland ripened in the Luffness garden, and hardly a year passes without a rich harvest of these, as well as Nectarines, Figs, Apples, Pears, soft fruits and every variety of vegetables. One of the Fig trees was planted to commemorate the great victory over the French at Waterloo.

Sir Alexander Hope's son John married Lady Frances Lascelles, a daughter of the Harewood family, but during their honeymoon in Florence he caught diphtheria and died. When the tragic young widow returned, she was received with kindness by her brother-in-law, the new Laird of Luffness. To console her, he had part of the old moat filled in and the garden extended, so that she might walk there when she pleased. It may be that the so-called Italian Garden took its name from this incident. This is a Rose garden, with a sundial at the centre, on the south side of the house, sheltered by Yew hedges.

The east front of Luffness, with its great recessed doorway and massive walls, is impressive. There is an ancient doocot by the carriageway, and a loupin'-on-stane (horse-block) for less agile horse-riders.

33 MAINHOUSE
꙳ Kelso

Kelso 4 miles, Morebattle 4
miles. Take road signposted
to Morebattle off B6351
Yetholm-Kelso road.
(MR & THE HON MRS SCOTT
PLUMMER)

This is a farmhouse, set in high-yielding agricultural land and dating, probably,
from the seventeenth century, with an additional wing built on in 1875. Though
the garden area is not large, it has been planned and planted with discrimination
and a refined taste, and the farmhouse walls, colour-washed white faintly tinged
with pink, make an effective backdrop.

The open situation receives some shelter from hedges of Beech, but the part
on the west side is mostly lawn with side borders of shrubs and alpines. The
heavy soil is a favourable medium for growing Roses and the garden's best
months are the mid-summer ones, when the Shrub Roses are in full flower. The
old Chinese perpetual 'Fellenberg' is well established against a house wall.
Amongst the alpines, planted for good drainage close to a retaining wall, one
finds *Euryops acraeus*, a dense silvery-leafed shrublet with yellow Daisy flowers.
Nearby, clumps of *Nerine bowdenii* with bright pink flowers make a brave show
far into the autumn.

A medium-sized Oak tree dominates the north end of the lawn, opposite a
small arbour, commanding distant views of the Cheviot Hills and the farmland
rolling towards the Border. Close at hand, and equally eye-catching, there is a
beautiful, shapely specimen of *Cornus kousa*, the flowering Dogwood, with
creamy-white bracts, followed by fruits of a strawberry shape, and vivid
autumn foliage.

Across the carriageway lies another garden where a long line of Scots Roses
conceals the vegetable area. Here the central point is an old statue of a goddess of
plenty, stationed beneath an Apple tree, with clumps of sweet-smelling *Daphne
retusa* about her feet.

34 MALLENY HOUSE
꙳ Balerno

From Edinburgh 8 miles on
the A70 road, and turn off to
Balerno.
(NATIONAL TRUST FOR
SCOTLAND)

Another of the National Trust for Scotland's smaller garden properties, which
came as a gift from Mrs Gore-Browne Henderson, herself a keen gardener and
rosarian.

The property has a fascinating history, especially concerning the house, and
the Scott family, who for many years inhabited it, but the garden and its
contents are fairly recent introductions by Mrs Gore-Browne Henderson. Sir
Herbert Maxwell included Malleny in his book, *Scottish Gardens*, with an
illustration of the garden as a frontispiece. Possibly it was the rather intriguing
historical background to the garden as much as anything which attracted Sir
Herbert's curiosity, and little wonder with the shield of a one-time owner, Lord
Rosebery, prominently displayed, together with a few of the figures wrought in
metal by a tenant of his, Sir Thomas Carmichael, whose particular interest and
hobby this was. To add further to enchantment, four large Yews — thought to
have been planted in 1610 — stand sentinel in a central position in the garden.

Basically the garden is a walled one, now with the fourth side open, removed
when the forecourt to the House was extended with the addition of the Georgian
rooms. It covers an area of approximately 4 acres. In addition there is a thin area
of woodland, effectively screening the house from a housing development in the

FIGURE 44
*Manderston, earlier in this
century*

neighbouring village of Balerno.

When Commander and Mrs Gore-Browne Henderson came to live at Malleny in 1960, the garden was by no means outstanding, and furthermore was greatly overshadowed by a further eight large Yews (together with those in the centre known as the Twelve Apostles), which were subsequently removed. At that time the enthusiasm of a neighbour, Roger Hog, had a telling effect upon future plans for the garden, and gradually more and more Shrub Roses were planted. Together with those the Trust have since added, they now form a good collection. It is a very cosmopolitan collection, without emphasis on any particular period, simply choosing what was felt to be the best of those available. They are associated with herbaceous and bulbous plants and shrubs such as Philadelphus, Kolkwitzia, as well as the smaller growing Potentillas, Thymes and Sages.

A recent improvement has been the development of part of the woodland garden, following a fairly substantial thinning and removal of several ageing and potentially dangerous trees. This offered the opportunity to provide colour for the early part of the year, which, of course, the Shrub Roses could not do, and by so doing to increase the general interest of the property.

A delightful garden in summer and especially for those who have a particular interest in shrub roses. It is open from 1 May to 30 September daily 10.00 a.m. to dusk.

35 MANDERSTON
❧ Duns
Signposted 1½ miles east of Duns.
(MR & MRS ADRIAN PALMER)

The entrance front to Manderston is twentieth-century, though deceptively like an eighteenth-century building. In fact, it replaced a house of the 1790s, built by Dalhousie Weatherstone. Richard Miller became the proprietor in 1855, bequeathing it five years later to his brother, William, a highly successful merchant who traded with Russia in hemp and herrings. He became a Liberal Member of Parliament, first for Leith, then Berwickshire, and was created a baronet on the recommendation of a grateful Mr W. E. Gladstone in 1874.

Sir William Miller's son, Sir James Miller, was anxious to impress his father-in-law, Lord Scarsdale, of Kedleston Hall, Derbyshire, and in 1901 engaged the eminent Scottish architect, John Kinross, to remodel Manderston in an imposing style. It has since been rated the finest Edwardian country house in Britain.

Four years later, Sir James and Kinross addressed their minds to landscaping the 56 acres of policies to a design more appropriate to the character of the rebuilt mansion, while retaining the spacious lawns and 1760 layout on the north side, stretching to the formal garden, and beyond to the earlier stables, the farm, the Marble Dairy and the ornate Scots baronial head-gardener's house and tower. Kinross designed the four terraces to the south and east of the mansion. They are laid out in a formal style, embellished with statuary supplied by a famous art dealer of that period, Lord Duveen.

The symmetry and regular lines of the south terrace are softened by parterres of Roses and Hostas. Four large stone vases, set equidistantly above the grass terrace on the east side, reiterate the disciplined architectural order of the gardens. Below there is a lavishly-wrought iron gate, between piers surmounted by stone griffons.

Beyond the south terraces, grass banks shelve down to a belt of Rhododendrons by the lake, and the eighteenth-century Chinese bridge leading to the Woodland Garden. The Woodland Garden was developed by Major Bailie, the present owner's father, from the mid 1950s onwards, and contains many rare specimens of Rhododendron and Azalea. Towards the top of the hill are peat beds, planted with no less than one hundred and eighty species and hybrid dwarf Rhododendrons. The south terrace looks across the Merse towards the Cheviot Hills.

The house was built between 1750 and 1754 by the last Earl of Marchmont, to supersede Redbraes Castle, 200 yards to the east. The semi-Palladian building was once thought to be designed by William Adam, for the 2nd Earl and built after the death of both of them by the brothers Adam; but it is now ascribed to Thomas Gibson. It is, however, a listed 'A' building, the large music room and fine plaster work in the main rooms being quite outstanding. A modernisation of the house was carried out in 1913-20 by Sir Robert Lorimer.

At 500 feet above sea level, it occupies an imposing site, in beautiful scenery, and has a commanding view of the Cheviot Hills. The climate is dry, with a prevailing west wind. Marchmont was a weather recording station for over a hundred years, one of the earliest to be instituted in Scotland.

The soil in Berwickshire is amongst the most fertile and highly productive in the country, a medium loam with a high pH rating. The 6-acre garden at Marchmont was first laid out in the mid eighteenth century by the 3rd Lord Marchmont, who built the house, with some extension and renewal being carried out during the Victorian era. There is a walled garden, most admirably situated for sun and shelter, and greenhouses, added in the early 1900s.

Lady McEwen planned and planted the Herb Garden; the remainder is mainly lawns and a Natural Garden, planted with spring-flowering bulbs, which have been regularly augmented over the years, and there are many Rhododendrons, Azaleas, and other fine shrubs and trees, including a Fern-leaf Beech (*Fagus sylvatica* 'Heterophylla'). There is also a cherished *Arbutus* × *andrachnoides*, a hybrid between the Greek *A. andrachne* and the Killarney Strawberry Tree (*A. unedo*), much admired for its cinnamon-red trunk and branchlets. The small, urn-shaped, pale pink flowers bloom in early to late winter, at the same time as the strawberry-like fruit appears, produced from last year's blossom.

Scotland is justifiably proud of Mellerstain, one of the great Georgian houses, commissioned in 1725 by Lady Grisell Baillie, daughter and heiress of George Baillie of Jerviswood and Mellerstain. She married in 1719 Charles, Lord Binning, eldest son of the 6th Earl of Haddington. The wings of the mansion

36 MARCHMONT
Polwarth
1 *mile from Polwarth,*
3 *miles from Greenlaw, on*
the A6105 Greenlaw-Duns
road.
(LADY MCEWEN)

37 MELLERSTAIN
Gordon

were built by William Adam, and the whole achieved in the period 1770–78 by his son Robert, appointed to the work by George Baillie, grandson of Lady Grisell. The interior has all the exquisite décor and furnishings associated with the younger Adam, and the exterior is equally impressive, possessing the symmetrical dignity and fine proportions of a richly endowed mansion of the period, seen to advantage in the light-coloured masonry.

MELLERSTAIN
(contd.)
6 miles north-west of Kelso, off A6089.
(LORD & LADY BINNING)

The house stands at an altitude of 600 feet, in a formal garden, laid out in 1909 by Sir Reginald Blomfield. This occupies an extension in raised terraces and balustrades and stairways of the house itself, with parterres on the upper levels planted with Rose bushes and conical-shaped Yew trees, descending to lawns and parklands, fringed with trees. The view, seen from the south front, includes a lake in the long strip of park, and the Cheviot Hills in the distance.

Plantings of Azaleas and Rhododendrons bring colour to the disciplined formality, and, in complete contrast, there is a thatched cottage with its own small, self-contained garden.

FIGURE 45
Mellerstain

Mertoun House was built in 1703 by Sir William Bruce for Sir William Scott of Harden. The Victorian additions were removed by the Duke of Sutherland (as Earl of Ellesmere) in 1954, the programme of reduction being put in the hands of the Scottish architect, Mr Ian G. Lindsay. This beautifully proportioned edifice, constructed of pink freestone, surveys wide parks and woodlands close to the great river Tweed.

38 MERTOUN
St Boswells
(THE DUKE OF SUTHERLAND)

Old Mertoun House, dating back to 1677, now accommodates the Mertoun estates gardener and his family, and has cellars for storing seeds, bulbs, and tubers; the management prides itself on its self-sufficiency, uses its own disease-free seeds and abstains from the employment of chemical pesticides.

The extensive glasshouses nearby produce many stove plants, flowers and fruit for marketing, including Figs and Peaches; while the orchard trees in autumn are bowed with the burden of their fruit. Further down the slope to the river stands the laird's doocot, erected in 1576. Once the bottom of the dell was covered with Phlox, all since removed.

Sadly, many of the old flower borders in the gardens have been grassed over or replaced with Azaleas and other shrubs, to save labour. On the other hand, specimen trees are being planted across the lawns — the Himalayan Birch (*Betula utilis*), Tibetan Cherry (*Prunus serrula*), Weeping Elms, the Willow-leafed Pear (*Pyrus salicifolia*) and orderly stands of Poplars (*eugenii*).

According to local records, the house of Netherbyres belonged in 1550 to a heritor by the name of Crow, or Craw, and his descendants retained possession for the next two hundred and sixty-four years. A landmark on the Merse, it is shown on a map of 1645 and on several subsequent ones, including that of 1771. William Crow of Netherbyres was respected for his mathematical and mechanical genius, and in 1747, three years before his death, he planned the Old Pier at

39 NETHERBYRES
Eyemouth
On A1107, ¼ mile south of Eyemouth.
(LIEUTENANT-COLONEL S. J. FURNESS)

Eyemouth and got it built by public subscription, an enterprise which increased the prosperity of the port.

The walled garden at Netherbyres was also the work of William Crow, and bears the stamp of a mathematical mind: the wall is elliptical, enclosing a mathematically-conceived design inside it, of division and sub-division. The oval wall is built of stone on the outside, and one half is faced with Dutch bricks. The second half was obviously lower when first constructed, and before the trees grew up it was probably possible to see into the garden from the house windows. Later it was built up to the same height as the rest of the wall, and the facing bricks are not the same as the earlier ones — probably still Dutch but of a later manufacture. Eyemouth exported wool and linen to Holland, and the bricks may have been brought back as ballast, to weigh down the empty ships' holds in heavy seas.

Captain Sir Samuel Brown, R.N., acquired the Netherbyres mansion and lands between 1822 and 1830. A man of the calibre and genius of William Crow, he built the iron suspension Union Bridge over the Tweed at Paxton in 1820, and also the chain pier at Brighton, for which achievements he was knighted by Queen Victoria in 1838. Brown demolished the old edifice of Netherbyres, but spared some outbuildings belonging to the same period as the Walled Garden of 1½ acres. The approaches to the new mansion were improved by the erection of Sir Samuel's own 'Tension Bridge' across the Eye Water. It had to be demolished in 1929 because of its dangerous condition.

The country hereabouts is richly fertile and the Ordnance map, surveyed in 1856, considered the garden at Netherbyres worthy of record. There was a fountain at the centre, and the front was landscaped with trees, shrubs and paths. Today the walled garden stands in a parkland of 40 acres. There is a nineteenth-century greenhouse with Vines, a very necessary adjunct for nurturing young plants in spring; the house lies close to the rugged Berwickshire coast, and the garden is much exposed to cold east winds off the sea.

40 ROYAL BOTANIC GARDEN
Edinburgh

Approximately 1 mile north of Edinburgh city centre, between Arboretum Road and Inverleith Row.
(DEPARTMENT OF AGRICULTURE & FISHERIES IN SCOTLAND)

The Royal Botanic Garden originated as a Physic Garden, founded in 1670 by Sir Andrew Balfour of Denmyln and Sir Robert Sibbald of Gibliston, who was King's Physician to Charles II. The first site of the garden was a small plot of ground in Holyrood Park, and its founders' intentions were to oppose the activities of vendors of quack medicines.

The space having become too restricting, the Garden was transferred in 1675 to an ampler locality close to the Old Trinity Hospital, where Waverley Station now is, Balfour and Sibbald being elected official visitors to the Trinity Hospital gardens. Their extent was about 300 feet from east to west, divided into six plots, three on each side of the canal which provided an outlet for the Nor' Loch. The plots were arranged according to plant genera and species.

One part of the garden, called 'The Dispensatoria', was intended for the instruction of medical students. James Sutherland, holder of the office of 'Intendant', catalogued two thousand plants in the garden in his *Hortus Medicus Edinburgensis*.

During the siege of Edinburgh Castle in 1689, the Nor' Loch had to be drained and water overflowed the Physic Garden, doing irreparable damage to many of the more tender plants. The garden was transferred in 1763 to Haddington Place, Leith Walk. It was moved again in 1820 to its present site on the west side of Inverleith Row, where it covered some 14 acres. (There are now approximately 70 acres.)

The modern development of the garden began in 1888, with the appointment of Sir Isaac Bayley Balfour as Regius Keeper. Soon thereafter it came under the control of Her Majesty's Office of Works. About this time the Arboretum was planted, the Rock Garden constructed, a new range of glasshouses erected, and the Laboratories reorganised and provided with new accommodation and equipment for botanical research and teaching.

Sir William Wright Smith, Balfour's successor, was mainly responsible for the creation of the Woodland and the Copse as they now are, for the construction of the Heath and Peat gardens, and the addition of two screes to the Rock Garden.

The main purpose of the garden is, of course, botanical research, especially research in taxonomy — that is, the accurate classification, identification and distribution of plants, work made possible by the collections in the modern Herbarium (containing over one and a half million specimens) and information available in the garden's Library, one of the wealthiest taxonomic libraries in the world.

These considerations apart, to the layman who cares for beautiful plants the garden is an earthly Paradise, and one of the brightest jewels in Edinburgh's crown.

The garden of the seventeenth-century Haddington House in Sidegate had become a grievously neglected orchard when the late Duke of Hamilton came to its rescue; he gave the ground to Haddington Garden Trust, a charity set up specifically 'to preserve the garden at Haddington House as an open public precinct and develop it as an old Scottish garden'.

41 SAINT MARY'S
PLEASANCE
Haddington
(HADDINGTON GARDEN TRUST)

These aims have been almost entirely achieved, and the old Haddington House Garden, re-named Saint Mary's Pleasance, has within its walls a number of interesting features.

The Sunk Garden, close to the house, resembles a knot garden, laid out in an intricate pattern of herbs and flowers. Beyond, and on the far side of the kitchen door, is the Rose and Herb Garden, full of fragrant Roses and culinary and medicinal herbs, and also containing a Medlar tree (*Mespilus*) and an Apricot against the brick wall — trees of a kind that were commonly seen in Scotland's gardens three hundred years ago.

The Apple House is a substantial stone shelter and a resting place. Inscribed on

FIGURE 46
Rhododendrons and Scots Pines in the Royal Botanic Garden, Edinburgh

FIGURE 47
St Mary's Pleasance, Haddington

an inside wall are these lines:

> Let the field be joyful and all that is therein
> then shall all the trees of the wood rejoice.

The Cottage Garden in front is a typical example of a simple country Scots village garden. A little further steps lead down to the Meadow Garden, filled with wild flowers and spring bulbs; and the Mount, a feature of ancient gardens, artificially constructed to provide a view of the surrounding countryside.

On the southern side of the Pleasance there is a flagged path. It leads through a boxed hornbeam alley and down the Laburnum Walk to the kirkyard of St Mary's, Haddington, a newly-restored medieval church, widely known as 'The Lamp of Lothian'. The brick wall between the Pleasance and the Kirk is reputed to have been built by French prisoners, taken during the Napoleonic wars.

An ancient flowering Crab, gnarled and stooped but still fruitful, overhangs the front entrance of Haddington House. It is the sole survivor of the orchard.

42 STEVENSON HOUSE
Near Haddington

2 miles from Haddington. Just east of town, turn right where signpost indicates 'Hailes Castle' and 'Stevenson'. Half a mile further on, 10 yards beyond entrance to Stevenson Mains, is the entrance to Stevenson Estate.
(DR J. C. H. DUNLOP *for the Brown Dunlop Country Homes Trust*)

There has been a house at Stevenson since the late thirteenth century when the property belonged to the Cistercian Nunnery in Haddington. All traces of earlier houses were destroyed in 1548 at the time of Hertford's invasion of Scotland.

The present house dates from 1560 and is designed on the well-known post-Reformation 'Grange Plan' — a four-square building round an open courtyard with spiral staircases in each corner. It is the only surviving inhabited house in Scotland built on this plan, which is still clearly discernible in spite of Georgian alterations in 1725 and 1820. These alterations left the house with an impressive staircase and two large reception rooms panelled in pine. At the same time the front facade of the house was streamlined and made symmetrical. The nineteenth-century garden, with Victorian layout, was derelict when inherited by the present owners in 1946. The whole has since been rehabilitated.

The walled garden is an interesting experiment. Distressed by the fate of so many country house kitchen gardens finally left uncultivated and with pigs running wild, the owners decided to try to see what could be made of such a feature without involving too much labour.

The layout was drastically altered by the present owners, advised by Mr Archibald Brockie, formerly head gardener at Tyninghame and head gardener at Stevenson for the last years of his active life. It was designed primarily as an ornamental garden, landscaped with trees and shrubs, but also allowing for the cultivation of vegetables in limited quantity. It was carefully planned so that it could be kept by one man with little or no additional help. The soil is heavy clay subsoil, but deep loam on the surface. The site is exposed to winds, despite good tree shelter. The walled garden (in the river valley) tends to be a frost pocket in severe winters.

The walled garden of 1¾ acres is landscaped with lawns, trees and shrubs. It also contains a herbaceous border and a small area which is intensively cultivated for vegetables. The garden in front of the house extending to 1½ acres is bordered by a copse planted with spring-flowering Aconites and Snowdrops. It has two large summer borders of herbaceous plants and Roses, and a spring border with bulbs and flowering shrubs succeeded by Astilbes and Hostas. There are also Rose garden and shrub borders. Throughout the garden there are good eighteenth-century stone statuettes.

The landscaping of the whole garden, and planting of fine shrubs and trees, have been the special interest of the present owners. The parks are being planted mainly with different varieties of Sycamore to give striking foliage effects in summer and autumn (*Acer Pseudoplatanus*, 'Crimson King', 'Leopoldii', 'Drummondii' and 'Worlei').

Tyninghame means 'the hamlet on the Tyne', but the house, park and gardens of the Tyninghame estate overlook the sandy Hedderwick Bay where the river Tyne flows out into the open sea.

Centuries ago the manor of Tyninghame, with the patronage of the church, belonged to the bishops of St Andrews, forming part of their regality on the south side of the Forth. But in 1553, as the storm clouds of the Reformation began to mass in the sky, Archbishop Hamilton, the last Catholic Archbishop of St Andrews, alienated the property to St Mary's College of the University.

In 1628, Tyninghame House and its lands were bought by Sir Thomas Hamilton of Binning, the wealthy Lord Advocate and confidant of James VI, who was known in Edinburgh among his familiars as 'Tam o' the Coogate' long after he had conferred upon him the grand title of 1st Earl of Haddington.

Thomas, the 6th Earl, married the Earl of Hopetoun's sister, and it was she who incited him to beome a tree-planter, beginning on Tyninghame Moor, site of Binning Wood, a forest of 400 acres, with thirteen rides, converging at four different points on a central glade. Later, he drew shelter belts along the enclosures of the estate's fields, and proceeded to experiment, in defiance of received opinion, with the planting of trees in sandy ground close to the sea shore. The plan succeeded.

Holly hedges were widely used in those days to provide shelter, and they became one of the most remarkable features of Tyninghame, standing 15-25 feet high and 10-13 feet broad at the base, and arranged in double rows, flanking walks and avenues.

The estate sacrificed much of its timber during the two World Wars, although on each occasion the depleted areas were quickly re-afforested. The great gale of 1968 inflicted further damage. The Holly hedges, once so trim, have now mostly disappeared, or survive as single trees.

The reduction in the number of estate workers has rendered some saving of labour in the gardens unavoidable, although Tyninghame is still a gardener's paradise, achieved over many years by a succession of able men. The woods provide good shelter, and the climate is sunny with a low rainfall. The soil is

43 TYNINGHAME
Dunbar
1 mile north of the A1, on the A198 to North Berwick.
(THE EARL OF HADDINGTON)

light, sandy loam, improved by large-scale dumping of peat, manure, compost and spent hops.

There is a walled garden of 4 acres, some distance from the house, and approached by the famous 'Apple Walk'. This was first planted in 1891 and became one of the garden's great delights. It was recently re-established, using the very pleasing hybrid flowering Crab-apples, such as *Malus* 'Golden Hornet' and *M.* 'John Downie'. Statues face each other from either end of the walk. Within the walls, the garden is formal in aspect, with high dividing Yew hedges, pedestalled urns, and classical statues set in embrasures cut in the Yew. A Florentine fountain stands at the intersection of paths.

Old herbaceous borders which needed so much labour have been cleared and replaced with one long, wide new border, planted with rare and exciting shrubs and trees. These include *Eriobotrya japonica* 'Loquat', a large-leafed shrub from Japan; *Paulownia tomentosa* from the same country; the Judas tree (*Cercis siliquastrum*); various rare Acers; the Oriental Plane (*Platanus orientalis*); the beautiful white-flowered *Stewartia pseudo-camellia*; and *Cornus nuttallii*.

The seventeenth-century Tyninghame mansion was enlarged by William Burn in 1828, and the gardens landscaped at the same period with a parterre, upper and lower terraces to the south, and shrubberies extending on each side of the house, to the west and the east. The parterre is laid out in a design of triangular Rose beds, cut into a square lawn. The Roses are all either white or golden — 'King's Ransom', 'Gold Jewel', 'Kerry Gold', and 'Iceberg'.

There are more Roses down either side of the long path by the south front — 'China Town' and 'Iceberg' planted opposite 'Felicia', 'Wendy Cussons', and 'Rosemary Rose', with Lavender for edging.

Steps lead down to a courtyard, planted with Hydrangeas, and many wall shrubs, such as *Ceanothus* 'Burkwoodii', Senecios, *Stranvaesia davidiana*, *Caryopteris* × *clandonensis*, and plants of *Agapanthus praecox*, a favourite of the gardeners. At the edge of the courtyard, a focal point is made by bushes of *Garrya elliptica* and *Carpentaria californica*. In the long herbaceous border, at the foot of the front terrace, there grows the Chatham Island Forget-me-Not (*Myosotidium hortensia*), a present to the Countess from the gardens at Inverewe.

What is known as 'Lady Haddington's Secret Garden' is a re-creation of an eighteenth-century French garden, containing old-fashioned Roses, Clematis, Tree Peonies, highly-scented 'Vestale' white Lilacs, and a row of pleached Apple trees. There is a bower, containing a statue of 'Summer', brought from Vicenza in Italy, and plants of pale blue Agapanthus beside the creamy-white, feathery plumes of *Cimicifuga racemosa*.

Through a gateway, a path leads to the woodland garden with beds of Camellias, Azaleas, Rhododendrons, *Philadelphus*, *Embothriums*, Shrub Roses and trees and shrubs selected for their autumn colours — *Parrotica persica*, *Sorbus sargentiana* and *Acer griseum*. In spring, the woods abound with Wild Primroses and Wild Hyacinths.

FIGURE 48
Agapanthus *and* Cimicifuga *in Lady Haddington's Secret Garden, Tyninghame*

**44 WHITCHESTER
🐾 *Duns***

*7 miles from Duns, among
the Lammermuir Hills, off
B6355.*
(MRS S. E. A. LANDALE)

The 7-acre garden is situated 850 feet above sea level, sheltered by Beech hedges and belts of trees. It is an outstanding plantsman's garden, full of rare shrubs and trees that are a challenge to the gardener's skill — Rhododendrons in plentiful variety, Eucryphias, various Acers, *Enkianthus campanulatus,* Magnolias, *Prunus serrula*, Embothriums, and *Hoheria sexstylosa* — to give a very abbreviated list. Most of these named are to be found in the Wild Garden, growing in light shade cast by the tree tops.

Two trained and long-serving gardeners are employed full-time, and the garden is run as a commerical concern, despite its distance from the large markets. Apart from the abundant produce from the kitchen garden, the trading is mainly concentrated on high-quality pot-plants — Cyclamen, Primulas, and Fuchsias (notably 'Rose of Castile') — and in exotic corsage and button-hole Orchids, Carnations, and Camellias.

In the greenhouse, two walls, each measuring some 8 feet by 15 feet are completely curtained by wire-trained *Camellia japonica* and *Camellia × williamsii*, producing exquisite flowers.

There is a mist propagating unit; the exotics produced include the Wax Flower (*Hoya carnosa*), trained along horizontal wires, *Streptosolen jamesonii*, another climber producing orange bell-shaped flowers hanging in lacy panicles, *Actinidia chinensis,* grown mainly for its cinnamon-brown fruits which are marketed as Chinese Gooseberries, and the beautiful, deep purple creeper *Tibouchina semidecandra.*

**45 WINTON HOUSE
🐾 *Pencaitland***

*Entrance drive of 1 mile,
starting in Pencaitland.*
(SIR DAVID & LADY OGILVY)

The twelfth-century landlords of Winton were the Setons. Their power greatly increased, and in 1620 the 3rd Earl of Winton commissioned William Wallace, the master mason whose name is associated with Heriot's Hospital in Edinburgh, to build the present Winton House (later Winton Castle). It remained unfinished until 1770. Meanwhile, the 5th Earl forfeited the estates in penalty for his Jacobite support in 1716, and they were sold to the York Buildings Company, being later acquired by Mrs Hamilton Nisbet, grand-daughter of James Hamilton, Lord Pencaitland. Her grand-daughter, Mary Campbell, married James, 5th Lord Ruthven in 1813.

The castle, notwithstanding these vicissitudes, is well preserved, a striking many-faceted edifice in the Scots style, with carved chimney stacks and ornately moulded plaster ceilings inside in the Renaissance manner.

On the south front, the formal garden descends to the level of the River Tyne in terraces, which are supported by the ancient retaining walls. The grey weathered stone makes a charming backdrop, shaded by a spreading Sycamore. The narrow flower borders contain herbaceous plants and shrubs — Magnolias, *Chaenomeles speciosa, Wisteria,* scented white and yellow winter Jasmines, Buddleias, old Species Roses, a *Ginkgo,* Lavender and venerable Yew trees.

In one retaining wall there is a stone, thus inscribed:
> 'Dounie Baugh,
> for eight years the faithful
> and affectionate companion
> of Lady Ruthven Winton. 1868'

Below, set in the river meadow, there is a formal garden, and at its centre a double wrought-iron peacock on a stone base.

114

MAP OF LOCATIONS

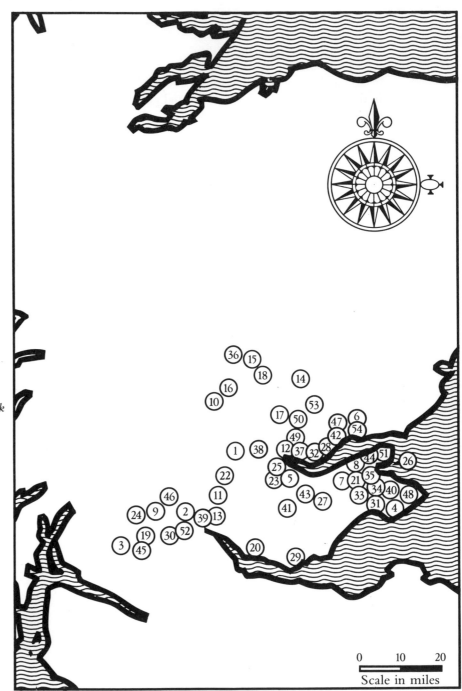

Scale in miles

EAST CENTRAL SCOTLAND

A stately old formal garden this, with long vistas down grass-grown alleys, overhung by drooping branches, and often ending in the darkness of the woods. Urns and statues from Greek mythology recall the grand style of Le Nôtre, as in a miniature Versailles, and there are stairways in the same formal mode leading from one grass terrace to the next. The small secret garden contains a curious sundial, carved with the date 1567.

1 ABERCAIRNY
Crieff

Crieff 4 miles, Perth 14 miles.
(MR W. S. H. DRUMMOND MORAY)

A broad central drive, also reminiscent of the sweeping approach to a French château, leads down to the site of the old House of Abercairny, usurped by a modern mansion, striking a discordant note after the dreamy antiquity of the garden. Beyond is a lake, and the valley of the Earn, and the distant Ochil Hills.

Maintained against great odds, the garden at Abercairny possesses the character and beauty of a faded dowager, defiant and proud of days long past, whose ultimate fate is increasing solitude.

The oldest part of Argaty, all of which is built of sandstone, dates from the late seventeenth century. At least six alterations and/or additions have taken place since then, the latest in 1935. The house enjoys wide views of the Gargunnock Hills, and south-westwards to the Ben Lomond area.

2 ARGATY
Doune

1 mile from Doune and 4½ miles from Dunblane. Signposted from the A820 Dunblane-Doune road.
(CAPTAIN D. S. BOWSER)

Most of the present garden was planted in the first half of the 1920s. Some of that has now disappeared, especially during the 1939-45 war and since. However, the main features survive, among them the Birk Wood with its Birches, Azaleas, flowering Cherries, Narcissi and Wild Hyacinths, where, within the last fifteen years, a number of exotic Conifers and Hardwoods have been planted. The walled garden includes a herbaceous border recreated in the last five years, and some interesting old Roses.

The full extent of the garden is approximately 20 acres, situated at 250 feet above sea level. It is exposed to the prevailing south-west wind, and liable to frost damage in almost any month of the year barring July.

Mrs A. Hope Henderson, grandmother of Captain Bowser and a former proprietor of Argaty, wrote a series of letters to *Gardening Illustrated* under the pseudonym of 'Grey Lady'. These were collected and published under the title *Garden Letters of 'Grey Lady'*, published in 1935 by Robert Grant & Son, Edinburgh.

Auchmar, with its view over Loch Lomond, is a garden created by the late Mary, Duchess of Montrose.

It was in 1935 that work began on the old eighteenth-century farmhouse at

3 AUCHMAR
Drymen

AUCHMAR (contd.)
*Milton of Buchanan, on
Drymen-Balmaha (B837)
road, 3 miles from Drymen.*
(THE MARQUIS OF GRAHAM)

Auchmar (the field of the Mar), to make it into a winter home for the Montrose family, in place of the over-large Buchanan Castle. Farm outhouses were turned into kitchen premises and garages, while an extensive new wing with windows facing Loch Lomond completely enveloped the old house. Work began later on the garden layout, under the Duchess's direction, and with the practised skill of MacKinnon the gardener; the aim was to make an autumn and spring garden.

A shelter belt of trees was planted, but they fell victims to the 1968 storm, uncovering a plantation of Pine trees, where the Willow Gentian (*G. asclepiadea*) now flourishes.

On the approach to the house, various species of colourful Berberis, mostly *aggregata* varieties, greet the eye, planted in a raised bed containing white Lilacs and *Prunus Cerasifera* 'Pissardii', the Cherry Plum with dark red foliage. This flanks the lawn, under the windows of the main rooms. Originally, the lawn ended in a ha-ha, cleared one day in a great long-jump by the Duke of York, later King George VI, when he and the Duchess were staying at Auchmar.

The lawns are the setting for the house, but the unique attraction of the site, besides the view, was the deep glen and waterfall on the Mar Burn to the south, many feet below. This is reached in stages.

First a grassy terrace was laid out along the south face of the house. Under the windows of the dining-room Scillas and early species Crocus flourish and seed. Below, and parallel to the house, a long low-walled garden was created, planted with autumn, winter and spring flowering shrubs, which include *Mahonia japonica, Viburnum farreri,* and *Kerria japonica* with its orange-yellow blossoms contrasting vividly with the royal blue *Pulmonaria azurea*, and patches of the brilliant red Kaffir Lily (*Schizostylis coccinea*) in autumn. In a corner, sheltered from the east and north, is *Ceroidiphyllum japonicum* with its autumn tints. Recently hybrids of *Paeonia lactiflorum* have been introduced.

On the south wall of this garden are trained several rose-flowered varieties of the Japanese Quince (*Chaenomeles japonica*), and also the climbing *Hydrangea petiolaris,* while outside the south-west corner a large specimen of the silver-leafed *Olearia macrodonta* is covered with daisy-like flowers in June.

The approach to the glen is through a small wrought iron gate, opening on to a grassy bank, which in spring is covered with a host of Daffodils. This leads on to a long line of steps running down to where the Mar Burn has cut a deep channel out of the hillside, and takes a right-angled turn, before tumbling over the waterfall, and on, out of sight. This ravine was obviously a delight and a challenge to the Duchess. In winter the Witch Hazel (*Hamamelis mollis*), planted on the bank, gives interest to the descent, which is caught at the bottom by a landscaped bed of Heaths and miniature Japanese Azaleas, among the rocks. Following the burn around, the path leads on to a bed of more Azaleas and, nearby, plantings of *Rhododendron* 'Praecox' and Japanese Maples, including the bronze-leafed *Acer palmatum* 'Dissectum Atropurpureum', Escallonia, a Bay tree, and Cherries with Heaths and Pulmonaria for ground cover. At this point, where the cliff ends with a promontory, a hump-backed bridge was built, leading to a small raised plateau, where species Rhododendrons were introduced among the trees.

Returning across the bridge, the eye is caught by the little raised wall in rough stone, flanking the burn, with pockets of Saxifrages which have survived the years. From under this wall a little stream was led off round below the cliff, under the new part of the house. Its banks were planted with Primulas, Hostas, the Dwarf Creeping Quince *Chaenomeles Speciosa* 'Simonii', *Narcissus cyclamineus,* and other treasures, including the spring and autumn flowering Cyclamens.

Unfortunately, the earth tremor of 1943, felt along the great fault of Scotland, caused a crack in the cliff under the house, and the base had to be shored up with rocks filling in the little stream at its feet. The top of the cliff then had to be cut out and bulldozed over the bank. This cutting can be seen today in the paved Rose garden, below the drawing-room windows.

Sadly, the Duchess died before she could plant the steep bank; but her grandson, the present Marquis of Graham, has planted Cotoneasters, Hypericum, heaths and other plants, which in time should make good ground cover and add interest to the view across to the waterfall, as seen from the house.

The last area to be developed by the Duchess after the war, with the help of Albert Sellar, was the spinney, to the west of the burn. A long grassy bank leads round and over the top of what is possibly an old burial mound, then down steep rocky steps to the foot of the waterfall. In spring, Daffodils and Rhododendrons and Azaleas flower beside this path, some brought up from Buchanan Castle.

Once again the windbreak of Fir trees to the west was brought down in a gale, and some of the more tender Rhododendrons have disappeared. But in spite of the shortage of labour and resources, the inspiration of the Duchess's garden, still tended by Albert Sellar, lives on.

Alexander III gave Ivor Cook a charter to the lands of Balcaskie in 1223. There was a castle of Balcaskie, purchased in 1663 from John Moncrieff by Sir William Bruce, the greatest Scottish architect of his day. He transformed the castle into a mansion and laid out the garden in terraces, remaining there with his family for twenty years. Part of that time, however, he spent building Kinross House, and his protracted absences from home caused his wife much annoyance.

Sir Robert Anstruther, third son of Sir Philip Anstruther of Dreel Castle, Anstruther, acquired Balcaskie in 1698, four years after obtaining the baronetcy.

Seen from the long, straight approach drive, the north front is most impressive, but there is no garden on this side. The south front, on the other hand, is homelier, the façade defaced with iron balconies, added in the nineteenth century. The garden immediately in front was originally an 'American Garden', made about a century and a half ago, when this was the vogue. The layout

4 BALCASKIE
Pittenweem
St Monance and Pittenweem 1 mile. Route B942.
(SIR RALPH ANSTRUTHER)

remains the same, but the contents are no longer exclusively American. Statues of Diana, the moon goddess, and Apollo, the sun god, contemplating each other from either end of a gravel walk, are part of the seventeenth-century design.

Beneath the verandah there is a Mexican Datura with trumpet-like white and purple flowers. It is said to be very ancient and deadly poisonous.

The stately stairways to the lower terraces were built by Gilpin *c.* 1850, and are overhung by Cedars and *Clematis montana* at each end. Against the retaining wall grow Magnolias, *Garrya elliptica,* Mount Etna Brooms and other shrubs and creepers. The upper ledge of each buttress supports busts of Roman emperors and classical heroes, and the Rose beds are interspersed with antique pedestalled urns and the palm-like New Zealand Cabbage Tree (*Cordyline australis*).

Balcaskie lies within a mile and a half of the sea, and on a sunny day the ambient light has a golden radiance reflected by the wide expanse of water.

As the M90 descends the northern face of the Ochil hills, five miles south of Perth, Balmanno can be seen off to the right, a tall white house nestling at the foot and lying on the edge of the wide flat lands continuing the carse of Gowrie.

This sixteenth-century tower house was surrounded by a brackish ditch in 1916 when Scotland's leading country house designer — Sir Robert Lorimer — came to restore it. The ditch, which was the clogged remains of a moat, was filled in to allow three walled enclosures to be provided beside the house, to give shelter from the wind sweeping along the hills from the west or inland from the North Sea.

Entrance is gained by a shadowy archway in the lodgehouse set athwart the drive which gives on to a long partly shadowed paved forecourt, softened only by a little grass, a few trees and shrubs, with the tall house rising luminously at the far end, like an ivory tower. Doors at either side of it give on to the large kitchen garden, to the north, and to the brightly lit pleasance overlooking the Ochils across low walls at the south of the house, and an open stair leads up to the *piano nobile* of the house.

Sir Robert was a master of surprise and the unexpected, and if he thought the garden should be a private arcadia roofed by heaven to one side of a house, he liked open countryside to sweep so close to the other side that the cows could peer straight in to the windows. This thinking is reflected at Balmanno, where the rose garden which opens from the last side of the pleasance is surrounded by high walls, east, north and south, allowing it to be enjoyed on those many clear sunny days which the keen breezes from the east would otherwise spoil, whereas the west of the pleasance steps down to wide lawns extending northwards along the west of the house and the kitchen garden beyond. Certainly the cows have been excluded, but then Lorimer's clients also had some say in these matters!

5 BALMANNO CASTLE
Perthshire
1½ *miles south of Exit 9, M90.*
(THE HON JAMES BRUCE)

FIGURE 50
The sundial, Abercairny

The planting is not without much interest but no original list of plants has come down to us. Lorimer had collaborated in earlier years on a number of houses in England with Gertrude Jekyll, its foremost garden designer at the time. If he was no horticultural expert, he had been interested in plants since his youth at Kellie Castle in Fife, and would also have learned a lot from her. She was particularly well known for her wild garden design, the only area of which at Balmanno is on the west and has been both much simplified and much added to since it was first laid out. Early photos of the herbaceous borders in the kitchen garden show plants massed as she would have done but elsewhere the arrangement of plants is governed by architectural considerations of balance. The tall yews in the rose garden are introduced to harmonise the beds of small rose bushes with the high wall with its niches which surrounds them, and the planting in the pleasance and forecourt, though sparse, is enough to enrich the bare walls but without cluttering the details or losing the fine proportions. Nature unconfined and kept well in check were combined at Balmanno, which is said to have been Lorimer's favourite commission.

FIGURE 51
The kitchen garden at Balmanno

Peter D. Savage

The farmhouse of Balmuir has so far escaped being engulfed by the rapidly advancing tide of Dundee's new industrial estates and residential areas, although the purposely planted screening trees cannot entirely hide the towering Trottick multi-storey flats, just south of the natural boundary of the Dichty Burn.

6 BALMUIR HOUSE
Dundee

2 miles north of Kingsway (Dundee bypass), beyond Trottick.
(MRS KENNETH BENTLEY)

The original farmhouse was erected in the sixteenth century on land owned by the Grahams of Claverhouse. It was rebuilt in 1780 and further extended a century later by Mrs Bentley's grandfather, to accommodate a family of Victorian proportions.

The 5-acre garden is an eloquent riposte against the brashness of the city which is poised to envelop it. Venerable Beeches, Oaks and Sycamores shield it from the cold east winds and Tayside haar rising out of the river valley, 200 feet below, and the land is gently inclined to the south. The soil is heavy, acidified with liberal additions of peat and leaf mould to encourage the many ericaceous plants. It is a natural garden, offering something of beauty throughout the entire year, beginning with fragrant Viburnums and Witch Hazels and early Rhododendrons in January through to winter-berrying Cotoneasters and Hollies and the bright golden yellow of Jasmine in December.

For the past forty years the owners have increased the numbers of flowering and attractively foliaged shrubs and ornamental trees. They now have an excellent garden which makes light demands upon them, and where the ground cover is mainly easily-mown, grass.

Barham was originally built as a thatched dower-house by Mrs Maitland of Ramkeilour in 1768. It was bought by the present owner's great grandfather in 1877, extended some years after that, and again by Sir Robert's grandfather in

7 BARHAM
Bow of Fife, near Cupar

1908. It was then that the garden — around 1 acre — was laid out in its present shape. Trellises were erected for Rambler Roses and flowerbeds planted up annually with bedding plants. In 1969, Lady Spencer-Nairn took over the garden and has since created the informal Rose and shrub garden that it is today.

Barham is very sheltered from winds, though unfortunately it is in a frost pocket, so tender plants do not thrive well. The soil is extremely sandy and tends to dry out quickly, for which large quantities of leaf-mould are the remedy, applied each springtime.

The soil conditions appear to suit the cultivation of *Meconopsis regia*, which may reach a height of 4 to 5 feet with branching candelabra of yellow flowers; Cowslips in late spring, and Roses, Peonies, Foxgloves, and Delphiniums in the early summer, though Roses need liberal additions of fertiliser. When the climate is favourable, Barham is an extremely sunny and sheltered garden.

The entrance to the estate is by an iron gate embellished with the Scrymgeour-Wedderburn coat-of-arms, overhung by a plantation of Beech trees of considerable height and beautiful pillar-like trunks, whence the carriageway declines between farmlands and woodlands to the mansion, above a bank that falls steeply to the Tay.

The old house of Birkhill, belonging to the Earls of Leslie, stood where once the Manor of Corby had been. The present mansion, built by Alexander Scrymgeour-Wedderburn in 1780, embodies part of the Leslie one, and was enlarged in 1858 according to plans by the Scottish architect, Mr Bryce. The present owner is Henry Scrymgeour-Wedderburn, P.C., 11th Earl whose claim to the Viscountancy of Dudhope was finally admitted by the Committee of Privileges of the House of Lords in 1952, and that to the Earldom of Dundee in 1953.

The windows at the front of the mansion look out across the Tay to the Carse of Gowrie, the Sidlaw Hills, and the far-away Grampian Mountains. The area here is all grass lawns, generously planted with spring Daffodils and Pheasant's-Eye Narcissi. These also flourish abundantly throughout the woodland, mingling with Primroses, Wild Hyacinths, Anemones, Celandine and Wild Garlic.

The land's worth lies mainly in timber: centuries-old Beeches, Silver Firs (*Abies alba*), Japanese Red Cedar (*Cryptomeria japonica*), and European Larch (*Larix decidua*). The Earl himself is a tree-planter, and may survey with satisfaction his own plantations of Larch and Hemlock.

The Yew hedge surrounding the family graveyard is of particular interest. It is over 50 feet high, gnarled and ragged. Some ascribe it to the Druids who venerated the Yew as a symbol of immortality; others to the early monks of nearby Balmerino Abbey, because the abbey forester lived at Birkhill (Corbie Hill) and may well have fenced his own garden with Yew hedging.

The Wild Garden occupies a steep-sided dene, through which a little burn

BARHAM (contd.)
On A91 Cupar-Auchtermuchty road.
(SIR ROBERT & LADY SPENCER-NAIRN)

8 BIRKHILL
🦌 *Balmerino*
Off the minor road which runs along the south bank of the Tay from Newburgh to Newport-on-Tay.
(THE EARL & COUNTESS OF DUNDEE)

FIGURE 52
Balcaskie

trickles down to the Tay. The shade provided by the canopy of Oaks and Beeches and Conifers and the permanently moist soil favour shallow-rooted shrubs, notably Rhododendrons. The list includes mixed species and hybrids such as *falconeri, fictolacteum, linearifolium, basilicum, lutescens, argyrophyllum, 'Penjerrick', wardii, campylocarpum, cinnabarinum blandfordiiflorum* and *fulvum*.

Among all these grow Eucryphias, Magnolias, Viburnums, Buddleias, Acers, Tree Heaths, and Flowering Cherries, underplanted with Azaleas, Pieris, Hydrangeas, and *Daphne retusa*. The ground cover is provided by woodrushes, grass and moss.

A wire fence preserves the Wild Garden as a bird sanctuary, by excluding the rabbits, hares, foxes and roe deer which inhabit the dense coverts of self-sown Beeches and Sycamores, Brambles, Bracken and Rosebay Willow Herb. Through this a track leads to the Walled Garden, for which a team of six to eight gardeners would once have been deemed necessary, but now there is just one aged gardener to do all the work. For that reason, the thorough cultivation and trimness of former days is no longer demanded; yet it is still a place of wayward but pleasing beauty, saved from the winds by screening trees and tall clumps of *Rhododendron arboreum* on the north side, and open to the full light and warmth of the sun.

Against that high south-facing wall flourish Magnolias, Viburnums, Ceanothus, and several Damson and Plum trees. Here too are the lean-to greenhouses, growing Grape-Vines, Kaffir Lilies, the pale blue-flowered *Plumbago capensis*, and many different ornamental pot plants. Generations have found joy in this garden, in its simple beauty and tranquillity, and have left their own imprint upon it: the Georgian sundial at the centre of an Ilex grove; the arbour, formed of a Yew hedge and opposing lines of pleached Cherry trees; the orchard of cankered Apples and Plums and Pears; the old Roses whose names no-one now remembers.

It has often been said, and rightly, that plants which would fail a mile or two to the east, succeed at Balmerino and Birkhill. The area is also noted for the longevity of its inhabitants. And when James V was seeking a place of convalescence for his delicate young Queen, Magdalen of France, his physicians recommended that 'the tender lady' be sent to Balmerino since it had, with St Andrews, 'the best aers of any places in the kingdom for her residence and abode'.

9 BLAIRHOYLE
Thornhill

On the A873
Stirling-Aberfoyle road,
3 ½ miles west of Thornhill.
(LIEUTENANT-COLONEL J. D. &
MRS PATTULLO)

Blairhoyle is located in the old parish of Port of Menteith, a rich carseland of good fertility and high culture. It is a modern replacement of a Victorian mansion, and from the balustraded terrace you may look out across the spacious lawns and trees to Flanders Moss, and beyond the Fintry Hills to the Campsie Fells.

When Colonel and Mrs Pattullo bought Blairhoyle in 1968, they found the 17 acres of garden and walled garden very overgrown and semi-derelict. They had been landscaped about the turn of the century by the owner at that time, Mr George Crabbie of Crabbie's Whisky, as advised by the Botanic Garden in Edinburgh. The Pattullos worked hard, restoring the gardens' beauty and good order, but they left the formal pattern of gravel paths, Box hedges and Rose beds, and the Rose arch leading down between extensive lawns to the lower terraces, practically unchanged. In fact, Crabbie's landscaping and his choice and allocation of shrubs and trees had been carefully thought out, providing colour in the garden throughout the whole year.

On the east side an avenue of old Lime trees, like the nave of a cathedral, leads through a veritable arboretum, planted with rare specimens such as the Eagle-Claw Maple (*Acer platanoides* 'Laciniatum'); the Yellow Birch (*Betula lutea*); the Chinese Necklace Poplar (*Populus lasiocarpa*); the Wing-Nut Tree (*Pterocarya caucasica*), which could be mistaken for a Walnut tree; and the 'French Tricolor' Beech.

All these trees provide good autumn colour. Another which is particularly decorative in this respect is the Katsura Tree (*Cercidiphyllum japonicum*); its leaves emerge a bright pink, turning in mid-October to a rich yellow and scarlet. The Sweet Gum (*Liquidambar styraciflua*) is no less brilliant at this time of year. Listing the Blairhoyle trees, one must not omit its Japanese Red Cedar (*Cryptomeria japonica*), nor the Cut-Leaf Beech (*Fagus sylvatica* 'Heterophylla'). From all this it must be obvious that Blairhoyle is a tree-lover's garden, and the International Society of Dendrologists visited it in May 1978.

The garden also contains many rare and beautiful shrubs. The Rose Acacia (*Robinia hispida*) is frequently remarked on by visitors; its leaves measure 10 inches long, and the deep pink flowers with rounded petals are borne in pendulous racemes. Another is the Chilean Lantern Tree (*Crinodendron hookeranum*) with rich crimson flowers in springtime, unless they are spoiled by frosts.

Some of the loveliest shrubs are the scented winter flowerers: the pale pink *Viburnum farreri*; the distinctive Witch Hazels (*Hamamelis mollis* and *H. japonica*) carrying bright yellow, twisted, strap-like petals on leafless branches; and Mezereon (*Daphne mezereum*), that wild native of our woodlands, with mauve or white blossom. The Cornelian Cherry (*Cornus mas variegata*) will also defy snow and ice, putting forth small acrid yellow flowers in February or March before its leaves.

The gardeners of the late Victorian and Edwardian period placed much reliance on Hollies for shelter. Blairhoyle has six or seven fine variegated Holly bushes. Another shrub which is kindred to the Holly in appearance is *Desfontainea spinosa*, an evergreen from Chile. It comes into flower in August, bearing long scarlet tubes tipped with yellow; this is something of an achievement here since it is partial to the seaside or hilly places.

Visit Blairhoyle in early spring. You will find Snowdrops in the woods, and the Corsican Hellebore (*Helleborus corsicus*), Crocuses of many gorgeous colours opening to the winter sun and the early bees, the Winter Heaths (*Erica carnea*) glowing pink; and the gold-ruffed Winter Aconites (*Eranthis hyemalis*) peeping from drifts of dead leaves beneath the trees. These very early spring flowers are the prey of the red squirrels, which scratch up the tiny tubers and devour them.

Early in April, a tide of golden Daffodils sweeps across the lawns, followed in May by the invasive and ubiquitous Wild Hyacinths (*Endymion non-scriptus*) and Primroses (*Primula vulgaris*) and the shy little Windflowers, the Woodland Anemones (*A. nemorosa*), forerunners of glorious June, the time of the Rhododendrons and Azaleas and the first Roses.

Commercially, Blairhoyle depends on its Heathers, grown on banks above the garden burn. Cuttings are propagated in one of the four greenhouses, and sold along with other produce, such as vegetables, tomatoes and pot-plants.

Colonel Pattullo and his wife both work very hard in the gardens. An engineer to trade, he has been engaged over a long time in clearing out the silted lochan at the south end of the garden; it was created artificially during the Crabbies' occupation. Mrs Pattullo is an authority on the rare trees and shrubs. She also propagates the Heathers and other cuttings, looks after the greenhouses containing the Vines and Peaches, and stocks the roadside stall.

When the Pattullos came to Blairhoyle in 1968, they received much help and advice from the daughter of a former head gardener, a trained gardener herself who willingly took employment with the new owners. She retired some time ago. They now have to do practically all the work of caring for these 17 acres themselves, with very little outside help.

10 BOLFRACKS
Aberfeldy

Approximately 2 miles out of Aberfeldy on A827 to Kenmore.
(Mr J. D. Hutchison)

Bolfracks is basically an eighteenth-century Scottish farmhouse to which a castellated Gothic front was added about 1830. There has long been a garden here, on a fairly steep north-facing slope, but the present one of 4 acres has been developed over the last fifty years by the present owner and his parents.

The soil is a good deep loam, on the acid side, in which ericaceous plants, hardy shrubs and perennials, and alpines, particularly Gentians, all do well. There is an annual rainfall of 40 inches, and it is a cold, rather late garden, subject to early and late frosts and vulnerable to north-west winds. The acreage is divided between shrub borders, peat walls, a wild garden containing bulbs, trees and shrubs, and a more formal walled garden.

11 BRACO CASTLE
Braco

Braco village 1½ miles.
(Lieutenant Commander G. R. Muir)

Figure 53
Azaleas at Branklyn

The Braco estate used to be owned by a branch of the Grahams, who were descendants of the 3rd Earl of Montrose, and baronets from 1625 to 1689. Part of the Castle dates from the fifteenth century, with later additions. The estate is well wooded and contains several small lakes or ponds. In the spring there are acres of Daffodils, many of which were originally grown for market.

The walled garden lies a short distance from the castle, reached by a Rhododendron walk. The site is 650 feet above sea level, but sheltered, and there are old Yew and *Prunus cerasifera* 'Pissardii' hedges, dividing the garden.

There is a traditional vegetable garden, much soft fruit, and greenhouses built

against the north wall and contining Lemons, Passion Fruit, Calamondin Orange, and flowering creepers, such as *Lapageria rosea,* and many Camellias.

The owners have specialised in shrubs, of which there is a wide range most of which they propagate themselves. The shrub borders are interplanted with Primulas, Meconopses and other plants. In the centre of the garden, a grass path with herbaceous borders leads down to a pond with a considerable collection of ornamental waterfowl.

12 BRANKLYN
Perth

¼ *mile from the Queen's Bridge, Perth, on the A85 (Dundee road).*
(NATIONAL TRUST FOR SCOTLAND)

If ever there was a case of outstanding success in gardening, achieved by endeavour and perseverance, the first prize must inevitably go to the late John and Dorothy Renton. When in 1922 the Rentons bought the land upon which they built Branklyn, they acquired about ⅔ acre of land. Being right next to the Dundee Road, understandably their first thoughts were to screen themselves from the noise of passing traffic — doubtless minimal compared to the present day. Through friends they were encouraged to acquire an additional piece of ground, where as Dorothy Renton wrote, 'We stepped into the pitfalls of many amateur gardeners by making all the orthodox things a garden should have'.

Very soon experience inspired confidence, which in turn led to ability, and the garden as we know it today began to take shape. There were two more acquisitions of land bringing the whole area to 2 acres, the present size. The Rentons were clever enough to retain several Apple and Pear trees from a former orchard; these contributed enormously to the character they gave to the garden.

Their interest at this time lay in alpine and ericaceous plants. The division of work was readily agreed — Dorothy being the gardener, plantsman and designer, John the willing labourer, as he described himself — and these rôles, once decided, were retained for the rest of their lives. In fact there was a minimum of design, for according to Dorothy Renton 'there was no pre-conceived rule of design about the garden. It has been evolved gradually and the principal aim has been to give plants the proper conditions — it is primarily a home from home for plants'. As a gardener and plantsman she excelled. In 1955 The Royal Horticultural Society acknowledged her excellence by awarding to her the Veitch Memorial Medal, one of the highest honours it can bestow.

Non-gardeners, and unfortunately many gardeners as well, think of a rare plant as an ugly oddity, a freak, which nature, being rather ashamed of her creation, restricted in number by way of compensation. Nothing could be less true as one may see in the beautiful and rare plants at Branklyn. There is a splendid collection of dwarf Rhododendrons, and equally impressive collections of *Primula* and *Meconopsis*, and countless alpines, dwarf trees and shrubs and bulbous plants. There are two screes, the largest and oldest being near the house; the other, of limestone, to cater for the type of plant which prefers alkaline conditions, is in the centre part of the garden.

Many of the smaller ericaceous plants are housed in one or other of the several peat beds situated at the far end of the garden. Here, too, you will find dwarf

Rhododendrons and other early summer flowering shrubs, for it is a period more than any other when Branklyn comes into its own.

When The National Trust for Scotland accepted Branklyn in February 1968, following the death of Dorothy Renton in 1966, and of John Renton the following year, many plants had disappeared through the enforced neglect caused by the owners' illness. Since then the Trust has added thousands of plants, including those which had been unfortunately lost. Several areas have been replanted, but in all work the greatest care has been taken to ensure that, as far as possible, the garden is still the same as that made by the Rentons.

The garden is open daily between 1 March and 31 October, from 10.00 a.m. to sunset.

Cauldhame is a castellated farmhouse, used in early days as a 'Cauld House' (a primitive inn) on the Drovers' Road from the Highlands to Stirling Fair. In it women and children were reported to have taken refuge and watched the battle of Sheriffmuir between the Jacobites and the Royalist army under the Duke of Argyll in the 1715 Rising. The house was celebrated in the ballad, 'The Braes of Cauldhame'.

13 CAULDHAME
Dunblane
On Sheriffmuir, 5 miles east of Dunblane opposite Sheriffmuir Inn.
(HON BERNARD BRUCE, MC)

In Victorian times it was purchased as a private dwelling. The tower and large room were added in 1860. It was later bought by Colonel Stirling of Kippendavie, step-father of the present owner.

The garden, described in the history of the Battle of Sheriffmuir as an orchard, existed in Victorian times, but was re-landscaped before the 1939–45 war by Mrs Stirling of Kippendavie, aided by Mr Roland Preece, the garden designer. It consists of 3 acres of wild garden, 1000 feet up on a moorland hillside. Rhododendrons, Azaleas, and spring bulbs make up most of the cultivated shrubs and plants, thriving in the acid soil despite the severely cold winters. Trees and shrubs provide natural shelter. Not surprisingly, the garden commands mangificent views of the Highlands.

The 2-acre garden at Cloquhat was created by the late Mrs Dunphie, from 1947 onwards. Colonel Dunphie has continued the work, making a terrace and a water garden, and extending the area after the great gale of 1953 which felled many trees in the surrounding woods.

14 CLOQUHAT
Bridge of Cally
6 miles north of Blairgowrie, 1 mile off A93 at Bridge of Cally.
(COLONEL PETER DUNPHIE, CBE)

The house stands on a hillside, facing south, with a view down to the 'ireful' Ericht, a turbulent river. At this altitude, 700 feet, the garden is partly exposed to winds blowing from the south and south-west, precluding the cultivation of tender plants.

The acid soil suits the growth of Azaleas and Rhododendrons, and Primulas and Meconopses flourish in shady situations and along the course of the garden's small burn. Potentillas flower over long periods, untroubled by the strong winds, and crevices in the terrace walls are filled with alpines and rock plants, revelling in their well-drained, sun-warmed situation.

The garden around Cluniemore, an early nineteenth-century house, blends so harmoniously with the surrounding scenery of mountains, moors and lochs as to appear a natural part of the whole. In fact, it had to be wrested from the rough woodland and a snipe bog, a prodigious feat undertaken by the late Charles Butter, beginning in 1910 and continuing for many years thereafter with the probable help of the Surrey nurserymen John Waterer & Sons.

15 CLUNIEMORE
*S Pitlochry
28 miles north of Perth on the A9 Pitlochry by-pass.
(MAJOR & MRS DAVID BUTTER)

Today, the 10 acres of house policies are established on an undulating terrain at 200 feet above sea level. The climate has been described as 'average'; but that, presumably, means severely cold winters in these highland parts, and the rainfall is 36 inches per annum.

There is a Rose garden, a rockery, a water garden, herbaceous and annual borders, a shrub garden, and a wild garden with ornamental trees.

Such is the selection and number of plants that there is interest and colour almost the whole year round, beginning with golden Winter Aconites, fragile purple *Iris reticulata* and Snowdrops, followed by *Tulipa kaufmanniana* and *I. fosterana* from Russian Turkestan, mingling with the Daffodils.

May and June are the best months for fragrance of Lilacs and Azaleas and old-fashioned Shrub Roses and the gorgeous colours of Rhododendrons; then follow the Hybrid Tea and Floribunda Roses, many Lilies and the first blooms in the herbaceous borders — blue Delphiniums, blood-red and pink Peonies, and the earliest Sweet Peas.

Roses flower throughout July, sometimes a dull month, except for the herbaceous borders; but August, with the first tinges of morning frosts and ling heather out on the hills, is a time for Dahlias, and butterflies fluttering between the white and lavender and deep purple Buddleias, and Phloxes in hues of pink and red.

For autumn colour there are many different Acers, Sorbuses bearing scarlet, pink or yellow berries, *Cercidiphyllum japonicum*, and Stranvaesias, glowing like torches throughout the short, late October days.

A visit to Cluniemore would kindle the enthusiasm of the most indifferent gardener!

Cluny in Gaelic means 'the meadow place' and by following the signpost on the Weem-Strathtay road you come to Cluny House, situated where the woodland of the steep slopes opens on to a grassy hillside. At this altitude, 600 feet above sea level, there are fine views taking in Ben More and Ben Lawers and the green valley of the Tay. Behind stand Bein Eagach, Farragon, and Meall Tairneachan.

16 CLUNY HOUSE
*S Aberfeldy
3½ miles from Aberfeldy, off the Weem-Strathtay road, north of the Tay.
(MR & MRS R. S. MASTERTON)

This part of Perthshire has often been compared to Switzerland, on account of the farmhouses and patchwork of fields and woods spread over the hillsides. The new garden at Cluny lies above the house, an open stretch of grassland still, similar in character and airy beauty to an upland meadow in Tyrol. It needs only the Gentians, the Autumn Crocuses, the Cyclamens, the Alpine Roses and the Wild Junipers to perfect the likeness.

FIGURE 54
Crocus nudiflorus *at Cluny House*

The house was erected in 1800, with additions in 1850; it originally had the character of a shooting lodge and was surrounded by 6 acres of its own land, now extended to nine. Mr and Mrs Masterton became the owners in 1950, and set about making a garden on the rough hill which slopes steeply to the river. What they have achieved since is a plantsman's garden, one of Scotland's best, containing many rare and beautiful shrubs and trees, imported from their native habitats in distant places.

At the outset the garden-in-the-making contained several trees that were over a hundred years old: two specimens of *Sequoiadendron giganteum,* a splendid Fern-Leaf Beech (*Fagus sylvaticum* 'Heterophylla'), and a Common Silver Fir (*Abies alba*). It was necessary to plant more quickly maturing trees as wind-breaks, yet the area had natural advantages: light, acid soil, some wet and some dry areas and natural deposits of peat, and an average rainfall of 40 inches. But winters in these parts are normally severe, and there are springtime hazards of killing frosts.

Each year more trees and shrubs were planted — Acers, Birches, Cherries, and several of the Sorbus (Rowan) species, and among these Rhododendrons, Magnolias, Enkianthus, Cotoneasters, Viburnums, Embothriums, Eucryphias, and other shrubs.

The garden has been planned so that serpentine paths through the woodland lead to many small constituent plots, screened from each other by natural coverts of trunks and foliage, and to openings that provide views of the surrounding hills and the river valley below.

The Regius Keeper of the Royal Botanic Garden in Edinburgh has described this garden as 'a treasure-house of rare Primulas'. Perhaps the most remarkable of these are the Asiatic, especially the *Petiolarids,* grown from seeds collected in the Himalayas and Western China. Yet the microclimate and soil conditions of the garden are such that the Himalayan *Primula sonchifolia* thrives and seeds itself in the damp areas, bearing a profusion of lavender-blue flowers.

The dappled shade and acid soil are appropriate to the successful cultivation of Meconopses of many shades of blue and yellow, and of the various Gentians, and *Nomocharis*, whose proper home is the high meadows of Western China, North Burma and south-east Tibet. On the verge of the wood and seeking the sun is the Giant Lily (*Cardiocrinum giganteum*), perhaps the most beautiful of them all.

In springtime, the lawns and other open places around the house bring forth colonies of Daffodils. Within the woodland, some Azaleas and Rhododendrons begin flowering in April, and sunlight filtering through the new upper foliage is sufficient to induce Trilliums and Fritillaries and Dog-Tooth Violets to blossom.

Embothrium coccineum (Norquinco Valley form) blossoms in late spring/early summer, its fiery tubular flowers the antithesis of the white petal-like bracts of the North American flowering Dogwood (*Cornus nuttallii*), and the delicate chalices of *Magnolia sinensis.* Some of the specimen trees were chosen for their beautiful barks — *Prunus maackii* (the Manchurian Cherry), *Prunus serrula* (the Tibetan Cherry), and the Himalayan Birch (*Betula utilis*).

Hoheria lyallii is uncommon in Perthshire gardens, though not in Argyll. Its hanging clusters of creamy-white flowers always draw favourable comment. New Zealand is its natural home. Another late-flowering shrub is the Angelica Tree (*Aralia spinosa*), from America, rarely seen in this country. The flowers are inconspicuous, but its leaves are sometimes as much as three feet long.

Autumn colour brings the garden's year to a spectacular close. Some of the shrubs and trees have been selected for their brilliant fruits — *Sorbus reducta* (the miniature Mountain Ash) and the other Rowans; Cotoneasters, Viburnums, and *Euonymus* (the Spindle tree). Others were chosen on account of their foliage — *Disanthus cercidifolius, Cercidiphyllum japonicum,* many species of *Acer* and *Betula* (Birch). The Spindle Tree makes fine autumn colour in its foliage too, also the *Enkianthus* and *Eucryphia* × *nymansensis,* though these are primarily flowering trees.

The garden was originally of a size appropriate to a country cottage, but following purchase by the present owner's grandfather in 1917 it was gradually extended, especially during the occupancy of her two aunts, both keen gardeners. Today there are about 2 acres, situated 450 feet above sea level, in a landscape that is open to the south and east, but sheltered by a belt of trees on the north-west. The soil is acid, light, and thin over rock, requiring constant feeding. As a remedy, mulches made up of equal parts of peat, leaf mould and garden compost are regularly applied.

The vegetable plot and a few fruit trees, aspects of the cottage garden, have gone and it is now entirely a flower garden. Long established spring Crocuses and Narcissi and autumn Colchicums never fail to make a fair show; but now they flower beside rare and beautiful species Lilies: *Lilium szovitsianum,* which has deep yellow waxy flowers and comes from the southern Caucasus and north-east Turkey; *L. paleyi;* one of the Bellingham hybrids with orange and red blooms, recurved in the form of a Turk's cap; *L. lakongense,* the White Trumpet Lily; *L. martagon* var. Cattaniae, a variation of the well-known Martagon Lily, with polished wine-purple flowers; the large and spectacular *L. giganteum,* now called *Cardiocrinum giganteum*; and the blue African Lily, *Agapanthus.*

The garden's greatest attraction is the collection of over 100 species and many unnamed Shrub Roses. Other rare shrubs include a *Carpenteria californica,* which has rose-like white flowers; *Hoheria sexstylosa*, with white flower clusters; and a *Eucryphia glutinosa,* for late summer blooming, the flowers pure white with golden stamens of a singular beauty.

This 250-300 year old croft came into the possession of Dr and Mrs Hewitt in the early 1970s. At that time it consisted of two crofts, with toolsheds at either end,

17 CRAIGANTAGGART
Dunkeld

4½ miles from Dunkeld. Taking the Blairgowrie road, turn right at Caputh and Snaigow signpost (i.e. leaving Loch of Lowes on left). 2½ miles up this road, turn left at signpost for Blackhill; Craigantaggart is on the left.
(THE HON MRS JOHN BOYLE)

18 CROFT CAPPANACH
by Pitlochry

but the whole building has been gutted and made into one house. Situated on a hillside, 650 feet above sea level, it commands magnificent views of the surrounding country with its moorland and mountains, and the rivers Tummel and Tay.

Creating a garden out of the neighbouring wilderness was an even greater achievement than the restoration of the buildings. Dr and Mrs Hewitt cleared the area themselves, made lawns and dykes, and planted shelter belts of trees, gradually establishing the garden with hundreds of plants, shrubs and saplings which they transported from their other garden south of the Border. Many of these would normally be regarded as too tender for such a lofty, exposed situation but the incautious approach has succeeded and the garden is now blooming and full of interest and changeful colour from early April until mid November.

There are, in fact, several small gardens within the whole. One area is planted entirely with Peonies. There are also many Hostas, Hellebores, *Alchemilla mollis*, and *Acanthus*, reflecting Mrs Hewitt's interest in flower-arranging; much favour has also been shown to ground-cover plants which will suppress weeds and other wild invaders, though bird- or wind-sown Foxgloves are cherished for their stately grace.

CROFT CAPPANACH (contd.)
Turn right on the Dalcapon road just north of Ballinluig, and left 2½ miles south of Pitlochry – off the A9.
(DR & MRS F. HEWITT)

This was a farmhouse originally, built in 1720. The conversion was carried out in 1925 by the well known architect John Keppie, R.S.A., with advice from the famous Scottish artist, Sir D. Y. Cameron (1865-1945), and Sir Gordon Russell of Broadway was responsible for the interior woodwork. It was at that time the property of the Drummond family.

The house stands in a garden of 5 acres, made by Miss Drummond, but opened up and the planting much increased by Mrs Alice Reynard. There are really several gardens within the whole — rock gardens on walls and scree, a white border, a yellow border, and an evergreen border, a border planted with different kinds of Liliums, an alpine house and a water garden. The soil is acid and highly suitable for the bountiful endowment of Azaleas, Rhododendrons, large and dwarf conifers and many other fine flowering shrubs.

There are magnificent views towards the Trossachs.

19 CULBUIE
Buchlyvie
Off the A811 Stirling-Drymen road. Coming from Edinburgh, turn left at end of village of Buchlyvie and drive 1 mile up hill road.
(MRS ALICE REYNARD)

Sir Edward Bruce, 1st Lord Bruce of Kinloss, built Culross Abbey House in 1608. When James VI left for London, Sir Edward accompanied him and was created Master of the Rolls.

His Culross property eventually passed to his kinsman Alexander Bruce, 2nd Earl of Kincardine, and on return from exile in Europe, he and his Dutch wife, Lady Veronica van Arsen, began to lay out the magnificent hanging or terraced gardens overlooking the Firth of Forth. A fine pavilion, dated 1674, bearing his Arms, faces the long border.

The soil is a deep friable loam, slightly acid, in which most plants thrive.

20 CULROSS ABBEY
    HOUSE
Culross
On a hill above Culross Royal Burgh.
(THE EARL OF ELGIN & KINCARDINE)

FIGURE 55
Culross Abbey House

Although the climate is mild, high winds from the south-west are a disadvantage.

The garden has always been a beneficial adjunct to the Abbey House. Figs used to flourish against the south-facing wall, where now there are ample Shrub Roses occupying the full length of the border, providing a splendour of rich colours and fragrance in early to mid summer. Tulips, planted by the Lady Veronica in the 17th century, seldom fail to gladden the garden in spring. The style is dignified and formal—close-mown terraced lawns, and a flagged terrace.

The garden is in the care of The Dowager Countess of Elgin.

21 DALGAIRN HOUSE
Cupar
½ mile outside Cupar, on the unclassified Cupar-Rathillet road.
(MR & MRS ROGER BANKS)

Dalgairn House stands high on a hill above Cupar in a sunny, west-facing situation. Its chief interest is the 2-acre walled garden which over a period has been allowed to go wild, providing space for the old cultivated trees, shrubs and perennials tenacious enough to survive, and for rare weeds, edible or poisonous, or considered worthy of preservation for their beauty or usefulness.

Digging is kept to a minimum; the garden is controlled by scything and winter pruning. There is no denying the beauty of this 'garden of weeds'. Many rare and lovely things have taken root and refuge here, blooming unstintingly, diffusing scents on the summer air.

Some territorial allocations have been made for disappearing wild flowers. An angle in the wall has been appropriated by aromatic herbs — Lavender and Rosemary, Wild Thyme and Peppermint. The old demarcations of the Rose border are still discoverable beneath obdurate, unpruned yet floriferous bushes of *Rosa rugosa scabrosa*, *R. alba* 'Cuisse de Nymphe Emue', *R.* 'Zephyrine Drouhin' and *R. foetida bicolor*.

A Eucalyptus tree, grown to giant proportions, has become inseparably entwined with Traveller's Joy (*Clematis vitalba*).

Swathes cut through the rampant growth end in coverts of native Broom, *Escallonia, Forsythia* and the Italian *Cytisus sessilifolius* with arching sprays of brilliant yellow. The reddish-orange Hawkweed 'Fox and Cubs' grows unchecked in the weedy gravel paths.

22 DRUMMOND CASTLE
Muthill
2 miles south of Crieff, on the Muthill road.
(GRIMSTHORPE & DRUMMOND CASTLE TRUST)

FIGURE 56
Drummond Castle from the air

Drummond Castle was founded in 1491 by John, 1st Lord Drummond. There is a legend which claims that Lord Drummond's daughter, Bonnie Margaret Drummond, was the unacknowledged wife of James IV. Whatever the truth, her relationship with the King was an obstacle to his marriage to Margaret Tudor, daughter of Henry VII of England, and she and her two sisters were murdered while the marriage treaty was being prepared. The Old Keep built by Lord Drummond is still standing, while most of the remainder of the Castle is a restoration, carried out by the 1st Earl of Ancaster about 1890.

The garden of Drummond Castle is one of the showpieces of Perthshire. It was first laid out about 1630 by John Drummond, 2nd Earl of Perth, who got the idea for the garden from his estate in France. James, 4th Earl (1648-1716),

formed the park around the Castle in an antique style of landscape gardening. He was appointed Lord High Chancellor of Scotland by James II of England, VII of Scotland, and followed the King into exile in France, being created Duke (titular) of Perth for his constancy.

FIGURE 57
Red Admiral butterfly on Sedum spectabile *at Drummonie House*

Around 1830, the castle gardens were landscaped anew according to plans drawn by the estate's factor and agent, George Kennedy. The steep slope under the Old Keep was terraced, and the flat area below took the design of a St Andrew's Cross, represented by borders of blue Lavender and white *Anaphalis*.

Today, the gardens are representative of the three great styles of European horticulture — the Italian, the French, and the Dutch. The central point on which all paths converge is a stone obelisk in the form of a sundial, which has about fifty faces for telling the time in most of the European capital cities. It was the work of John Mylne, Master Mason to Charles I.

There are Italian statues set in arbours at different points throughout the garden, contributing along with the parterres of Roses, the conical clipped Yew trees, and the brilliance of the peacocks to a most pleasing sense of ordered beauty and peace.

Lawrence Oliphant built Drummonie in 1697 as the dower house of Kilgraston, giving it the original name of Pitkeathly House. The discovery of mineral springs at Pitkeathly led to the establishment of Pitkeathly Wells and the growth of Bridge of Earn as a popular holiday village in the eighteenth and nineteenth centuries.

23 DRUMMONIE HOUSE
Bridge of Earn
1 mile west of Bridge of Earn; turn left off B935.
(MR & MRS MICHAEL GOW)

Pitkeathly House was then converted to an inn and renamed Drummonie, but later the proprietor had to forfeit it in satisfaction of a gaming debt. The Earl of Moray was among the subsequent owners.

The quiet byways of Dunbarney, Forgandenny and Forteviot were bustling then with visitors to the Wells, out for leisurely drives in horse-drawn carriages. Many drew rein at Drummonie for refreshments, and to admire the gardens, especially the Tulip Tree on the lawn, alas no more.

Today Drummonie House is a dignified white-harled building with crow-stepped gables, standing in a sheltered, gently wooded situation. The main door looks down a short Beech and Horse Chestnut drive, planted for spring with Lilies and Wild Hyacinths. The gardens are informal and natural, with surrounding hedges of Beech and Cypresses. There are beds of mature Azaleas, and groves of Lilacs, Weeping Willows and Flowering Cherries. The present owners have plans for the re-landscaping and renewal of the gardens.

Duchray Castle is a forbidding-looking tower house, part fifteenth- and part sixteenth-century, commanding a ridge on the right bank of the Duchray Water, 3 miles west-south-west of Aberfoyle. It was a stronghold of the Grahams, notorious as the murderers of King James I of Scotland at Blackfriars Monastery in Perth on 20 February 1437. On 23 February 1671, a christening

24 DUCHRAY CASTLE

24 DUCHRAY CASTLE (contd.)

near Aberfoyle
*Off the A81 running south
from Aberfoyle, up the
Forestry Commission road
for 2½ miles.*
(MRS A. C. RAMSAY)

party of Grahams from Duchray Castle met in bloody conflict with their kinsmen, led by the Earl of Airth and Menteith, on the old bridge at Aberfoyle.

The castle has mellowed slowly with the passage of time. For many years it served as a shooting lodge. There was then little or no garden, but some sheltering trees and shrubs were planted after 1860. The garden extends to 3-4 acres. It is surrounded on all sides by wild open country, much of it under its own and Forestry Commission plantations.

Sensibly, no attempt has been made to alter the character of the terrain, but suitable plants have been chosen for the natural environment of outcrops of rock, wet and dry areas of acid soil, scraggy grass slopes changing to lush margins by the river, alpines for where there are collections of scree. It is chiefly a garden of Rhododendrons, Azaleas, Heaths, Heathers, and other plants which thrive in moist, lime-free soil. There is a small water garden, and the meadows by the river have a wealth of Daffodils in Spring.

The tower used to be mantled with Ivy. This has been torn down and replaced with flowering climbers. The Filberts likewise, for which Duchray Castle used to be noted, have disappeared. One relic of past days is the fine, very old Box hedge, still the best of our native evergreens and better than Yew or Holly for dividing lines near the flower garden.

One of the disadvantages of gardening in this remote, wild country is the near presence, seen or unseen, of herds of deer. They come down to forage in hard winter weather, and are no respecters of rare garden plants.

25 DUNBARNEY

Bridge of Earn
*½ mile north-west of Bridge
of Earn, off B935.*
(MR A. M. GOMME-DUNCAN)

Dunbarney House is to be found amid the beautiful, sparsely populated, abundantly fertile eastern area of Strathearn, only half a mile south of the river Earn's serpentine course. Chiselled into the stonework of the west front gable is the date 1697; the eastern wing was not added until 1780. There have been distinguished lairds of Dunbarney — Robert Craigie (1685-1760), who was Lord President of the Court of Session, and his grandson, Lord Craigie (1754-1834) of the same name, also an eminent judge.

During the eighteenth century, the curative properties of Pitkeathly waters were officially recognised, and so great were the crowds visiting the five wells that the village of Bridge of Earn was built to accommodate them. There was a well on the site of the old village of Dunbarney; it is suspected that when the old village was demolished much of the masonry went towards extending the laird's domain and his walled garden, including the belfry from Dunbarney Auld Kirk, which now graces the roof of the potting shed.

The long Beech tree avenue leading to the mansion is in keeping with its venerable character and dignity; so too is the doocot, with the date 1697 carved on its lintel, containing stone nesting boxes for over 1,100 pigeons. The old conical windmill, a little way to the south, used to grind local farmers' corn.

The mansion is constructed of Old Red Sandstone, which imparts a mellow, sun-soaked appearance, and the surrounding garden blends harmoniously into the tranquil farmland of Strathearn — six clipped Yew trees, spaced out across the lawn; an ancient sundial of the same stone as the house; beds of summer annuals, and herbaceous borders.

The walled garden has an atmosphere of assured fertility. Trained against the walls are Plum, Pear, and Apple trees, bowed with their autumnal abundance, the fragrance of their fruits mingling with the tang of wintering Potato haulms, and full-flowering Chrysanthemums, Dahlias, and Michaelmas Daisies. To complete the delights, there is a little grove of Sycamores surrounding a statue of the goddess Diana, who holds a bow and arrow and a dead bird.

FIGURE 58
The courtyard and wellhead at Earlshall

FIGURE 59
Herbaceous border, Falkland Palace garden

26 EARLSHALL
🐞 *Leuchars*
1 mile from Leuchars.
Route A919.
(MRS ARTHUR PURVIS)

Earlshall estate in the fourteenth century formed part of the barony of the Duke of Albany, brother of King Robert III. The castle was started in 1546 by Sir William Bruce, but completed as a magnificent fortified house by his great-grandson of the same name in 1620.

After many vicissitudes and a period of neglect in Victorian times, it was acquired in 1891 by R. W. R. Mackenzie of Stormontfield, Perthshire, a dyer to trade. Since his family were on friendly terms with Professor and Mrs Lorimer of Kellie Castle, Mr Mackenzie decided to give young Robert Lorimer a chance in the restoration of Earlshall. It was the first commission for the famous Scottish architect and restorer of old houses.

Lorimer's style is very evident in the layout of the front courtyard, the wrought-iron well-head, plant troughs and flagged paving. The old dovecot has been preserved, and the garden is formal with much topiary, Yew hedges and stone terracing. The herbaceous border on the south side is particularly fine, and there are interesting shrubs, choice Roses and a most rewarding kitchen garden. The latter contains a little belvedere, known as 'Mary, Queen of Scots' house', though this hapless queen is not known ever to have crossed the threshold of Earlshall. The house and gardens are not open to the public.

FIGURE 60
The topiary garden at Earlshall

27 FALKLAND PALACE
🐞 *Falkland*
Turn onto A912 off A92 from Edinburgh, or off A91 from Stirling.
(NATIONAL TRUST FOR SCOTLAND)

Being a Royal residence, at one time a home of Mary, Queen of Scots, Falkland has a long, well recorded history. The fact that the Palace served as a Hunting Lodge, and consequently was used primarily for less formal occasions, does not seem to have discouraged the making of a large formal garden, such as one might confidently expect to be associated with a building of this importance. In fact most of the references in statistical accounts are to the kitchen garden, frequently about the inability of the gardener to meet his obligations to fulfil the requirements of the household.

The work of John Sharp in 1502 seems to have been the beginning of a new lease of life for the garden, for ten years later the wooden trellis enclosing the garden was replaced by a stone wall, which marked the start of several improvements. Specific details, unfortunately, are not given, but as in the past, efforts would appear to have been concentrated on culinary rather than Elysian pleasures.

There is little information about anything which may have happened during the seventeenth century, and indeed up to very recent times. During World War II the garden did service as a forest nursery. Almost immediately afterwards the then Captain, Constable and Keeper of Falkland, the late Major Michael Crichton Stuart, engaged Percy Cane to design a new garden with a character suited to its distinguished past. It was then that the National Trust for Scotland became owner by being appointed Deputy Keeper.

By comparison to others, Falkland garden is not large, being no more than 7 acres in total. Cane very skilfully contrived to accentuate the length and breadth by creating borders around the perimeter with a series of large beds set away

from the walls to establish broad grass walks around the outside, and a large expanse of grass in the centre, which carefully conceal the limits of the small area.

The planting shows the very great talent of which Cane was capable. There are two herbaceous borders, the main one on the east side of the garden in which there is a strong sense of colour, then a smaller border where colours have been restrained and confined to pale shades of blue and pink and large quantities of silver and white.

Trees and shrubs range from the potentially large Cut-Leaved Beech and Purple Sycamore which stand as specimen trees in the lawn, to small shrubs, Roses and a good variety of climbing plants which adorn several walls. In all it provides an interesting selection to give a primarily summer display.

As a contrast to the colour of the main garden, the small north garden is perhaps almost too severe in the lack of it relying, as it does, upon foliage contrasts for effect.

To the west of the garden is the orchard, now largely a collection of old gnarled trees, which may be very inefficient fruit-producing plants, but do provide a glorious spring display, quite splendid enough to encourage one to make a special journey just to see it.

The gardens are open from 1 April–31 October, Mon–Sat 10.00 a.m.–6.00 p.m., Sunday 2.00 p.m.–6.00 p.m.

28 FINGASK CASTLE
Rait, by Erroll
Off A85, on the back road between Glendoick and Kinnaird.
(MR MARK S. MURRAY THREIPLAND)

The front tower of Fingask was built in 1594, the central portion is older still, and there is a 1674 addition with pepper-box turrets at the angles. As a one-time fortified tower-house, it occupies an advantageous situation, 200 feet above the Carse of Gowrie, on the west side of a nicely wooded glen.

The Threipland lairds were strongly Jacobite and on the night of 7 January 1716 the Old Pretender, after a good dinner, occupied the 'state room' of Fingask. The estates were forfeited following the failure of the 1715 Rising, and the Castle was plundered by Hanoverian dragoons on at least two different occasions. However, Sir David Threipland's son, Stuart, after years of banishment in France, returned and became a successful Edinburgh physician, amassing enough money to buy back his rightful inheritance in 1783. The baronetcy was restored in 1826.

The 5th baronet, Sir Patrick Murray Threipland, died without issue in 1882, and was succeeded by his cousin, William Scott Kerr, who assumed the name Murray Threipland together with the baronetcy. His grandson, Mark S. Murray Threipland, bought back Fingask and its 90 acres of policies from the family Gilroy in 1967. The policies consist of woodlands in the main, sloping from the sixteenth-century castle to St Peter's Well, deep in a ravine, and to the remains of an old Apple orchard on the floor of the Carse.

Broad lawns on the south side have neatly clipped Yew trees posted along a line where the land begins to drop steeply into the glen, and also on the braes

FIGURE 61
Topiary at Fingask House

above the Castle. Some have been clipped into fantastic shapes, yet it is the placing of these trees — some three hundred and twenty in all — that is such a striking feature of the policies.

A small enclosed garden rises in a series of formal terraces to the west of the Castle. Trained against the sheltering castle walls are Magnolias, Camellias and Fuchsias. There are closely planted Roses, herbaceous plants, and low-growing shrubs such as Mexican Orange Blossom (*Choisya ternata*), *Hydrangea macrophylla* and border hedges of Lavender. Potentillas and Japanese Acers, Hellebores and Auriculas and vivid clumps of Heaths and Heathers provide interest and colour throughout the seasons, well-nourished by the heavy, made-up soil.

In the walled garden stands an old sundial and a canopied water tap. A few steps away stands the pillar of Perth's Auld Mercat Cross, restored after its mauling by Cromwell's soldiers in 1651. There is also an assembly of near-life-size statues of characters from Scottish poetry, mossy with age but still startlingly life-like.

Mark Murray Threipland is a farmer with a keen interest in silviculture. His estate is rich in Giant Beeches, Sequoias, Larches, Douglas Firs, and to these he has recently added plantings of Oaks, Paper-bark Birches (*Betula papyrifera*), Raoul (*Nothofagus procera*), and *Ginkgo biloba*.

Azaleas and Bamboos flourish in the ravine, and there are great clumps of Rhododendrons along the driveway and on the braes around the Castle. They are preyed on by roedeer, which come in from the woods; the deer prefer the blood-red flowers of *R. arboreum* var. *roseum* — in excellent taste!

N.B.   The public are not admitted to this garden.

29   FORDELL CASTLE
Inverkeithing

From Forth Road Bridge, take 2nd turning on left (A92) towards Kirkcaldy, then 1st left (B981) towards Cowdenbeath. Gates to Castle 2 miles on right.
(NICHOLAS FAIRBAIRN OF FORDELL, QC, MP)

Fordell Castle was the seat of the Mercer-Hendersons, but passed in 1881 to Edith Isabella Mercer-Henderson, wife of the Hon Hew Adam Dalrymple Hamilton Duncan, 2nd son of the 1st Earl of Camperdown. Undeterred by his already lengthy name, he added Mercer-Henderson to it, and the escutcheons both of the Hendersons and of Viscount Duncan of Camperdown appear on the Castle walls.

One of the best preserved sixteenth-century castles in Fife, it was visited by Mary, Queen of Scots in 1567. The private chapel in the grounds was erected in 1630; you can still see the brazier which held the beacon fire, one in the chain of warning signals reaching from end to end of Scotland.

Coal mines on the estate were begun in 1600, and the 4-mile long 'Fordell Railway' used to carry the product from the pit-heads to the former coaling port of St David's, 1½ miles east of Inverkeithing.

The Castle today stands in 5 acres of wooded parkland, perched above a 50 feet deep ravine through which flows the Keithing Burn. The gardens, once pronounced 'unsurpassed in Scotland', had long been neglected, but have recently been re-made by the present owner. They are formal in style, with parterres, Rose gardens, a water garden, rockeries and a herbaceous border.

The plantings continue while the established spring bulbs, Azaleas, flowering Cherries, Rhododendrons and Potentillas provide a magnificent display throughout the months of April, May and June. There is an ancient Cedar in the garden which, legend declares, some knight brought back from the 5th Crusade (1217-21) and planted within the fair woods of Fordell.

The original Gargunnock Peel was built to guard a ford over the river Forth. During the first phase of the War of Scottish Independence, the English invaders succeeded in capturing it, but not for long: the Scots, led by Sir William Wallace, mounted an attack on the captured stronghold, vanquished the enemy garrison and demolished the peel-tower.

At one time the northern part of Gargunnock parish and some of the land to the south was covered by the ancient Caledonian Forest. With the degeneration of the trees, this area became a deep, swampy moss of no worth. In the eighteenth century, however, the bog was reclaimed and became a highly fertile carseland.

Gargunnock House developed out of the sixteenth-century L-shaped tower-house, reflecting the area's new-found prosperity in its fine Georgian south front, completed in 1794.

Sir James Campbell of Ardkinglass was laird in the mid eighteenth century and added the walled garden, now abandoned. Traces of the embellishments of more spacious days can still be seen — the boundaries of the wider eighteenth-century park, the garden walks, the pavilion that once stood beside the lake.

The nineteenth-century flower garden, recently re-made and lying close to the mansion, contains a fine selection of bulbs, heaths, herbaceous plants and shrubs, selected for ease of cultivation and an attractive display. Campbell of Ardkinglass's sundial is there too, inscribed with the year 1731 and his armorial crest.

During the 1745 rising a Jacobite garrison occupied Gargunnock when Prince Charles Edward passed eastwards from Fords of Frew, and the hulk of a tree which he rode under can still be seen.

In 1848, Frederic Chopin, the Polish-born composer, accompanied by his pupil and benefactress Jane Stirling of Kippendavie, visited Gargunnock House in the course of his tour of Scotland.

The estate is planted with many rare and beautiful trees, some centuries old. A fine cut-leaf Beech (*Fagus sylvatica* 'Heterophylla') deserves particular mention. Also, among the shrubs, a very old bed of *Kalmia latifolia*. Acers and other shrubs, planted among the immense Redwoods that line the drive, colour brilliantly in the Autumn; and provide coverts for the many wild birds that find a safe habitation here.

Gargunnock soil is basically red till over Old Red Sandstone. It needs generous additions of dung and leaf mould, but the resultant acidity is suitable for the cultivation of the ericaceous plants that predominate in the gardens.

30 GARGUNNOCK HOUSE
near Stirling

Off A811 *Stirling/Drymen, 7 miles west of Stirling, down unclassified road to Gargunnock village, then east to Gargunnock House, ¾ mile.*
(*Trustees of Gargunnock Estate, per* MISS V. H. C. STIRLING OF GARGUNNOCK)

31 GIBLISTON

   Colinsburgh

1½ miles north-east of Colinsburgh. 10 miles south of St Andrews.
(MR CHRISTOPHER LORIMER)

Sir Robert Lorimer, well known architect of the Thistle Chapel and the Scottish National War Memorial at Edinburgh Castle, purchased Gibliston in 1916 as his country house.

The ½ acre of garden, 250 feet above sea level, is situated in the fertile East Neuk of Fife. Its formal lawns, Yew hedges, shrubberies and Rose garden were planned and planted by Sir Robert Lorimer in 1918. His son, Christopher Lorimer, added more flower beds in 1965. There are grass parks around it, with trees and a glen traversed by a stream.

Significant of the climate is the fact that Mimosa (*Acacia decurrens* var. *dealbata*) blooms here from January until mid March under unheated glass.

32 GLENDOICK

   Glencarse

8 miles east of Perth, off the A85 dual carriageway, between Perth and Dundee.
(MR PETER ALFRED COX)

A fine Georgian mansion such as Glendoick House is sure to have a colourful history; so it is with no surprise that one learns that one dark night in the year 1745, a rowing boat put out from Carpow, on the south bank of the Tay, carrying Prince Charles Edward across to sup with the Laird of Glendoick, the Rt Hon Robert Craigie, a Lord President of the Court of Session.

Today, Glendoick is of greater interest to plant collectors, botanists, horticulturists and gardeners generally than to historians, for here is one of the world's comprehensive collections of Rhododendrons, assembled throughout a life-time by the late E. H. M. Cox, and still being added to by his son, Peter Alfred Cox, the present owner.

The eighteenth-century house occupies a most desirable situation, at the end of a half-mile drive, where there is sun and shelter, in the lee of the Braes of the Carse of Gowrie, and great peace, away from the blare and the fumes of traffic along the dual carriageway between Perth and Dundee.

The Carse of Gowrie is the 'Garden of Scotland', for reasons obvious to all who know it, and many years ago it used to be famous for its Apples. The market gradually contracted and died after the arrival of the railways and the establishment of a regular ferry service between Glasgow and the English and Irish ports, which supplied well packaged and easily marketable fruit, of a good quality and appearance.

Like the stretches of reed beds by the Tay, old orchards, twisted and bowed with years, remain one of the characteristics of the Carse, though the appleyard at Glendoick, to the east of the mansion, is in good heart. The walled garden, on the west side, contains a plant nursery, kitchen garden, a long double-sided herbaceous border, and a Rose garden. Behind this lies the main area of interest, the Wild Garden, established in a wooded glen with a stream running through it, and steep, south-facing banks planted with Rhododendrons and Azaleas.

The soil at Glendoick is light to medium loam, low in organic matter, well drained yet moist because of an underlying bed of clay in this part of the estate. The trees provide shelter from the winds, and some shade in summer. In winter, they protect the blossom from the harmful effects of hard frost and early morning sunshine occurring together, the Rhododendrons — both species and

FIGURE 62
Dahlias at Hill of Tarvit

hybrids — have flowering periods spread throughout nine months of the year. Lengthy periods of drought are dangerous if these shallow-rooting shrubs cannot reach reserves of moisture. Sometimes sprinklers have to be turned on, but this is not often necessary.

The trees are mainly Beeches, Oaks — which give good leaf soil — Larches, *Eucalyptus,* grown from seed collected in Australia, and some less desirable Elms which are greedy for moisture, provide poor leaf mould, and are prone to crash in high winds, damaging the plants underneath. There are also mounds of *Rhododendron ponticum* on the fringes of the wood.

The nursery for Rhododendrons, Azaleas and similar shrubs lies beyond the Wild Garden, encircled by hedges of *Cupressocyparis leylandii.* Here much additional peat is used. The collecting and hybridising of Rhododendrons, it has been said, is a mania that has changed the pattern of gardening in Britain. But it takes five to eight years to produce a small-flowering plant from seed, while the large ones will take twenty years. Stock can be increased by cuttings or layering.

At Glendoick also are Magnolias, Camellias, *Pieris* in variety and many other Ericaceae, some growing in the West Garden: *Magnolia stellata* and *M. soulangiana,* dwarf Azaleas and Meconopses, Viburnums and *Hamamelis* (the Witch Hazel); *Staphylea holocarpa* × *pinnata*, a small tree from the Caucasus bearing clusters of white flowers in May; the low-growing *Hebe fairfieldii* with its pale mauve flowers, culled from the sea cliffs of New Zealand; and, trained against the wall, a pale pink Clematis, *C. spooneri* var. *rosea*.

Many of the rare plants in the garden at Glendoick were brought back by E. H. M. Cox from his plant-hunting expeditions across the world, made in the company of other celebrated collectors such as Reginald Farrer. His son Peter Cox is continuing the good work. The Glendoick Garden Centre is located at the end of the drive, beside the main Dundee-Perth dual carriageway.

33 HILL OF TARVIT
Cupar
Off the A916, 2½ miles south of Cupar.
(NATIONAL TRUST FOR SCOTLAND)

This is yet another property which owes much to the work of Robert Lorimer. The formal area south of the house is basically as designed by him, when he remodelled the house and garden for Mr F. B. Sharp in 1906. Sharp was evidently a keen and knowledgeable gardener himself, and although he made several additions to Lorimer's plan, they were carefully enough done so as not to intrude, and in fact blend well with the original Lorimer conception.

As so often is the case where landscape is involved, it is the view from the garden which is attractive, rather than the garden itself. It is certainly so at Hill of Tarvit. The garden is divided by two approach roads into the upper garden, with a steeply sloping southerly aspect, and the lower, formal layout to the south of the house.

Both areas have only a limited amount of colour, supplied by a shrub border along the top of the garden, a fairly recently introduced herbaceous border, and a Rose garden at either side of the house, which were part of the Lorimer design. The remainder is maintained as grass with a very elegant pair of steps leading from one level to another south of the house. At one time a number of interesting trees had been planted in the surrounding woodlands, a few of which have survived, such as the August-flowering *Eucryphia glutinosa,* an exceptionally good *Parrotia*, a few good Rhododendrons, a *Garrya* and so forth. Several more had been smothered by saplings from the encroaching woodland.

There is also a sizeable walled garden, some 2 acres in extent, now let for commercial use, and a range of glass, very typically Victorian in combining a central conservatory with growing-houses at either end.

Despite there being little to attract a keen gardener, Hill of Tarvit has an undeniable charm. Possibly it is the view from the garden, or an even more dramatic one from the viewpoint on a hill behind, or just the pleasantly peaceful atmosphere of well-maintained grass and trimmed Yew hedges; something there certainly is which will remain a very happy memory of one's visit. In addition, the house is open to visitors and has a notable collection of porcelain, pictures and Chippendale furniture. The grounds are open all year, daily 10.00 a.m. to dusk. The house is open from 1 May to 30 September.

Hillside is a two-storey house, originally a cottage but added to at the end of the nineteenth century. The garden used to be correspondingly long and narrow, in keeping with the cottage's dimensions. In 1947, however, the adjoining field was bought by Mr and Mrs Peterkin, the area of cultivation was extended, and shelter belts of Larch and Scots Pine were planted.

34 HILLSIDE HOUSE
Ceres
In Ceres village, by Cupar.
(MRS W. C. G. PETERKIN)

There are 3½ acres of good land on a gentle slope. Both house and garden face south to south-west, with a view over the village of Ceres and the surrounding, richly fertile countryside. The garden soil is neutral, requiring peat for ericaceous plants, and the climate is good with west winds prevailing, though winters can be severe.

The style of the garden is natural, with rock borders around spacious lawns, and Heath and Heather areas diversified by the colour of flowers and foliage, and also by the many dwarf conifers of different shapes, growing habits, and shades of green and yellow — a garden to enjoy throughout the whole year.

Few houses have such an enviable site as Hilton. It is built on a low shoulder of Kilmaron Hill, and faces south with an uninterrupted view of Cupar, and the Howe of Fife, stretching to the Lomond Hills. A magnificent avenue of Beech trees, between two and three centuries old and like a cathedral's pillars, leads up from the lodge to the late eighteenth-century farmhouse, with its dignified proportions and fine ashlar stone.

35 HILTON HOUSE
Cupar
1 mile north of Cupar on the Hospital road.
(MRS M. M. WILSON)

Mrs Wilson's late husband planted thousands of Daffodils and Narcissi each year in the grass beneath the Beeches, a sea of pale yellow and green in April. The spring blossoming is followed by Cherry trees, then Rhododendrons, vivid against the tender green of the trees' new foliage.

A gateway into the formal walled garden is arched over with *Rosa* 'New

Dawn', and early and mid summer brings a concerted flourish of Roses throughout the garden. Then interest switches to the herbaceous borders, designed in the form of a cross, with the intersection opposite the main gate. The delphiniums are particularly fine. Part of the walled garden is used for vegetables and fruit. There is a large greenhouse, divided into three, the heated part for pot plants, the other two for Vines and Carnations.

36 HOUSE OF URRARD

Killiecrankie

On A9, ½ mile north of Killiecrankie village.
(MR & MRS CHARLES FINDLAY)

The House of Urrard was erected about 1831 by William Burn, close to the river Garry. Built of stone with Dutch gables, it is an extension of an older house, while the back is modern.

The walled garden was made about a century ago. It includes 'Dundee's Mound' and the old well where Graham of Claverhouse, Viscount Dundee, was shot in the course of the battle of Killiecrankie in 1689, though it was a victory for his Highland clansmen. The bullet which killed him is reputed to have been fired from a window of the old House of Urrard.

The owners modestly make no great claims for the 'botanical excellence' of the garden, yet it commands some fine views that include the deep gorge of the river and the high mountains on all sides. Much of it is enclosed within the walled garden, but there are lawns bright with Daffodils in springtime, and midsummer sees the Rhododendrons and Azaleas in bloom.

By the path through the woods from the garden to Killiecrankie village you will pass two of the original Larches, brought back in 1738 from the Tyrol by Menzies of Vuldares.

37 INCHYRA HOUSE

Glencarse

On main Perth-Dundee road; 5 miles from Perth, 16 miles from Dundee.
(LORD & LADY INCHYRA)

Inchyra House was built *c.* 1800-1810 in the Georgian style. The architect, it is thought, may have been Gillespie Graham, one of the creators of Edinburgh's New Town. The garden, extending to approximately 5 acres, plus greenhouses, is formal in the immediate vicinity of the mansion. The walled garden lies some way off, at the end of an avenue of young Horse-Chestnut trees, a pretty sight at any time, but especially so in spring and autumn.

Brick-making is a Carse of Gowrie industry, and the red bricks of the walled garden were almost certainly made at the Inchcoonans brickfield. Their reddish colour makes a pleasant backdrop for the flower borders and cordoned fruit trees.

The formality of the garden is sustained by patterned Rose beds, sentinel Yews and Cypresses. A raised Lily pond makes a focal point at the centre. The garden is typical of the Carse country, having light sandy soil and clay in places. The climate is fairly mild here, in the lee of the Braes, without much frost or snow. Roses and Rhododendrons thrive, and Peaches ripen out of doors against sunny walls.

38 KEILLOUR CASTLE GARDEN

Keillour Castle was built in 1849 on the site of a previous castle, burned down about 1640. It stands at a height of 500 feet above sea level on a peninsula between two dens, facing south-east and overlooking the broad valley of the Earn towards the Ochil Hills.

Apart from mature specimen trees, established around 1860 and later, the garden was made by Major Knox Finlay between the years 1946 and 1970 and has since been maintained by the present owner. It is not open to the public.

There are about 15 acres divided between a rock garden, Rose garden, water garden, kitchen garden, lawns and a Rhododendron den. Spread throughout these is a good collection of trees, shrubs and herbaceous plants, including choice Primulas, Meconopses and various Lilies. The garden at Keillour Castle is generally regarded as one of the best in Perthshire, admired especially for its Rhododendron den with the burns merging at the foot.

The lands of Keir were acquired in 1448 by Lucas of Strevelyn. His descendant, Sir William Stirling-Maxwell, Bart (1818–78), an authority on Spanish art, spent a great deal of time and money on the property. In landscaping the grounds he believed that the attractions should be gradually revealed, and that at every turn there should be something specially fitted to attract the eye — a noble tree, a peculiarly constructed vase, or a far-reaching vista.

The gardens are woodland in character, extending to 45 acres, and at a height of 300 feet above sea level on average. They overlook the Carse of Stirling and the Gargunnock Hills. The climate is typical of central Scotland, with reasonably mild winters, although there are exceptions. Tender shrubs such as *Drimys winteri*, *Crinodendron hookeranum,* and *Desfontainea spinosa* survived the recent severe winters with little damage.

Keir is famous throughout Britain for its vast collection of trees and shrubs, including Rhododendrons and Azaleas, and its magnificent herbaceous borders. In such an extensive, lavishly planted garden, there is always something of interest and beauty, throughout the entire year.

In the course of its history, the garden has received many distinguished visitors: Benjamin Disraeli, Lord Beaconsfield, planted a commemorative Cypress tree, and Frederic Chopin, the Polish-born composer, came in 1848.

The lands changed hands after eighteen Stirlings had been lairds of Keir. The family loft remains in Lecropt church, one mile north-west of Bridge of Allan.

Compared to big brothers such as Brodick, Crathes and Inverewe, Falkland may be small, but Kellie is positively tiny. But if ever there was a doubt about the truth of there being good things in small parcels, Kellie would confound agnostics.

The garden is just over 1 acre, enclosed by high stone walls, and is situated on the north side of the castle, thus denying a quarter of this scrap of land from any direct sunlight.

The origins of the castle began as long ago as 1360, but the greater part was a later addition of about 1600. From the Seward, or Siward, family it was sold in

---

KEILLOUR CASTLE GARDEN (contd.)
Perthshire
Half-way between Perth and Crieff; first turning on right after passing through Methven village.
(Mrs MARY W. KNOX FINLAY)

39 KEIR GARDEN
Dunblane
Entrance 50 yards from Keir roundabout on M9, on the road to Doune.
(Under the control and management of BLACKFORD FARMS LTD)

40 KELLIE CASTLE
by Pittenweem
On A917 between St Monans and Anstruther.
(NATIONAL TRUST FOR SCOTLAND)

FIGURE 63
Kinross House – aerial view; (inset) the view from the house

1613 to Thomas Erskine, who became the 1st Earl of Kellie. It was abandoned in the early nineteenth century, and purchased in the 1870s by Professor James Lorimer, whose son Robert's architectural achievements are now an essential part of Scotland's heritage. So too are his gardens.

From an old print it is known that a very formal garden did exist at one time, but a further drawing made in 1880 by the then sixteen-year-old Robert shows the basis upon which the present garden was developed. Young Lorimer's maxim of 'a garden within a garden' is illustrated in the restored 'Robin's Corner' at the north end of the garden, and again in the south-east where there is a Yew enclosure, also of Robert's design. By the time the Trust acquired the property in 1970, the garden had obviously suffered from neglect and lack of management, but with the help of Hew Lorimer and others who knew the garden, plus the helpful account of the garden by Gertrude Jekyll following her visit at the end of the nineteenth century, it was possible to restore much of the former glory of the garden; the mixture of gay flowers, fruit and vegetables which Robert noted as 'one of the characteristics of Kellie'.

It is a very difficult task to attempt to restore the old-world, informal gaiety of a late Victorian garden such as Kellie; in this case it would have been impossible but for the sympathetic help of George Knox, the experienced and very skilled craftsman the Trust is fortunate enough to have as a gardener at Kellie.

The object was to recreate, as far as possible, the almost 'cottage garden' scene depicted by George Ellwood in the picture used to illustrate the account by Gertrude Jekyll in the second edition of the book *Some English Gardens*. First there was a considerable amount of fundamental clearing up to be done before restoration could really begin. Bishopweed was rampant, the grass coarse and weedy, but in time the battle showed signs of being won. Roses, especially Shrub Roses, were an important element of the garden, and again there were reasonably clear indications of what had been grown. The pattern for the main borders was gleaned from an illustrated article which appeared in the July 1906 edition of *Country Life*. Apparently the main components had been Hollyhocks, Roses and a wide edging of Pinks, and most of these were replaced, although after one glorious year the Hollyhocks have never since been quite so outstanding.

To see the garden to best effect, a visit during August is recommended, at which time most of the annual and perennial flowers are at the height of their flowering period; but in fact it is well worth seeing from mid June until the garden officially closes.

Gardens open from April to September, daily 10.00 a.m. to dusk.

41 KINROSS HOUSE
🐾 *Kinross*
Kinross ½ mile.
(SIR DAVID MONTGOMERY, BT)

Magnificent Kinross House stands on a peninsula between Kinross town and Loch Leven. It was built between 1685 and 1692 by Sir William Bruce, architect of the later portions of Holyroodhouse, for his own use and not, as has been claimed, for the Duke of York (later James VII). In the eighteenth century, it was

the seat of the Grahams of Kinross, passing by marriage to Sir Graham Graham Montgomery, Baronet of Stobo Castle in Peebles-shire, of whom the present owner is a descendant. The house lay empty during much of the nineteenth century, and thus escaped alteration.

The entrance gates are in the town, and there is a drive through the park, with the mansion constantly in view, up to the main doorway. The gardens, on the far side, are landscaped in the grand style. A good vantage point is the Fish Gate, looking back to the great house down a central pathway, with the bowl of the fountain intervening. The view in the other direction is of Loch Leven and Castle Island, where Mary, Queen of Scots was imprisoned.

Long herbaceous borders and Rose beds, wide lawns and Yew hedges form the garden which is walled on all sides, its formality further enhanced by statues and summer houses in stone.

42 MEGGINCH CASTLE by Errol

Midway between Perth and Dundee, on the main A95 dual carriageway.
(Captain Humphrey & The Hon Mrs Cherry Drummond)

Megginch Castle surmounts a 50 foot rise above the flat, richly fertile Carse of Gowrie, an area acclaimed as the 'Garden of Scotland'. Centuries ago it was surrounded by the Tay estuary's marshes. The name means 'Beautiful Island'.

Sheltering clumps of Yew, 60 feet high and an estimated thousand years old, suggest that the place may have had Druidic associations — the Yew being their symbol of immortality. But the first Megginch garden was almost certainly made by Christian monks and the tiny 17th-century family chapel, embosomed in Yews, replaced a pre-Reformation shrine, dedicated to the Blessed Virgin in the Fields, burned down by John Knox and his angry rabble of Protestants.

Entrance to the 10-acre policies is gained through a castellated gateway, erected by Captain Robert Drummond in 1798, whence a carriageway ¾ mile long sweeps up to the Castle between plantations of mature Oaks, Beeches, and Geans. The grass verges in springtime are deep in Daffodils.

Parts of the turreted Castle date from 1460. The first Baron of Megginch was Peter Hay, second son of Edmund Hay of Leys. He added to it considerably in 1575 and made the old walled garden. In 1664, Sir George Hay of Megginch sold the Castle and lands to John Drummond, 8th Baron of Lennoch in Strathearn. It has remained in Drummond hands ever since. Successive generations of Drummonds have left their own imprint, not just on the Castle, but on the garden and grounds, landscaping them with care, planting trees for posterity, and introducing new plants, many from distant places.

The top walled kitchen garden, made in 1575 by Peter Hay, is still in use. The walls are made of red bricks from Inchcoonans, providing a lee for a brown Turkey Fig, Nectarines, Peaches, and also White and Red Currants, planted here in 1793 and still cropping abundantly.

In the days when coal was cheap, gardeners sometimes employed ducted heat in which to nurture 'stove plants' and other exotics. Megginch gardeners resorted to this method and one can still see the flues in the brick walls through which hot air rose from the ovens.

FIGURE 64
The doocot, Megginch

Captain Robert Drummond built the bottom walled kitchen garden in 1800. He returned from adventuring in China with a fortune, and numbered plant-collecting among his particular interests. A flowered walk runs through the entire walled garden, passing beneath the boughs of an aged Pear tree. This makes a good vantage point for looking back at the Castle's dramatic skyline.

Returning to the Castle, one passes through a wicket into a paved Rose garden. It is quite small and intimate, and was created by Mrs Colin Drummond about 1760 in a delicate and very feminine mode. She apparently preferred Shrub Roses like *R. damascena,* the White Rose of York, the Jacobite Rose associated with Prince Charles Edward, and *R.* 'Souvenir de la Malmaison', all interspersed with clumps of verdant Boxwood.

Lady Charlotte Drummond, daughter of the 4th Duke of Atholl and wife of Admiral Sir Adam Drummond, made the formal garden in 1830. It remains almost unaltered. Flower beds, edged with Box, contain Lavender from Drummond Castle, near Crieff, and 'Coltness Gem' Dahlias in jewel colours. Milk-white doves flutter down from sunny perches to drink at the fountain, and peacocks pick their stately path across the lawns. Mrs Malcolm Drummond, grandmother of the Hon Mrs Cherry Drummond, was responsible for the topiary, silver and gold Hollies and Yews clipped into fantastic shapes. There is a sundial, put there in honour of King Edward VII; and a remarkable Crown Imperial, shaped from living yellow and green Yews, commemorates Queen Victoria's Golden Jubilee of 1887. As it is hollow, one can look inside and admire how each component branch and twig has been trained to a wooden frame.

The Lime tree avenue was planted by Mrs Colin Drummond before she departed for Canada in 1767. So tiny were the baby trees that she could envelop them entirely with her pocket handkerchief. In May and June white and purple Lilacs spread their sweet fragrance through the garden, and the clumps of *Rhododendron campanulatum*, introduced from the Himalayas in 1825 and planted at Megginch shortly thereafter, are a mass of mauve and white flowers.

It was about 1807 that Captain Robert Drummond, sailing his East Indiaman the *General Elliot*, returned from China with the first white Banksian Roses and the first double pink Camellias. Some he presented to his friend, Sir Joseph Banks (1743-1820), the naturalist and first unofficial director of Kew Gardens, and some he planted at Megginch. They survive to this day, but rarely flower.

The garden also contains plants brought back from Macao, Southern China, in the late eighteenth century, and Roses and bulbs imported very cheaply from Holland in 1702. Lord Strange, Mrs Cherry Drummond's father, planted the Birch trees in 1921, and Lady Strange the *Cupressus macrocarpa* in 1965.

The Gothic courtyard behind the castle is built of reddish brick and stone, with rose-shaped and Gothic windows. A dovecote, like a pagoda, is a reminder of Captain Robert Drummond's interests in China. It is topped by a model of his East Indiaman, the *General Elliot*. The clay urns beneath the arches are planted with pink and scarlet Pelargoniums.

When James I of Scotland was held prisoner in England 1405-24 the English page who attended him was a young squire called Robert Coxwell. On his return to Scotland, the King rewarded Coxwell with a pension, paid out of the Edinburgh customs, and with possession of the South Quarter of Auchtermuchty including the area known as 'The Myres'. He also appointed Coxwell as his mace bearer, and for centuries thereafter the office of Myres Macer was heriditary to the proprietor of the Myres estate.

The old parts of the castle date from 1530, when it was the property of John Scrymgeour, Master of the King's Works, who was responsible for the building and repair of Holyrood Palace.

With a serenity that matches its antiquity, the castle stands in its own park and gardens, looking out over the richly fertile Howe of Fife. The paddock in front was planted in 1906 with three thousand Daffodil bulbs and the whole area is a mass of yellow in April. They sweep around a Spanish Chestnut tree, said to have been planted by Mary, Queen of Scots on a visit to Myres in 1563.

The walled garden on the west side of the castle is subdivided by Yew hedges, some of which date from around 1890. The 'garden rooms' are planted with vegetables, soft fruit bushes, and choice plants include Lilies and Gladioli. Sweet Peas thrive in the rich loam, and Lily of the Valley increases undisturbed. Beyond the line of Beeches, planted in 1760, are two specimens of *Magnolia grandiflora*, grown from seed brought back from Madeira.

There is a small Lily pond, visited by pigeons from the two doocots; the octagonal one also came from Madeira. The pottery water fountain on the garden wall is another Portuguese feature of the garden. The most impressive aspect of Myres is the avenue of arched Lime trees, with clumps of Rhododendrons about their feet, and the ancient castle tower looking down the carriageway.

Among the first landowners of Naughton estate were Norman barons of the name of De Lasceles. The ruined castle of Naughton, however, was built by Robert de Lundon, William the Lion's natural son, in the early years of the thirteenth century. The list of subsequent owners is hardly less impressive, including the Hays of Errol, Sir Peter Crichton (Master of the Robes to James V), the Hays of Durdie, the Morisons (Dundee merchants), and a grandson of Admiral Viscount Duncan of Camperdown.

The present mansion was built by James Morison in 1793. The policies extend to 48 acres, including a walled garden of 1½ acres. The owner, Brigadier H. N. Crawford, was born in New Zealand and many of the contents of the garden are natives of that country, yet they thrive in Naughton's douce climate.

The shell of the castle makes a delightful 'secret garden' containing fragrant herbs and old Shrub Roses, Veronicas, Viburnums, Mexican Orange Blossom (*Choisya ternata*), Jerusalem Sage (*Phlomis fruticosa*), New Zealand Cabbage Trees (*Cordyline australis*), the evergreen *Griselinia littoralis*, and its compatriot

---

43 MYRES CASTLE
Auchtermuchty

On outskirts of Auchtermuchty, on the road to Falkland.
(CAPTAIN DAVID & MRS FAIRLIE)

---

44 NAUGHTON HOUSE
Balmerino

4½ miles north-west of Newport-on-Tay on the road to Balmerino.
(BRIGADIER H. N. & MRS CRAWFORD)

from New Zealand, the spiky wild Spanish Spear Grass (*Aciphylla*).

The walled garden, made in 1900, is no longer under cultivation, apart from the fruit trees — Peaches, Greengages, Victoria Plums, Conference Pears, and various Apples. The greenhouses too stand empty, owing to the prohibitive cost of fuel for heating; however, the 'forced' Daffodils and Narcissi they once contained continue to bloom in their thousands year by year, providing occasion for 'Daffodil teas' and 'open days', which raise funds for Balmerino Church.

Several rare trees make the wild garden a place of special interest — evergreen Pittosporums, Incense Cedars (*Libocedrus decurrens*), Japanese Umbrella Pines (*Sciadopitys verticillata*), the not uncommon Monkey Puzzle (*Araucaria araucana*), and the Maidenhair tree (*Ginkgo biloba*).

A garden house, thatched with Tay reeds, and a doocot, with crow-step gabling and the date 1750 on the lintel, contribute to Naughton's ambience of tranquillity and wholesome living.

45 OLD BALLIKINRAIN
Balfron
On Fintry road (B818),
some 2 miles from turn-off
on Killearn-Balfron road.
(MR & MRS WILLIAM CUTHBERT)

There has been a dwelling of one kind or another at Ballikinrain since the mid fourteenth century, when Donald, Earl of Lennox, granted the lands to his kinsman, Cilestine MacAlowne. The MacAlownes later, and for reasons unknown, became Napiers, and the lands of Ballinkinrain remained with them for five centuries. The oldest part of the present house was built by James Napier some time before 1750. In 1862 Ballinkinrain was purchased by Mr Archibald Orr-Ewing, Sir Archibald as he was to become; in 1870 he built Ballinkinrain Castle on the Campsies, and the former mansion became known as Old Ballinkinrain.

It is situated in Strathendrick Glen, close to Endrick Water, with an upward view to the Campsie Hills. The climate in such a low-lying area is often unfavourable, with frost pockets occurring even in June and September.

The 5 acres of garden, not counting the woodland walks, are dominated by beautiful old trees, mainly Beeches, and consist of formal and semi-formal areas. The original 'mixed Scottish' garden, situated some distance away from the house, has been made into an organic vegetable garden. New borders have been introduced together with a main 'shrubbery', and the lawns extended so that they give access to the estate's burn and the woodlands. An interesting feature is the herb garden, made in an erstwhile open-air squash court.

The shrub garden contains a diverse collection of ground-cover and shade-loving plants — Hostas, Day Lilies (*Hemerocallis*), Astilbes, Lady's Mantle (*Alchemilla mollis*), Spurges (*Euphorbias*), Irises, *Epimediums*, and Torch Lilies (*Kniphofia*). The acid soil and woodland shade provide favourable conditions for Rhododendrons and Azaleas, their flowering season following that of the Daffodils, of which there is a good display in early spring.

The former main entrance, facing south, has been transformed by the addition of a conservatory in the style of an eighteenth-century orangery, containing Fuchsias, Geraniums and potted Begonias. The doors open on steps leading down to the formal paved Rose garden, with borders of Lavender, Honeysuckle and *Ceanothus* growing against the adjacent house wall. The woodland garden contains a replica of Michelangelo's 'David'.

The sight of ponies grazing in the paddock accords well with the serenity of the garden.

The Roman Camp Hotel is said to occupy the site of an advanced post for the legionaries of Antonius Pius in AD 142. The house was built in 1625 as a hunting lodge for the powerful Drummond family, and their motto 'Gang Warily' appears carved in stone above the doorway.

46 ROMAN CAMP HOTEL
Callander
Within the town of Callander, on road to Doune.
(MR & MRS G. A. WOOD)

Following the defeat of the Jacobite Rising of 1745, the Drummonds forfeited their estates, but a younger branch of the family succeeded in buying them back later. The property passed to the wife of the twentieth Lord Willoughby D'Eresby, then to her descendants, the Earls of Ancaster, who in 1908 sold the Roman Camp to the 2nd Viscount Esher, an adviser to Queen Victoria. His diaries are full of references to the Camp, and the pleasures he derived from its ownership. It was later bought by Lady Wilson, a friend of the Esher family who, rather than see the house fall into disuse, had it turned into an hotel. She was also responsible for landscaping the 20 acres of garden. The present owner, at considerable expense, has now restored the buildings and gardens to their former glory.

The gardens are approached by a narrow road, flanked on either side by Lime and Horse Chestnut trees, and at the bottom of the gardens flows the River Teith. The fine walled garden contains at the centre an Italian-style wishing well, decorated with an acanthus-leaf and rope design, and the crowned eagle and the rose, and two lions on opposite sides. The remainder is mainly herbaceous border and Rose beds.

Tame peacocks strut the wide lawns in a haughty, proprietorial manner, disappearing into coverts of Maples, Rhododendrons, and other ornamental shrubs and trees. There are walks through the woods, and walks by the Teith where fishermen wait patiently under the Alder trees.

The so-called Monk's Garden is modelled on the knot garden, with small borders edged with Box and filled with scarlet Salvias or spring bulbs, an ancient sundial at the centre, and the whole surrounded and divided by high Yew hedges.

It is thought that the River Tay once came up to the foothills of the Sidlaws and later retreated, leaving the Carse of Gowrie with flat areas of fertile blue clay, and what had been islands of dark clay loam, locally known as 'black land'.

47 ROSSIE PRIORY
Angus
North of A85 dual carriageway, 15 miles from Perth, 6 miles from Dundee. Signposted to 'Rossie Priory'.
(LORD KINNAIRD)

In 1170 King William the Lion showed favour to Radulphus Rufus by conferring upon him the barony of Kinnaird in Gowrie. His descendant Reginald de Kinnaird increased the family's wealth and status by marrying Marjory, daughter and heiress of Sir John Kirkcaldy. Throughout the Cromwellian period, George Patrick Kinnaird remained loyal to the house of Stuart, in recognition of which Charles II knighted him in 1661. In 1682, he was raised to the Scottish peerage as Baron Kinnaird of Inchture.

In 1807, the old mansion of Drimmie, which had been the Kinnairds' seat, was pulled down to make way for Rossie Priory — there are in fact no monastic connections — designed by Atkinson for the 8th Lord Kinnaird. It stands about 130 feet above sea level, on the south-facing slopes of Rossie Hill (567 feet), so with the surrounding woodland the situation is quite sheltered. However, much of the great house was demolished in 1946, making space for a new garden within the original nineteenth-century one.

The back road to Rossie Priory passes close to a row of estate workers' cottages. Built of red sandstone, each has the initials A.K. and the year 1880 carved above its door, and all face across a little stream with closely mown grass banks. Each cottage has its flower borders on either side of the front door, and they present a pretty picture from early spring till autumn.

The estate's kitchen garden was made on the enviable 'black land', open to the full sun, and sheltered on every side by high red brick walls. Entry is through either of two large, opposing and most impressive wrought-iron gates. Much space is devoted to vegetables of every kind, soft fruit, cordoned apples, and flowers suitable for marketing in cut bunches. There is also much wall-trained fruit, and greenhouses growing Grapes, Figs, Carnations, *Cymbidium* Orchids, and the beautiful evergreen creeper *Lapageria rosea*, with its pendulous, bell-like flowers, blooming all the summer. Areas of garden wall are clothed with *Actinidia kolomikta,* a deciduous climber with fragrant greenish-white flowers, yellow fruit, and blotchy pink, white and green foliage, turning an all-over pink in autumn.

A gravel path leads through the far gateway into the flower and woodland gardens beyond, with their beautiful specimen trees, a Pinetum, archways of Yew, and a water garden where a fountain replenishes a pool surrounded by pink Astilbes, Primulas, Ligularias, Rodgersias, and Gunneras.

48 St Adrians
Crail
On the road down to Crail harbour.
(Mr & Mrs Oswald Wynd)

St Adrians house and garden occupy a narrow, underlying shelf of rock between the yellow sandstone cliffs and the sea wall, washed and pounded by every incoming tide. Often, under the weight of the sea's fury, the house can be felt shuddering, and spindrift in great clouds drenches the garden, the house, and the lane behind. It was flouting Nature's laws to make a garden on such a site, yet Nature favours the courageous, and there is a certain wild beauty here.

The house is estimated to be three to four centuries old, but its predecessor was erected on land which Countess Ada, mother of Malcolm IV and William the Lion, bestowed on the Cluniac Benedictine monks who had their monastery on the Isle of May, 6 miles off the Crail shore.

The Hungarian missionary, Adrian, was murdered by Danish sea-robbers on the Isle of May in 875. 4th March, the day of his martyrdom, was piously observed all along the East Neuk coast; and, at the heart of this old house in Crail, an ancient stone fire-surround is engraved with the entreaty, 'Sancte Adriane, ora pro Nobis'.

It is as though the garden enjoyed the saint's lasting beneficence. A headland, once occupied by the ancient Crail Castle, shelters it against the north wind, and it receives a full share of the sun's brightness and warmth. Moreover, the tides cast up on the low-lying grassy areas enough seaweed to maintain the garden in good fertility.

In no respect is this an impoverished garden. Instead, plants thrive with a kind of bold defiance — New Zealand Cabbage Trees (*Cordyline australis*), pink Nerines from South Africa (*N. bowdenii*), Corsican Hellebores, and *Hebe* 'Autumn Glory' with deep violet-blue flowers. Roses flourish in shallow beds of soil, even scaling the cliff face where cantankerous fulmars, uttering guttural chuckles, brood their eggs on sun-baked ledges. Scented Carnations flower in winter under glass, and perennial Scandinavian Wallflower (*Erysimum alpinum*), Daffodils and Tulips herald spring's arrival — but only briefly before east winds off the sea end their short-lived beauty.

There is beauty, too, in the garden's stones — the texture of the cliff, the ancient house walls, and the mellow red Dutch pantiles, used as ballast by merchantmen returning to Crail after exporting 'Crail capons' (sun-dried herrings) to the Low Countries.

Among St Adrians' previous owners was the sister of Francis Campbell Boileau Cadell, R.S.A., R.S.W. (1883-1937). She had the shutters made to order in France, and painted them a bright marine blue.

The present owner is Mr Oswald Wynd, the novelist.

The crowning place of Scotland's early kings, and one-time guardian of the Stone of Destiny, Scone is certainly one of our most historic centres. Scone Palace incorporates the great house erected by the Earls of Gowrie in 1580, but much enlarged in 1803-8 by William Atkinson for the 3rd Earl of Mansfield and restyled in the Gothic manner as a reminder of the mediaeval Abbey which once stood at the east end of the Palace terrace. It is surrounded by parks and woodland, bordering the east banks of the Tay for over 2 miles, and including Scone Race Course.

49 SCONE PALACE
Perth
2 miles north of Perth on the A93 Perth-Blairgowrie road.
(THE EARL OF MANSFIELD)

The Pinetum, started in 1848, contains one of the finest collections of rare conifers in Britain, among which is a Douglas Fir (*Pseudotsuga menziesii*), raised from seed sent home from America in 1827 by the traveller and botanist, David Douglas, who was born on the estate and worked for a time as an undergardener at the Palace.

Giant Cedars of Lebanon (*Cedrus libani*) crowd around the family chapel of the Mansfield earls on Moot Hill, an artificial mound of earth on which in ancient times Scotland's chiefs stood to swear fealty to their king at his coronation.

There is a delightful small garden at the south of the Palace; and paths

meandering among Rhododendrons and Azaleas lead to the Monks' Playgreen and the Friars' Den, and the Chantry Gait where brethren of the Abbey used to forgather to chant their evening hymn.

Stobhall consists of a group of four fourteenth to seventeenth-century buildings, situated on a high tongue of land, on the wooded left bank of the Tay, 8 miles north-east of Perth. It was the principal seat of the powerful Drummond family until they moved to Drummond Castle in 1491.

The buildings are grouped around a grassed courtyard with one single, but most effective, ancient Yew tree in the centre. Daffodils bloom in the spring around the boles of the mature Beech trees forming one side of the approach. There is a seventeenth-century topiary and Rose garden and the ravine below contains fine shrubs and trees, chief among them being Maples, Rhododendrons and Azaleas. Steps cut in the steep bank lead down to the river Tay, whence a path strays through beautiful woods to Campsie Linn (scene of Conachar's death in Scott's novel *The Fair Maid of Perth*), where the river plunges in a cataract over rocks.

According to legend, James IV met and courted the beautiful Margaret Drummond among these woods, close to her father's castle of Stobhall, 'when the river bank was bright with spring blossom and the blackbird sang blithely among the trees'.

Before World War I, Tayfield had an extensive and fine garden, including a dene walk with Tree Ferns. This is now either woodland or wild garden, and altogether quite beautiful, bringing great pleasure to all who know and love Tayfield.

The estate at one time formed part of the barony of Inverdovat, held in turn by the Leightons of Usan and the Crawford Lindsays of Balcarres. Mr John Berry, whose wife came from another local family, the Nairnes of St Fort, bought Tayfield around 1790. The present house was begun that year, with extensions to the south and west made between 1828–30, in the Tudor style, to plans by John Smith (*alias* 'Tudor Johnnie').

Some old accounts show the cost of planting the Den in 1792. Harry Clark, William Culdross, James Elsdale and Robert Taylor received £3:2s:1d. between them for casting 4144 iron fence posts, or 1/6d per hundred; while Cosmo Hepburn earned one guinea for twenty-one days' work in the garden.

The estate has long been noted for its mature specimen trees, referred to in nineteenth-century books on Fife. Today there are: a hollow Locust Tree (*Robinia pseudacacia*), much favoured by tree-creepers and woodpeckers; a *Fagus sylvatica* 'Heterophylla' (Cut-Leaf Beech); and about thirty species of *Eucalyptus*, some grown from seed given to Dr Berry by the Professor of Forestry in Canberra University in 1970.

There are two sizeable ponds, frequented by exotic waterfowl, including

50 STOBHALL
by Perth
On A93 Perth to Blairgowrie road, eight miles north of Perth.
(THE EARL & COUNTESS OF PERTH)

51 TAYFIELD
Newport-on-Tay
Within the burgh of Newport.
(DR JOHN BERRY, BBE, DL)

FIGURE 65
Astilbes in the water garden, Rossie Priory

free-flying Mandarins and Carolina duck and wild geese. Many migrant and breeding birds are attracted into the sanctuary by the diverse and sheltering terrain.

FIGURE 66
Beech trees at Tayfield

From 1420 until 1928 Touch House was held by a branch of the Setons, one of Scotland's grandest old families, and within the garden is Mary Seton's Bower, composed of Box hedging. She was one of Mary, Queen of Scots' 'four Maries', her personal attendants.

52 TOUCH
🐿 *Cambusbarron*
Off A811. Cambusbarron 2 miles, Stirling 3 miles.
(MRS BUCHANAN & MR & MRS P. B. BUCHANAN)

The house contains a tower, built around 1450, and other parts dating from the sixteenth century. The beautifully proportioned front, attributed to John Adam, was built in 1749. During the 1745 Rising, Prince Charles Edward slept the night at Touch, prior to the battle of Prestonpans.

The situation looks deceptively sheltered, facing south towards the Touch Hills, but the gardens and woodland suffered severe damage during the 1968 storm. Clearings in the surrounding woods are being replanted with *Rhododendron* species and other shrubs, such as *Stranvaesia davidiana* and *Parrotia persica*, both of which will provide brilliant autumn colours.

The walled garden, on a gentle east-facing slope, is sub-divided, one half woodland garden, the other formal garden, contents of particular interest being the Shrub Roses including *Rosa moyesii 'Geranium', Magnolia stellata,* espaliered Apple trees against the red brick walls, and the plots of dwarf Rhododendrons. The greenhouses are being used for propagating Rhododendron cuttings and bringing on other valuable shrubs. There are ancient Yew hedges, and a large and handsome Silver Fir (*Abies*) at the entrance to the garden strikes a dominant pose.

The original Tower was founded about 1570 by Sir David Herring (Heron) of the family of Herring of Drumlochy, probably as a keep and/or hunting tower. The walls of the original buildings are of great thickness, and the apartments stone-vaulted. It appears to have been surrounded by a moat; the dell part of the present garden to the west is formed from a section of the moat, with a stately backdrop of Beech trees. These Beeches were once clipped to form a hedge similar to the celebrated one at Meikleour. Extensive additions in the Scottish Baronial style were made to the Tower in 1885, using the same warm-tinted old red sandstone from a quarry on the estate.

53 TOWER OF LETHENDY
🐿 *Meikleour*
2½ miles from Blairgowrie on the Blairgowrie-Kirkton of Lethendy road (A984).
(LETHENDY ESTATES LTD)

The garden consists of 30 acres of level, well-drained soil. It faces south and the main feature is the variety of old mature trees: Limes (*Tilia*), Beeches (*Fagus sylvatica*), Douglas Firs (*Pseudotsuga*), and other conifers predominating. There are also two very old and beautifully shaped Sycamores (*Acer pseudoplatanus*) at the south end of the main lawns.

The Dell is thickly planted with numerous hybrid Rhododendrons, a great variety of Azaleas, Camellias, other ornamental shrubs and herbaceous plants. There is also a large rock garden and a water garden. The walled garden, containing the kitchen garden and greenhouses, is used as a preserve for the cultivation of herbaceous plants, annuals, and shrubs.

54 WESTER BALRUDDERY
Invergowrie

3 miles from Invergowrie. ½ mile from Invergowrie roundabout on Dundee-Perth road, A85, take turning marked Benvie and Fowlis; then turn left at sign to Flocklones. Immediately after the farm, turn right, following a wall. Take entry on right marked 'Cats' Hotel', go up the drive. The garden is on the left, by a red-roofed house.

(Lt.-Col. & Mrs J. Anderson)

The garden is located in a wooded glen with a burn. The setting is peaceful, although only 7 miles from the centre of Dundee, and sheltered from most winds. Here the land is rising gently towards the Sidlaw Hills, and the view from the house front is across the Tay to Fife. The garden comprises approximately 4 acres and was started in 1964 by the present owners, who also designed it. They had ease of maintenance as one of the main considerations, and no outside help is required.

The style is natural, but with two rock gardens containing a wide range of alpines. These do well in this locality, which is subject to quite severe frost, with very rarely any protective snow blanket.

The soil is on the acid side, and thus suitable for ericacious plants such as Rhododendrons and Azaleas. Meconopses and Primulas, especially the Asiatic varieties, provide an excellent display. In fact, from May until July the garden is full of colour, with June as the peak time for Meconopsis and Primulas, and Embothriums and Rhododendrons still in flower.

The garden is not open to the general public, but small parties or individuals are welcome by appointment (telephone Longforgan 209).

172

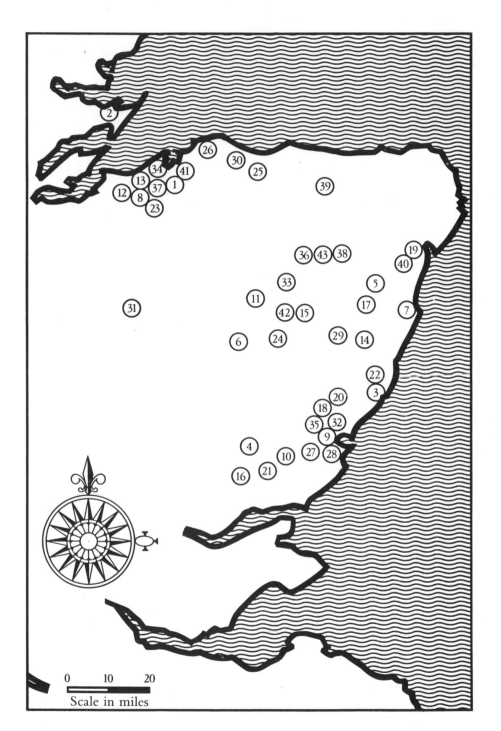

Scale in miles

SECTION 3

THE NORTH EAST

The modern house stands in a garden, landscaped by Sir William and Lady Gordon Cumming twenty years ago with lakes and islands artificially constructed by dumpings of rubble and masonry from the old, demolished Altyre House. The nucleus of mature shrubs and trees, needed to form the basic outline of the new garden, was transferred from the old one.

The Altyre Burn, rising on the south-west slope of the Hill of Glaschyle, flows past Altyre, falling at last into the bay at Findhorn, one mile west-south-west of Kinloss. Wooden bridges cross the waterways to islands that are bosky with spring-flowering shrubs — Lilacs, great clumps of Forsythia, Flowering Currant, Sea Buckthorn, various Willows, Rhododendrons and Azaleas, and hedges of Copper Beech (*Fagus sylvatica* 'Purpurea').

The soil is light loam, and the climate very mild for north-east Scotland, the rainfall only 22 inches per annum, and the wind prevailing south-westerly.

Hugh Rose had this house built in 1780 for his wife, Arabella. She was by all accounts a great beauty, and was painted by Romney. The building is in keeping with the prevalent eighteenth-century style, being bow-fronted, white-harled and with a parapet roof, and the additions are in keeping. The outlook is pleasant and satisfying, across the garden and farmlands to the Hill of Nigg.

The garden was designed to complement the house, with spacious lawns and fine trees. It remains little altered, except that Sir John and Lady Dick-Lauder sold off the walled garden at the rear when they created the main flower garden and orchard in 1938, reducing the total extent to 6 acres.

Here, at sea level, the climate though variable is often warm and sunny, due in part to good shelter from the prevailing north or south-west winds.

Spanish Oaks (*Quercus* × *hispanica*) flank the driveway, with Rhododendrons growing about their boles, and where it ends by a curved sweep of lawn before the front of the house there are Spanish Chestnut, Walnut and Ash trees and also two very beautiful old Limes.

The garden is formal in parts. Much of it is given to lawns, areas of rough grass sown with naturalised Snowdrops, Daffodils and Narcissi, and plantings of Rhododendrons and Azaleas and other flowering shrubs which succeed in the lime-free clay soil. Some, like the ornamental trees, have obviously been chosen with an eye to good autumn leaf-colour. There are also Floribunda and Climbing Roses in abundance.

A water-lily pond and a fountain in the shape of a small lion make a charming focal point.

---

1 ALTYRE

Forres

3 miles south of Forres on the A940 Forres - Grantown-on-Spey.

(SIR W. GORDON CUMMING)

2 ARABELLA HOUSE

by Tain

Take A9 from Inverness to Kildary. At Kildary and opposite Ken's Garage, a signpost to the right says 'Arabella 2 miles'. The house is 2 miles along there, on a straight stretch.

Wrought-iron gates to drive.

(VICE-ADMIRAL SIR JOHN & THE HON LADY HAYES)

Home of the Arbuthnott family since 1190, the site was occupied by a fortified dwelling-house, later enlarged into a castle and courtyard in the fifteenth century. After further modifications in the sixteenth century the 3rd Viscount of Arbuthnott made additions to the house between 1680 and 1690 and created its garden. A classical façade of local sandstone was added in 1754; the graceful porch and fanlight are nineteenth-century refinements. The drawing room ceiling is a remarkable example of seventeenth-century plasterwork.

Perusals of old account books would indicate that the garden was designed and made *circa* 1685, conforming to the style of that period. The site forms the south-facing side of the valley sloping steeply down to the river Bervie, with diagonal paths linking the grass. The overall pattern, as seen from the other side of the river, resembles that of a Union Jack. The soil is poor, shallow-rooting plants are difficult to establish, and much labour is expended over the provision of peat, mulches of leaf mould and compost; and long periods of drought can be a serious hazard.

Lady Arbuthnott is a keen gardener and despite its disadvantages the garden prospers, verdant with old Yew and Box hedges, flowering shrubs, herbaceous borders and nut-bearing Hazels on the lower slopes. Among the surrounding tree tops there is a much patronised rookery, ever clamorous.

This garden was formerly the property of the late Major George Sherriff, plant collector and explorer. Mrs Sherriff, who shared his life-interest in plants and the Ascreavie garden, died in 1978. It is widely famed for the collection of Meconopses and Primulas, as well as other rare Himalayan plants, made by Major Sherriff and his wife, and established here. They are the subject of Harold R. Fletcher's book, *A Quest of Flowers – The Plant Explorations of Frank Ludlow and George Sherriff.*

There are between 3 and 4 acres of garden, situated on the lower foothills of the Grampians at a height of 800–900 feet, from which one obtains an excellent view of Strathmore, to the south. The climate and peaty soil suit the cultivation of Himalayan plants, although the leaves of the Rhododendrons are sometimes scorched in winter by cold blasts from the east.

The garden is formal, and great care has been taken to recreate as nearly as possible the wild nature of the plants' conditions in their native habitat. It is frequently described as an alpine garden. The Sherriffs laid out the front of the house garden first of all, extending it later to incorporate a Primula Garden. They subsequently made the Rhododendron Glade on the west side, a task which took between six and seven years. Further alterations and changes were made, with various Rhododendrons and Azaleas being established alongside the driveway approach to the house.

From time to time, enquiries have been received from other countries, seeking to obtain rare plants growing in the Ascreavie Garden to add to their own botanic garden collections. Some of the Sherriff discoveries are identifiable by their names, notably *Meconopsis sherriffii,* a very beautiful pink *Meconopsis*, a new Lily, *Lilium sherriffiae,* and Mrs Sherriff's 'Dream Poppy'.

Balbithan House is situated some two miles from the River Don, surrounded by farmland. It was built around 1560 by the Chalmers family, and later belonged to the Earl of Kintore. During the time of the Covenanters, the Marquis of Montrose and his henchmen made this a rendezvous. Following their defeat at Culloden, adherents of Prince Charles Edward came knocking on the door at dead of night, asking for food and refuge; or so it is said.

Balbithan is an L-shaped house with corner turrets; the roof was lowered in 1803 and it now stands only three storeys high. Mrs McMurtrie re-styled the garden when she bought the property some twenty years ago. She had the old stone wall, which used to run down the centre of the area, rebuilt, and hedges of Yew and old Shrub Roses planted to enclose the lawn. Against current conventional styles, she retained the original straight line paths of a typical Scottish garden.

The soil is acid, with heavy clay in parts. Belts of trees shelter the 2-acre garden from cold winds blowing up the river valley from the east. Winters in these parts can be severe, and frost pockets form in the garden hollow.

Old stone cattle troughs, provided with good drainage, are used to charming effect for Saxifrages, and there are raised beds planted with spring-flowering Alpines. Space is generously provided for old favourite cottage-garden flowers such as sweet-smelling Pinks, Auriculas, Scotch Roses and Daffodils, and there is a small pot planted with fragrant culinary and medicinal herbs.

5 BALBITHAN HOUSE
Kintore
2 miles south-east of Kintore, off the B977.
(MRS M. MCMURTRIE)

The personal home in Scotland of Her Majesty the Queen stands on a strip of level meadow, bounded on one side by a sweeping curve of the Dee and overlooked by Craig-Gowan.

Balmoral is Gaelic for 'majestic dwelling' and there had been previous castles on the same site before the estate was purchased in 1852 by Prince Albert, consort of Queen Victoria. The Prince engaged William Smith, the then city architect of Aberdeen, to draw up plans for the royal residence. With certain modifications, made by Prince Albert himself, it was built of light grey Invergelder granite, quarried on the Balmoral estate, and completed in 1855.

Queen Victoria called Balmoral 'this dear paradise' and she and the Prince immediately began making a garden about the Castle and planting the grounds with rare coniferous and forest trees. Queen Mary added the sunken Rose Garden in 1932, and since 1953 the Queen and Prince Philip have made other improvements and extensions, the latest being the Water Garden, made in 1979 close to Queen Victoria's Garden Cottage.

The soil is light, and the 3 acres of garden are vulnerable to west winds and extremely cold winter weather. Plants for the herbaceous borders around the perimeter of the Castle are obviously selected with these adverse conditions in

6 BALMORAL CASTLE GARDENS
Crathie
Turn off A93 Aberdeen-Braemar road at Crathie.
(HER MAJESTY THE QUEEN)

mind, and also to provide a colourful display of flowers when the Royal Family are in residence, from mid-August to October.

Throughout the grounds there are statues and cairns in memory of Queen Victoria's family and their descendants, and also specimen trees, labelled with the names of the visiting dignitaries who planted them.

There is some formality, but the gardens are mainly natural in style and eclipsed by the Castle's own character and situation beside the Dee, set against a background of bottle-green deer forests, purple heather moors, and the grandeur of the mountains.

7 THE BEECHGROVE GARDEN
Aberdeen

In the grounds of Broadcasting House, Beechgrove Terrace, Aberdeen.
(BRITISH BROADCASTING CORPORATION)

The garden was created from empty ground behind Broadcasting House in Aberdeen; work commenced in the spring of 1978.

The popular BBC Scotland Television Gardening Series, based on this garden, and titled 'The Beechgrove Garden', was first transmitted on Friday, 14th April, 1978. It was presented by George Barron and Jim McColl, who were responsible for designing and laying out the garden.

The area is modestly sheltered and open to high winds. Aberdeen has a fairly harsh climate and winters are often severe.

The garden is in existence for the sole purpose of servicing the series of TV programmes, yet it makes an excellent demonstration garden, incorporating many aspects of horticulture and both long-established and new methods and ideas.

Visitors are admitted on nominated open days and by arrangement with the BBC in Aberdeen, when they can see for themselves how the garden is organised and planted.

There are traditional rotational vegetable crops alongside unusual ones, as well as fruit trees, ornamental trees, herbaceous plants, greenhouses with Peaches and Vines and a large selection of pot and florists' plants, container-grown plants, various varieties of hedging, rock gardens, and exhibits of the different types of paving and patio designs.

8 BRACKLA HOUSE
Cawdor

1 mile from Cawdor, 4 miles from Nairn on B9101.
(MAJOR GENERAL & MRS I. A. ROBERTSON)

Built in sight of Cawdor Castle, Brackla was erected in 1812. The garden has been created by the present owners over a period of thirty years on the site of a Victorian garden.

It is close to the Moray Firth, noted for its temperate climate, which is here normally windy, yet dry and sunny. Most hardy shrubs do well in the sandy loam, as do Lilies. One of the garden's striking features is the long herbaceous border, backed by a brick wall, providing a sheltered situation for Climbing Roses and Delphiniums of particular beauty.

There are about 3 acres in all, some of it lawn, planted with Flowering Cherry Trees, and many Daffodils, these boon companions of Spring.

Both modern Hybrid Tea and Floribunda Roses are used to good effect, and so are the sweet-scented, old-fashioned Shrub Roses, cherished over many years, and having the added attraction of colourful autumn foliage and fruits.

The garden has beautiful Beech hedges, freshly green in springtime, brilliant in autumn, and retaining their pale brown leaves throughout the long winter months.

Brechin Castle stands on a rock above the South Esk river. It was built in 1711 by Alexander Edward on the site of a much older fortress, which in 1303 withstood seige by the army of Edward I of England for three weeks, until the death of its defender, Sir Thomas Maule, ancestor of the present owner, the 16th Earl of Dalhousie, K.T., G.B.E., M.C. Further additions were made in 1854 and 1863 by John Henderson of Edinburgh.

9 BRECHIN CASTLE
Brechin
In Brechin Castle policies, just west of City of Brechin.
(THE EARL OF DALHOUSIE)

There are 40 acres of garden within the castle policies, situated on a terrain of Old Red Sandstone, partly sloping towards the south. They are very well wooded, many old trees having been planted during the early eighteenth century by Lady Panmure, who was also responsible for building the walls round the heart-shaped garden. Their curved form has always aroused comment.

Others who determined the character and layout of the gardens were the 11th Earl and 14th Countess of Dalhousie. The present Earl landscaped them as they now are; he also greatly improved communication between castle and gardens by making new woodland walks, lined by Rhododendrons and Azaleas.

The soil is inclined to be heavy and rather too alkaline, so large quantities of leafmould and peat are regularly added. Ancient Holly and Yew hedges 14 by 14 feet, Rhododendron mounds, and stands of mature Beech, Oak, Douglas Fir, Cedars and *Sequoiadendron giganteum* all help to make this a sheltered garden, although the tree nursey is unfortunately open to the winds and needs constant attention.

200 feet above sea level and 9 miles from the sea, the coldest winter temperature so far recorded is 0°F. Severe cold threatens the survival of the Embothriums, grown from seed in the garden, although Magnolias do well. There are Rhododendrons of many different species, Azaleas, decorative wall plants, and collections of ornamental shrubs and specimen trees.

The hundred-year-old glasshouses contain Peaches, Figs and Grape-Vines, and also such exquisite flowering plants as *Lapageria rosea,* the Passion-Flower (*Passiflora caerulea*), Cymbidium hybrids, and a variety of tender Azaleas and Rhododendrons, a prize exhibit being *Rhododendron dalhousiae* named after Lady Dalhousie, wife of a Viceroy of India; it is a species from Nepal. The leaves are pale green and the lime-green flower buds open to huge greeny-yellow trumpets. The scent is delightful and it makes an excellent greenhouse plant.

This is one of the best of our Scottish gardens.

Brigton House is a listed building, as are its stables, east gates and doocot, but there has been a domain here since the sixteenth century, if not before.

10 BRIGTON
by Forfar

BRIGTON (contd.)
*On the B9127, off the A94
Glamis to Forfar road.*
(MAJOR & MRS MACMILLAN
DOUGLAS OF BRIGTON)

The Strachans were the first lairds, succeeded by the Lyons of Glamis Castle, then by the 'Red' Douglases whose ancestors included 'Bell the Cat' and Janet Douglas, Lady Glamis, and who purchased Brigton and its lands from John Lyon, a younger son of the Earl of Strathmore, in 1743.

The Howe of Angus, in which Brigton lies, had been Douglas country ever since 1329, when an earldom of Angus was created in their favour. As Robert Bruce lay dying, he made his old comrade, Sir James Douglas, promise that he would take his heart to the Holy Land, because he himself had not been able to fulfil his vow to lead a crusade against the infidel Turks. 'Good' Sir James died on the way to Palestine, and a crowned heart has remained the emblem of the 'Red' Douglases.

When Robert Douglas of Brigton added a walled garden to the policies in 1743, he designed it in the shape of a Douglas Heart, with walls on two sides, a ha-ha on the third, and a planting of trees to represent the crown. This garden was ploughed up ten years ago, but the walls remain.

The advent of less plentiful times has curtailed some of the garden's old splendour. Gone are the wide herbaceous borders, Rose beds and flowery nooks. But still there is beauty in Brigton's bright emerald lawns, graced by an old sundial, and sloping gently down to the banks of the Kerbet Water, head-long in its course, prone to winter spates before it flows into first the Dean, then the Isla. In spring Daffodils cover the lawn, followed by golden showers of Laburnum, and the brilliance of Rhododendrons and Azaleas.

11 CANDACRAIG
Strathdon
*Approximately 45 miles
west of Aberdeen, on the
B973.*
(MR & MRS FALCONER
WALLACE)

Gardening at Candacraig, at an elevation of 1000 feet amid the hills of Strathdon, is beset with climatic hazards — high winds, particularly at the spring and autumn equinox, and long winters of killing frosts and heavy falls of snow that weigh down and break the stoutest branches.

Nevertheless, gardeners have persevered here since the building of the first Candacraig House in the sixteenth century. A kailyard and a doocot were contained within its ample policies. With the arrival of doucer and more plentiful days, the 'auld hoose' had to be reconstructed and enlarged. The man hired to draw up the plans was John Smith from Aberdeen, widely known as 'Tudor Johnnie', because he generally chose that English style; in fact, the second house of Candacraig was a mixture of the Tudor and Scottish Baronial. The walls were of granite, quarried on the estate, and very thick, but fire destroyed most of this mansion in 1955. Its successor is in the traditional Scottish domestic style, designed by Marshall MacKenzie of Aberdeen.

The family of Anderson, lairds of Candacraig since the last quarter of the eighteenth century, made a walled garden about 1820. We may be sure that the produce of fruit and vegetables from its 2 acres kept the 'big hoose' kitchen well supplied. But the modern housewife requires more from her garden than filling for the larder, and in 1920 it was decided to extend the Candacraig garden beyond the constraints of the walled area. Field stones were wheeled into the

FIGURE 68
*Herbaceous border, Cawdor
Castle*

steading for the making of a wild rock garden and new paths were laid, leading to plantations of ornamental shrubs and trees, chosen for their autumn colour.

At that time of cheap labour, every country mansion had its long, carefully colour-schemed herbaceous borders. But the old sweetly-scented Shrub Roses were yielding space to beds of Hybrid Tea Roses, and the new Hybrid Poly-anthas were just beginning to appear, many of them from the Rose gardens of Svend Poulsen in Denmark.

Despite its harsh upland climate, the Candacraig garden is chiefly admired for its Roses, blooming in a sequestered environment, close to the Don, which flows full and fast after its meeting with the Nochty Water, draining down off the Ladder Hills.

12 CAWDOR CASTLE
by Nairn
5 miles south-west of Nairn, by B9090.
(EARL CAWDOR)

Shakespeare used an older Cawdor Castle as the scene of the murder of Duncan by Macbeth; the central tower, surrounded by seventeenth-century buildings, tends to corroborate the ghastly details of the plot.

Cawdor's pleasant gardens, however, and the flower garden in particular, contain many delights. The style is formal, Rose beds hedged around with blue Lavender, the delicacy of Lilies against the sombre green of venerable Yews, and *Clematis* and Climber Roses entwining with fruit tree branches.

All is contained in a sheltered haven, surrounded by walls and towering Limes, Oaks, Sycamores, Horse Chestnuts and Yews. There is a walled kitchen garden (closed during alterations), as well as woodland walks, a wild garden, and good facilities for tourists, including open-air games, a snack bar and restaurant.

13 THE CONSTABULARY GARDEN
Nairn
Off Nairn High Street.
(ELIZABETH, COUNTESS CAWDOR)

The Constabulary Garden used to be the site of the old Cawdor Castle, erected on this mound to guard a ford across the river Nairn. At one time the sheriffs of the town were *ex officio* wardens of the castle; however, the office of sheriff and constable of the castle became in the fourteenth century hereditary to the Cawdor family, and remained so until the abolition of hereditary jurisdictions in 1747. The present house was built in 1870, as home for the factor of Cawdor Estates and as the Estate Office. A century and a year later, it became the Dower House.

Elizabeth, Countess Cawdor, is a keen gardener, and within a few years she has transformed a dull area of rough grass and forlorn river-bank into a charming garden. There are fine lawns at various levels, a new and remarkably mature-looking Yew hedge, beds of Roses and brightly coloured annuals and herbaceous plants, Climbing Roses and *Clematis* and Jasmine obscuring the old grey walls, and shade-loving Hostas and Bergenias and Periwinkles flourishing on the wooded terraces.

14 CRATHES CASTLE
Banchory

Crathes Castle and garden, in the care of the National Trust for Scotland, is one of the loveliest and most interesting properties on Deeside. Of particular interest in the garden is the Walled Garden, which adjoins the castle on the south-east side, the oldest part being that nearer the building and divided into four compartments by veteran Yew hedges, some 280 years old.

CRATHES CASTLE (contd.)
16 miles from Aberdeen on the A93 Ballater road, 1 mile east of Banchory.
(NATIONAL TRUST FOR SCOTLAND)

The policies, or parkland, were at one time noted for their arboretum, and although there remain several trees of importance, the majority were lost in early 1968 as the result of a severe gale. Both policies and garden owe their origin to the late Sir James and Lady Sybil Burnett of Leys, who started at the beginning of the present century to develop a rather indifferent and unremarkable garden into one which is now acknowledged as one of the best of its kind in existence. Of the eight small gardens which form Crathes garden, all but two were completely altered or remade — the four on the lower level were designed and made by the Burnetts themselves. One has only to look at the garden to realise that they must have been skilled designers as well as practical gardeners to achieve such perfection. Fortunately, their skills and interests were complementary — Sir James in his love of trees and shrubby subjects, Lady Sybil finding expression in herbaceous plants and a very remarkable flair for colour combinations.

All eight gardens conform to one theme or another. This may be a colour, as in the case of the blue garden, or a specialised interest, such as the Rose garden, the upper pool garden in which the design was based on three colours, red, yellow and bronze or purple, or the trough garden which simply derives its name from the large stone trough in the centre. Although it may not be immediately obvious, there are good collections of genera such as *Viburnum*, Roses, Hydrangeas and Hostas, not grouped together, as so often is the case, but distributed throughout the garden.

Outstanding in every way are the herbaceous borders. The June borders, normally best at the end of that month, are a very gay mixture of colours, such as one might imagine in a cottage garden, and quite the reverse of the white borders, which depend upon white flowers with grey or silver foliage for effect. The main borders have bold groups of strong colours, broken by fairly generous groupings of grey foliage, while the west border is confined to more delicate shades of blue and pink.

The gardens are open daily all year, from 9.30 a.m. to sunset.

The house has a magnificent prospect of the far Grampian mountains. The gardens were set out in 1911 by Lady MacRobert with spacious lawns in front and, on the west, a Rose garden and herbaceous borders containing a good collection of clear yellow, deep coppery orange and bronze-red Heleniums.

15 DOUNESIDE HOUSE
Tarland
1½ miles from Tarland, off the A97.
(MACROBERT TRUSTS)

The dene, on the east side, is deeply shaded by mature hardwood trees and there is a burn, spanned by an ornamental timber bridge, with bog plants growing on the banks. The acid soil and plentiful supply of leaf mould make an excellent medium for the many dwarf Rhododendrons, Azaleas, Heaths and Heathers, all growing on a sunny mound of rocks.

FIGURE 69
Herbaceous border, Crathes Castle

16 DRUMKILBO
Meigle

1 mile outside Meigle on A94 Coupar Angus-Glamis road.
(LORD & LADY ELPHINSTONE)

The house of Drumkilbo was originally a fortified tower, added to in 1811, in 1920 to 1922 by Sir Robert Lorimer, and again in 1963.

The garden was created by the 17th Lord Elphinstone between the years 1950 and 1970. There are some 10 acres of it, making a delightful setting for the house. It enjoys the favourable climate of the low country of Strathmore, sunny and sheltered with trees and bosky shrubs. Such conditions and a naturally acid soil suit the many Rhododendrons and Azaleas and the heath border.

There is a small stream garden, and several rare and very beautiful shrubs, including the North American Flowering Dogwood (*Cornus florida*), conspicuous among the others by reason of its white petal-like bracts, turning flush pink as the flowers age. As the autumn deepens, the leaves turn yellow and scarlet.

The late Lord Elphinstone took a keen and active interest in his garden at Drumkilbo, and its beauty and graceful informality bear tribute to him.

17 DUNECHT HOUSE GARDENS
Dunecht

1 mile from Dunecht village. Reached by routes A974, A944 and B977.
(THE VISCOUNT COWDRAY)

One of Scotland's stately homes, Dunecht House is a very imposing edifice built in 1820 of local granite in a Grecian style, but with a number of additions, the latest being made in 1877 to 1881, from designs drawn by G. E. Street, R.A.

The drive up to the great house passes through huge wrought-iron gates, remarkable — like the house itself — as reminders of the bygone affluence of the landowners and the craftsmanship at their command.

The garden is part formal, part natural. To the front roll acres of lawn with twin fountains, guardian beasts in stone, and a belvedere of granite in a far right-angle of the garden wall.

The lawn is flanked on either side by long borders of herbaceous plants, growing in broad bands of the same species for colourful effect, a magnificent tapestry when all are in full flower.

A stone staircase in the same grand style, with statues on either side, leads from the formal garden into the wild garden which is almost entirely devoted to Rhododendrons and Azaleas and other flowering shrubs, spaciously set out under an airy canopy of trees and all easily accessible along grass paths.

There can be little doubt that Dunecht's wild garden of Rhododendrons is its main attraction, and there is usually an opportunity for the public to visit it in early June.

18 EDZELL CASTLE
Edzell

About 1 mile west of Edzell village, off the B966, Brechin to Fettercairn road.
(SCOTTISH DEVELOPMENT DEPARTMENT)

Ouchterlony of Guinde (*circa* 1683-1722) described Edzell Castle thus:
'It is ane excellent dwelling, a great house, delicat gardine, with wall sumptuously built of hewen stone, polisht, with pictures and coats of armes in the walls, with a fyne summer house with a hous for a bath on the south corners thereof, far exceeding any new work of thir times.'

The Great Hall of Edzell was once the most splendid castle in Angus; built by the Stirlings of Glenesk in the sixteenth century as a defence against the caterans coming through the glens from Tanar, Birse and Cromar to lift their cattle, it passed by marriage to the Crawford Lindsays. In point of strength and solidity it is little different from similar tower houses, but its garden enclosure or pleasance, added in 1604, is one of the rare responses Scotland made to the Renaissance in Europe.

The builder of the pleasance was Sir David Lindsay, later to become a Lord of Session and Privy Councillor. He was the elder son of the 9th Earl of Crawford, by his second marriage, and unfortunately for him and his brother, who became Lord Menmuir, the title reverted to the direct heirs of the 8th Earl, so the Lindsays of Edzell were deprived of much land and rent money. The widowed Countess of Crawford, however, determined that her sons should nevertheless receive the best possible education, and sent them both to the Scots College of the Sorbonne in Paris, in the company of a tutor, James Lawson, who kept her Ladyship informed as to how he had spent their allowance, on Greek and Latin lexicons, candles to study by, sweetmeats and condiments, and wool with which to darn their hose.

Within a few months of their arrival, the Massacre of St Bartholomew took place, and because of the continuing armed conflict between Catholics and Protestants in the streets of the city, Lawson was advised to remove his protégés to a safer place. They all returned to Britain and the students resumed their education at Cambridge University.

When Master Davie finally returned home to take up the burden of duty of Laird of Edzell, he had travelled more widely than most of his contemporaries, had gained much book learning, and shown himself to have considerable practical skills, so that 'the sword, the pen, and the pruning hook were equally familiar to his hand'.

And, instead of carping against the uneventfulness of life in a remote Angus countryside, he bent mind and body towards exploiting the untapped wealth of his inheritance, clearing and cultivating the heathery wastelands of Glenesk, sowing and reaping an abundance; planting and selling sapling trees from his own nurseries; and establishing a weekly market for farm produce in Edzell.

Following the Reformation, much of the wealth of the Old Church had been acquired by the landed aristocracy. During the brief period of comparative peace between Church and State, these showed a certain flamboyant exuberance, a desire to flaunt their prosperity and make use of their leisure to cultivate the ampler life. This trend no doubt influenced Sir David Lindsay, and after discovering that deposits of gold, silver, quicksilver, copper, lead and tin could be mined on his estates in Glenesk, he embarked on an extravagance: the building of a pleasance adjoining the south wall of the Stirling Tower. He engaged highly-skilled stone-masons to carry out the work, and no expense was spared. The completed work reflects the interests of a gentleman, both wealthy and learned, whose pleasure it was to take his ease and discourse with his friends in the beauty and peace of his flower garden.

Like many of his contemporaries, Lindsay was keenly interested in natural

astrology; he tried to read his destiny in the stars, consulted lists of 'blessed' and 'evil' days prior to making decisions, and was a student of Greek and Latin writers on the subject.

On the east wall of the pleasance vesica-shaped panels represent the seven planetary deities (Saturn, Jupiter, Mars, the Sun, Venus, Mercury and the Moon). A charming little stone summer-house intervenes, then along the south wall we find the seven liberal arts (Grammar, Rhetoric, Dialectic, Arithmetic, Music, Geometry, and Astronomy). There is a well at the south-west corner, and a door leading out to the Laird's bath-house. On the west wall the seven cardinal virtues complete the theme (Faith, Hope, Charity, Prudence, Temperance, Fortitude, and Justice). These, it was suggested, were the foundations of a happy and prosperous life. The planets gave heavenly guidance, the arts wisdom, and the virtues strength of character.

The heraldic carvings between the panels represent the stars of the Stirlings of Glenesk, Sir David's ancestors; while the chequer-board pattern of recesses, intended for red, white, and blue-flowered plants, are designed to resemble the fess-chequy of the Lindsay arms.

Unfortunately, the making of the pleasance cost more than Sir David had budgeted for. The mineral wealth of Glenesk did not match his expectations, and his son's involvement in the accidental death of Lord Spynie resulted in heavy financial reparations. Sir David, Lord Lindsay of Edzell died in penury on December 1, 1610. The making of the pleasance, which was his undoing, remains today as his memorial.

The Gordons of Hallhead and Esslemont have been Aberdeenshire landowners since the fourteenth century. They began at Hallhead, a small property near Alford, then removed in 1728 to the fifteenth-century Castle of Esslemont, now a ruin, 1¾ miles west of the town of Ellon.

Fervently Jacobite in sympathies, the defeat of the 1745 Rising forced them into temporary exile. On their re-instatement at Esslemont in 1760 they decided to build a new house, about a ½ mile north-east of the Castle, where the castle garden had been.

Apart from the advantages a new domain possessed over the draughty old fortalice, the change was probably dictated by a desire to be closer to the kailyard, an important contributor to the larder, and to the grange buildings. But the surrounding countryside is flat, windswept, and bitterly cold in winter, and as nothing was gained by the removal in the way of improved shelter, belts of trees and the first of the Yew hedges — which are a feature of Esslemont — were planted when the Georgian house was erected, in 1760.

A hundred years later, the house was rebuilt in an imposing mid-Victorian style, the walls constructed of seven different kinds of local granite. Then the garden boundaries were pushed outwards, and a second shielding Yew hedge was planted, though the garden gates remained some 150 yards from the

19 ESSLEMONT
Ellon
2 miles from Ellon, on the A920 towards Oldmeldrum.
(CAPTAIN & MRS R. WOLRIGE GORDON OF ESSLEMONT)

FIGURE 70
The formal garden at Edzell Castle

mansion, the correct separation according to received opinion of the day. Old plans, drawn before these changes, show the farm steading east of the outer Yew hedge. The old well today is on the far side of this hedge, while the water pump remains within the garden itself.

Successive generations of Wolrige Gordon have planted and re-planted the Esslemont garden; the process continues today, and with its rich fertility and in the shelter of the Yew hedges it yields abundantly.

For ease of maintenance, however, much space has been turned into lawn and borders of hardy shrubs, and it is likely that the already large beds of Roses will be enlarged still further. The list includes 'Rob Roy', 'Lively Lady', 'Honeymoon', 'Iceberg', 'Silver Jubilee' and 'June Aberdeen Europeana'; also the Climbing Roses 'Ritter von Barnstead', 'New Dawn', 'Seagull', 'Mme Alfred Carrière', 'Mermaid', 'Étoile d'Holland', 'Rosy Mantle', and 'Park Director Riggers'.

The recommended months for the Esslemont gardens are May, when the Daffodils are in flower, late June and July for Roses, Azaleas, Potentillas, *Philadelphus*, Delphiniums, Peony Roses and the various Brooms, and August for the smaller herbaceous borders.

20 FETTERCAIRN HOUSE
🐾 *Fettercairn*
Fettercairn village ¼ mile.
(MRS PETER SOMERVELL)

The lands of Middleton were held by the Middleton family for upwards of five centuries. Charles II honoured General Middleton at the time of the Restoration by creating him Earl of Middleton, and Lord Clermont and Fettercairn, and the present house was built by him in 1666, in the Jacobean style. It was enlarged in 1829 by Sir John Stuart-Forbes, and again by Lord Clinton in 1877.

This area forms part of the Howe of the Mearns, and after driving over the hazardous Cairn-o'-Mount from Banchory it seems sedately rural. But winter in these parts is often severe, and the garden at Fettercairn is a prey to very damaging frost pockets, and high winds.

For this reason, there is little in the way of a flower garden in front, but two large beds, let into the lawn, contain closely planted 'Dreamland' pink Hybrid Tea Roses (grown by the late Alex Cocker, of Aberdeen). Also, that vigorous rambler, *Rosa filipes* 'Kiftsgate', has climbed into a full-grown Holm Oak, taking it over completely — a beautiful sight in July and August when it is covered with hundreds of creamy-white Roses, as fragile and delicate as Cherry Blossom.

The back door of the mansion gives direct access to the walled garden, where much use has been made of Yew hedging, to screen off the vegetable area, and also to form charming little 'garden rooms', each one different in content and character from its neighbours. Striking effects are achieved with grey-leafed plants, beds of Fuchsias and scented Stocks, Euphorbias and *Veratrum nigrum*.

Such elaborate gardens are becoming uncommon in these days of scarce skilled labour and high costs. However, the owners do most of the work themselves, apart from occasional help from the estate foresters.

After he visited Glamis Castle in 1765, the poet Thomas Gray wrote to a friend: 'The house, from the height of it, and the greatness of its mass, the many towers a-top, the spread of its wings, has really a very singular and striking appearance — like nothing I ever saw'.

Gray's visit took place just before 'Capability' Brown re-designed the park at Glamis, when the old gates down the central drive were removed, and also the old parterres and formal gardens and topiary work, and walls replaced by ha-has. Sir Walter Scott greatly deprecated these changes. 'A disciple of Kent', he wrote, 'had the cruelty to render this splendid old mansion more parkish, as he pleased to call it; to raze all those external defences, and to bring his mean and paltry gravel walk up to the very door, from which, deluded by the name, we might have imagined Lady Macbeth issuing forth to receive King Duncan.' Be that as it may, the simple dignity of the long main carriageway, with the Castle looming at the far end, is very effective, comparable with the most distinguished of the French châteaux.

Most of the frontal areas are laid out in lawn, but there is a Dutch garden by the east wing, made between 1907 and 1910 by Claude and Cecilia, the 14th Earl and Countess of Strathmore and Kinghorne, parents of Her Majesty Queen Elizabeth The Queen Mother. It is a sunken garden of Rose beds, edged with Boxwood, in a formal pattern, with gravel paths between and a small fountain to provide the focal point. Further eastward one comes upon the 'Shrubbery', a triangular woodland of specimen trees and shrubs.

The 2-acre Italian Garden has as its most attractive feature a pleached Beech walk. There is a herbaceous border along one side of the enclosing Yew hedge; and on the other a terrace furnished with seventeenth-century style gazebos, and carved stone flower-pots and summer seats, made by local craftsmen.

Patrick, 3rd Earl of Kinghorne and 1st Earl of Strathmore, erected two lead statues of Charles I and James VI; also the sundial, standing over 21 feet high with eighty-four dials.

The main feature of this garden is the long and very decorative nineteenth-century conservatory. It was designed by Moncrieff of Edinburgh around 1870, carrying the traditional 'thistle' décor.

There are about 2½ acres of garden, including lawns and wooded policies, with the Pilketty Burn running through to join the River Bervie at the ford below Glenbervie House, an ancient Douglas stronghold which still retains its gunloops, arrow slits, and iron yett.

The herbaceous borders contain many old and interesting plants such as *Veratrum nigrum* (White Hellebore), *Gillenia*, a neglected perennial from North America, and *Kirengeshoma palmata* from the mountains of Japan, with long drooping bright yellow flowers in autumn. There are separate borders of Delphiniums, Phloxes, and Hemerocallis hybrids.

The garden is at its best in springtime, with masses of naturalised Daffodils

21 GLAMIS CASTLE
Glamis
(STRATHMORE ESTATES
(HOLDINGS) LTD)

22 GLENBERVIE
Drumlithie,
Stonehaven
1 mile off A94,
8 miles south of
Stonehaven.
(MRS P. M. BADENACH
NICHOLSON)

and Narcissi flowering amid *Claytonia sibirica, Cardamine bulbifera* (Coralroot), and Doronicums (Leopard's Bane). Spring comes late, however, owing to the severe frost pockets which form in the lower regions of the garden. Apart from this disadvantage, most hardy plants grow well in the light loamy soil.

23 GLENFERNESS
Nairn
14 *miles from Nairn, route*
A939.
(LORD LEVEN)

The approach road to Glenferness House runs through a Heather-carpeted Fir forest, reaching neatly clipped Beech hedges and mounds of Rhododendrons, a sign that the house is not far away. It was built in 1844 by Mr Robert Dougall, as a family mansion. Two wooden wings, in the Norwegian style, were added in about 1895. The front faces east, across wide, well-kept lawns. There used to be Rose beds on the west side, but these were converted to lawn because of frequent visits by roe deer which came from the surrounding woods to consume their favourite delicacy of Rose bushes. The situation of the house and grounds is a flat clearing in a Highland forest. There are hills on all sides, and nearby is the Findhorn, thrashing its way to the sea through a deep gorge.

The 1-acre garden, only a step or two from the front door, has high walls on three sides, and a low wall surmounted by iron railings on the fourth. It is formal in style, laid out in herbaceous and bedding-plant borders, the kitchen garden and wall-trained fruit trees on the west side screened from view.

The garden is not open to the public, apart from one day a year when it is opened for charity.

24 GLEN TANAR
Aboyne
4½ *miles up a side road off*
the B976 Banchory-
Ballater road.
(THE HON MRS JEAN BRUCE)

The road up Glen Tanar has for company the turbulent Water of Tanar, tumbling down off the slopes of Hair Cairn (2203 feet) in Glenmuick parish. Queen Victoria visited the Glen with Prince Albert and their daughter, the Princess Alice, and described the drive in her Journals as 'through a beautiful and richly-wooded glen'.

In early Victorian times, Glen Tanar was out of sight of human habitation, and the wealth of its forests could not be tapped because of the unapproachable sites of the trees. All this changed with the making of the Glen Road, and today there is even a Visitors' Centre, encouraging people to discover for themselves the beauty of this area, once part of the ancient Caledonian forest.

The garden of Glen Tanar House has been made on an alluvial haugh of good gravelly loam, overlying drift and rough sand. Alas, marauding herds of deer steal down from the hills, so it is of necessity a walled garden, containing a small, burgeoning orchard, an arboretum, vegetables, long borders of shrubs and herbaceous plants, and greenhouses for Figs, Tomatoes, and the usual indoor flora.

The house is of a modern design of considerable character. The frontage overlooks rough grass, beyond which lies the water garden, fed by the river and overhung by Alders and Horse Chestnuts. One path leads to the small chapel of St Lesmo, others into the darkness of the forest, emerging on the drovers' Firmounth Road across the mountains to Glen Esk.

FIGURE 71
Autumn leaves in the water
garden, Glen Tanar

25 GORDON CASTLE
Fochabers
(LIEUTENANT GENERAL SIR
GEORGE GORDON LENNOX)

Today, the Tower-house and East Pavilion are all that remain of Gordon Castle. The original castle, called Bog-of-Gight, was founded by the 2nd Earl of Huntly about the end of the fifteenth century, at a time when the 'Cock of the North' (the nickname of the Earls) was all that it implied.

This fortress was almost entirely rebuilt towards the close of the eighteenth century by the 4th Duke of Gordon, acting through John Baxter, mason to William Adam. A place of great splendour, the battlemented front stretched along 600 feet, including a four-storied centre, connected by galleries with the two-storied east and west wings, and incorporating the old Bog-of-Gight tower.

In 1937 some 90,000 acres of the Gordon estates were sold to the Crown; and, beginning in 1950, the great eighteenth-century castle was gradually reduced to its present fairly modest proportions. The official approach is through the lofty battlemented archway between two domes in Fochabers, whence the carriageway sweeps on between broad grass verges, shrubberies and woods to the Castle.

Visitors look in vain for the awful splendour with which the 'Cock of the North' liked to surround himself. Instead there are broad sweeping lawns — part of the old 1300-acre deer park — stone balustrades, an orangery, a modest garden of Roses, herbaceous plants and a few vegetables, and a water-lily pond and stone fountain carved with the date 1540.

Around the fringes of the woodland are many beautiful flowering shrubs and trees: Rhododendrons, Acers, Eucryphias, *Enkianthus*, and the various fragrant Viburnums. There is a large walled market garden some distance from the house, containing several glasshouses, fruit trees, soft fruit, and acres of vegetables.

**26 GORDONSTOUN
SCHOOL**
Duffus, near Elgin
*Duffus 1 mile. Route
B9012 Elgin-Hopeman
road.*
(GORDONSTOUN SCHOOL LTD)

Gordonstoun — originally Bog o' Plewlands — was built by the 1st Marquess of Huntly in 1616. In those days treacherous marshes cut it off from other centres of habitation; but the isolation suited the 'Cock of the North' since it allowed him to pursue unmolested his intrigues with Catholic Spain; give hospitality to recusant Papist priests; and, if real danger threatened, escape abroad from his harbour at Covesea. In 1638, the 2nd Marquess was obliged to sell Plewlands House to his cousin, Sir Robert Gordon of Kynmonowie. In time, the new laird had Plewlands recognised as a barony and, in 1642, renamed Gordonstoun.

The 2nd Baronet, Sir Ludovick Gordon, formed a trading partnership with his factor, operating a shipping commerce between Findhorn and Rotterdam. Out of the profits he drained the Bog o' Plewlands by excavating an ornamental lake, and landscaped his house policies in the decorous style of the period.

Today, much of this area comes within the category of a wild garden. There are few formal flower-beds, but Daffodils flourish at Easter by the lake and in the woods; summer sees the Rhododendrons in bloom, and the Wild Cherry and May; autumn adds fiery lights among the Beeches and the Horse Chestnuts.

Roads and pathways radiate from the main school building to the various residences and buildings of historic interest: to the Michael Kirk, shaded by tortured Beech trees; to the Round Square, built by the 3rd Baronet, known as 'The Wizard', as a place of magic proportions where he could find sanctuary when the Devil called to claim his own; and to the several doocots erected by the 4th Baronet, 'Ill' (vicious) Sir Robert Gordon, so close to the boundaries that the birds often fed on his neighbours' cornlands, and seldom on his own.

Guthrie Castle is a battlemented pile, standing close to a broad stretch of the Lunan Water. The Guthries were actively prominent in Scotland's affairs from at least the thirteenth century, and obtained a charter to their lands from James II. The most distinguished was Sir David Guthrie, Baron of Guthrie, who held numerous high offices during the reigns of James III and James IV, amassing a large personal fortune. In 1468, he was granted a licence to erect the present tower, and also the iron yett which forms the gateway between the walled garden and the wild garden. The mansion attached to the tower was built in 1818, and the tower had additions built on in 1848.

27 GUTHRIE CASTLE near Friockheim
On A932 Friockheim-Forfar road, 1 ½ miles west of Friockheim.
(MR & MRS DAVID GUTHRIE)

The wild garden is magnificent in early summer with massive clumps of Rhododendrons and Azaleas in contrasting colours growing under the wild Cherry, and Silver Birch trees amid the vivid green grass and the Wild Hyacinths. There are woodland clearings planted with Welsh and Himalayan Poppies and glades bright with Primroses and Wind Flowers.

According to records still in existence, it was in the year 1730 that 'Mr Ogilvy built himself a fine new house' at Pitmuies. When the household moved into the new habitation, they left the old house extant, and this was joined with the white harled, three-storied dwelling much later.

28 HOUSE OF PITMUIES Friockheim
1 mile from Friockheim, on the A932.
(MR & MRS FARQUHAR OGILVIE)

Contemporary with the old house is the curious doocot, standing near where a ford used to cross the Vinny Water. The date 1643 and the Guthrie/Ogilvy coat of arms appear on the north wall, for in 1599 the property had belonged to Patrick Guthrie of Guthrie and formed his daughter's dowry at the time of her marriage to David Ogilvy, younger son of Lord Ogilvy.

Three years after taking possession of the new House of Pitmuies, David Ogilvy died, leaving his widow Margaret with three offspring. The lady did not remain inconsolable for long: in 1734, Mr Carnegy of Lour fell off his horse while crossing the ford and, being sorely doused, 'stepped ben to dry his claes' in front of Mistress Ogilvy's cosy ingle. He remained at Pitmuies for ten years. Eventually, Mistress Ogilvy of Pitmuies became Mistress Carnegy of Lour, a decision forced upon her when young Master Ogilvy came of age, in 1744; this profligate lad died a pauper in foreign parts, leaving his affairs in such disorder that all his effects had to be sold to clear his debts.

The new owner, Mr Pearson, purchased the neighbouring estate of Balmadies during his tenure, but only survived for two years, dying in 1763. His

initials, 'R.P.ESQre', appear on the sundial of the flower garden.

It is thought likely that the next laird of Pitmuies, James Mudie, had married a sugar heiress from the Caribbean; he was certainly well off, and greatly improved the property. A lawsuit which he filed against the Lyells of Gardyne rid him of the ford and the noisy commotion of traffic passing in front of Pitmuies House. He then went ahead with the erection of a new range of farm buildings and estate workers' cottages, and the extension of the mansion itself.

The steading and farm cottages remain today unaltered; their roof slates of stone, held down by wooden pegs, are encrusted with moss and ferns, and their antiquity is borne out by date stones of the 1770s and 1780s, and a weathervane with Mudie's initials 'I.M.' and the date 1773. Mudie also built the 'Gothick wash house', outside the formal garden, near the Vinny Water, which might easily be mistaken for a chapel. The 'bleaching green' in front is thickly planted with Snowdrops and all the different Crocuses, making a vivid tapestry in early spring. Against the low garden retaining wall there is a full hedge of Shrub Roses — 'Frau Dagmar Hastrup', and 'Blanc Double de Coubert', entwined with a pink *Clematis*.

James Mudie followed the example of the landowning 'improvers' of his day and planted trees that are still the pride of the estate, especially its magnificent Beeches, both green and copper, Spanish Chestnut, various conifers, and the avenue of Lime trees, beginning by the doocot.

There were three generations of Mudies, and the last bequeathed Pitmuies to his friend, Lord Lyell, in 1877. Lord Lyell continued to reside at Kinnordy, near Kirriemuir, and the House of Pitmuies was generally let for the summer months, and its grass parks throughout the year, to a succession of tenants. It was sold in 1919 to Major Crombie. The Crombies re-created the long-neglected garden, and planted the first Delphiniums for which Pitmuies became quite famous. They were exhibited regularly at flower shows in London and throughout the entire country, winning many prizes.

Major and Mrs Ogilvie bought the House of Pitmuies and its lands in 1945, and continued to enhance the gardens and policies, planting many shrubs and trees. The house is now the home of their son, Mr Farquhar Ogilvie, and his family. Much has been done to modernise the house, and maintain the eighteenth-century steading and farm cottages in good repair. Mrs Farquhar Ogilvie is the daughter of Mr Gerald Annesley, the owner of one of Ireland's most beautiful gardens, Castlewellan in County Down, and takes a particularly keen and active interest in the garden at Pitmuies.

The Delphinium Border at Pitmuies remains a remarkable feature. Mrs Ogilvie had the happy thought of edging it with different coloured Irises, which bloom before the flowers in the central bed, leaving a foil of green foliage to set off the brilliant pale blue, dark blue, and white Delphiniums.

Broad herbaceous borders, divided by grass walks and a low-cut hedge of 'Purple-Leaved Plum' (*Prunus cerasifera* 'Pissardii') run the full length of the

FIGURE 72
The wild garden at Guthrie Castle

garden, one of them consisting of blue and white flowers only.

At the centre of the Rose garden there is a Lily pond, with a stooping cupid on an 'island' in the middle. The surrounding beds contain Hybrid Tea and Poly-antha Roses — 'Iceberg', 'Prima Ballerina', 'Paprika', 'Firecracker'; the less common Shrub Roses, such as 'Châpeau de Napoleon', 'Hebe's Lip' and 'Goldfinch', occur throughout the garden. A tall Yew hedge gives welcome shelter from the prevailing west wind, and many fine shrubs flourish against the east wall — Eucryphias, Stranvaesias, Embothriums, Magnolias, all under-planted with many different Hellebores, Meconopses, Fritillarias, Hostas, and dwarf Rhododendrons.

29 INCHMARLO
ᶄ *Banchory*
1 mile west of Banchory, route A93.
(A. H. BOWHILL, ESQ)

Inchmarlo is a classical eighteenth-century mansion with a balustraded parapet. A third storey was added in the mid-nineteenth century. It occupies a com-manding situation, overlooking the north bank of the river Dee.

The garden, enclosed and a short way from the house, was made in a beautiful, open woodland of tall, well-spaced conifers, mostly Douglas Firs and Redwoods, with some Copper Beech and self-sown Silver Birch. The natural beauty of the wood remains supreme, enhanced by ornamental trees and shrubs and herbaceous subjects, and is never excessively darkened by the overhead canopy of branches and foliage. Blue Meconopses, Rhododendrons, Azaleas and *Pieris formosa* flourish in the dappled shade, while the thick carpet of Ling, Blaeberry, Mosses and cultivated Heaths and Heathers safeguards their shallow roots against summer drought. There are red and gold Acers, providing patches of brilliant autumn colour, and Eucryphias and Embothriums, both natives of South America, yet blooming freely in this Scots wood. Here, too, Australian Gum Trees (*Eucalyptus*), thrive. The light shade and good leaf-soil suit the low, spreading, purple-plumed *Astilbe chinensis*, the white Buddleias, and *Hydrangea paniculata*.

A path leads obliquely up through the woodland to a clearing, where there are greenhouses, and a formal garden of Roses and herbaceous plants, the whole enclosed by a hedge of the purple-leafed *Prunus cerasifera* 'Pissardii'.

The garden at Inchmarlo was planned, planted and tended by the late Mrs Bowhill. It remains her memorial.

30 INNES HOUSE
ᶄ *Llanbryde, Elgin*
3 miles north of Llanbryde (which is 4 miles east of Elgin on the A96 to Aberdeen).
(CAPTAIN IAIN & LADY MARGARET TENNANT)

The Edinburgh master-mason William Aitoun designed Innes House, built 1640-53 for Sir Thomas Innes. The property was in the possession of the Inneses, a powerful Morayshire family, from the twelfth century until 1767, when Sir James Innes, the 6th Baronet since 1625, sold it to James, 2nd Earl of Fife. The Fife earls carried out alterations, as did the Tennants more recently. The magnificent building consists of two four-story wings and a central tower, all constructed of stone of a fine quality and texture, embellished with Renais-sance ornamentation.

The formal garden was created in 1912, with subsequent changes made by the

grandfather and father of Captain Tennant, and by his wife, Lady Margaret. The style is simple yet stately, the area sub-divided by Yew hedges. The main allée leads between twin borders of choice plants down a flagged path, past an ornamental sundial, to the door in the tower. The deciduous creepers, *Actinidia kolomikta* and *Vitis coignetiae*, adorn the lower area of the tower walls, both producing rich autumn colouring.

A stone wall with Gothic-style gateways surrounds the garden. The narrow borders on either side of it contain Hostas and regularly spaced plants of Rue, or Herb of Grace (*Ruta graveolens*), a small aromatic, evergreen shrub with glaucous leaves and clusters of yellow flowers. The plantation of shrubs and trees in the immediate vicinity of the garden was planted in the 1930s. It contains Rhododendrons, Shrub Roses, Maples and Flowering Cherries under a canopy of Limes, Elms and Oaks.

The 12-acre park is hundreds of years old and contains many trees of matching antiquity.

31 INSHRIACH NURSERY

Aviemore

If coming north, turn off the new A9 just north of Kingussie on to the A9152 (old A9) to Kincraig. Turn right at Kincraig and follow the Inshriach sign. If going south, turn off the new A9 just north of Aviemore, drive through Aviemore and turn left on to the B97 ski road, then follow the Inshriach sign. The Nursery is 5 miles from both Kincraig and Aviemore.

(MR JOHN C. LAWSON)

Inshriach Nursery was set up by Jack Drake. After six years working in the family firm of sugar brokers, he came to the conclusion that city life was not for him, and decided to go in for horticulture. He became an apprentice with the firm of W. E. Th. Ingwersen Ltd, during which time he accompanied Will Ingwersen on a plant-hunting trip to the Canadian Rockies, Vancouver Island and the Olympic Mountains. At last, in February 1939, he was able to set up his own Nursery at Inshriach. It had to be closed during the 1939-45 war, but it eventually became nationally famous for its alpine plants.

Situated in the Spey valley, between the Cairngorms and the Monadhliath mountains, amid a natural wood of Silver Birch and Juniper and close to the river, the Nursery has more of the appearance of a wild garden, and a very beautiful one too. A highland burn makes gentle water music as it twists and turns through the 4½ acres, and a circular pool under the Birch trees reflects the glancing sunlight like a jewel.

Speyside has its own, unpredictable climate, and at an altitude of 760 feet winters in these parts are generally severe. The soil is acid, poor, and gravelly but highly suitable for alpines and most rock plants, while Meconopses and Primulas of many different kinds flourish in drifts by the roadside and in glades throughout the garden.

Mr Drake is now retired, and John Lawson, his former partner, is now the proprietor.

32 KEITHOCK

Brechin

Keithock House dates from around 1800. It was later enlarged and its grounds spaciously landscaped in the grand manner with wide lawns, avenues, parks and a dene. A genuine ha-ha divided the lawns from the 30-acre park.

Some 9 miles from the sea and in the lovely low country of Strathmore, this is an area of rich fertility and a kindly climate. Further shelter is provided by the magnificent trees, many of them around two hundred years old, and clumps of Rhododendrons. The fine Copper Beeches are particularly remarkable. There is a double-sided herbaceous border, each side 90 yards long and 3 yards broad. Three large Rose beds lead the way to the glass-houses, one of which contains a highly productive Peach tree and other fruits. There is also a walled garden of 2 acres.

This is a garden to visit in June, when the Rhododendrons are in bloom and the trees are freshly in leaf.

KEITHOCK (contd.)

Off the Edzell (B966) road, 150 yards from the north end of the Brechin by-pass, down an avenue on the east side.
(MR H. J. KENNAWAY)

Kildrummy is a scattered community rather than a village, but there is a church, school, shop, an inn and a hotel.

Colonel James Ogston, a soap manufacturer, purchased the Kildrummy estate in 1898. He built the English Tudor-style house in place of the old Gordon lodge, bridged the Den with a replica of the Auld Brig o' Balgownie in Old Aberdeen, and made a new approach road through the policies.

Across the Back Den stands the thirteenth-century Kildrummy Castle, a fortress erected by Alexander II to keep apart the Picts and Moray men. Besieged and temporarily captured by Edward I during the Wars of Independence, it was in the custody of the Lords Erskine, Earls of Mar, and for many years served as the administrative capital of the Mar and Garioch districts.

The Earl of Mar hatched plans for the 1715 Jacobite Rising within Kildrummy Castle walls, and his support for the Old Pretender lost him the ownership. In 1731 the Gordons of Wardhouse bought the estate from another Erskine. Their descendants planted Silver Firs, Larches and Hemlock Spruce around the Den, forming a sheltering screen within which Colonel and Mrs Ogston began the Kildrummy gardens. Japanese landscape gardeners helped them construct the Water Garden, using the burn flowing down through the Back Den, while the foot of the ancient sandstone quarry in the Den provided the right conditions for an alpine garden, planted by Backhouse's of York in 1904.

General Ogston succeeded his brother at Kildrummy, and continued with the making of the gardens. In the course of the work, he collected the old millstones, querns, Pictish stones, and other items of interest which, since 1970, are on display in the small museum in the Den. The Ogstons' niece, Mrs R. I. B. Yates and her husband continued the work of planting the gardens with rare and beautiful plants and shrubs and specimen trees. The rock garden was begun in 1936, using glacial boulders found on the hills of Strathdon, and planted by Messrs Gavin Jones in 1937. Interesting stones are continually being added to the rockery.

The great gale of 1953 wrought havoc in the gardens, but the cleared areas provided scope for new plantations of shrubs and trees. The high sides of the Den afford some protection against the winds, but frost pockets sometimes form in the disused quarry. While snow may provide a welcome blanket against cold blasts, weighty accumulations can break the sturdiest branches.

33 KILDRUMMY CASTLE GARDENS

Kildrummy

On A97, off A944 Aberdeen/Huntly at Kildrummy.
(*Kildrummy Castle Garden Trust, Hon Gardens Director* — MRS HYLDA SMITH)

Interesting trees, shrubs and Alpines are continually being added, and plants have also been collected overseas to bring interest throughout the growing season.

In the gardens today, there is no formality and little attempt at grouping for effect. Instead, plants are situated where they are most likely to succeed.

34 KINCORTH HOUSE
Forres
Signposted from the A96, at a point 2 miles west of Forres.
(MRS A. D. MACKINTOSH)

The garden at Kincorth House is open to the public from late May until the end of August. It lies in the Laigh of Moray, a beautiful, flat, high-yielding seaboard plain. One authority described the house as 'an old-fashioned manor'. The date on the door lintel is 1797, but the older part was erected in 1520. During the seventeenth century it served as the episcopal manse for the parishes of Dyke and Culbin, and one of the incumbents became Bishop of Moray. The house was for long in the ownership of the Grants, a well-known powerful Morayshire family.

Some of the Beech trees encircling the garden on the south side are at least two hundred years old. There is a wide lawn between them and the house, with island beds of *R. rugosa scabrosa* and Azaleas, with Lilies pushing up through the foliage, and cushions of dwarf Rhododendrons. The closely cultivated area is on the north side. Apples, Pears, and even Peaches — for this, be it remembered, is the Laigh of Moray, an area with a mild climate — ripen on the south-facing wall. There is a greenhouse in the same vicinity.

Parts of the herbaceous borders have been underplanted with creeping Thyme, purple-flowered and fragrant. The best of these makes the long border, against the west wall, a rich tapestry of contrasting colours in late summer with Ligularias, Japanese Anemones, *Monarda didyma*, Phloxes, Lady's Mantle, Shasta Daisies, Japanese Stonecrops, London Pride and many other favourite flowers of Scotland's gardens.

35 KINNAIRD CASTLE
Brechin
4 miles south of Brechin. Route A933.
(THE EARL OF SOUTHESK)

Duthac de Carnegie acquired the lands of Kinnaird by purchase and marriage in 1401. He fell at the battle of Harlaw ten years later, and his son Walter, for fighting against Earl 'Beardie' at the battle of Brechin in 1452, had his castle of Kinnaird burned down by the Lindsays. Sir Robert Kinnaird, an ambassador to France, rebuilt the castle in 1550 and it was visited in subsequent years by James VI, Charles I, Charles II and the Chevalier.

Mostly rebuilt again about the beginning of the nineteenth century, it was enlarged and remodelled 1854-60, to designs by David Bryce, in a style reminiscent of a French château, with many towers and turrets, stone balconies and balustraded terrace walls.

There is a formal garden surrounding the Castle, laid out by the 9th Earl of Southesk in 1854, but the chief interest is the 1300-acre deer-park, enclosed by a high wall where it is not bounded by the river South Esk, and containing many fine old trees. There are Rhododendrons growing in the woodland, and the autumn colouring of the trees is particularly fine.

FIGURE 74
*The water garden,
Kildrummy Castle*

Leith Hall is typical of the many smaller gardens which came into being in the early part of the present century as a result of the interest in gardening which an abundant amount of plant material and a plentiful supply of gardeners had stimulated. Frequently, inexpert hands could produce the most bizarre results, while in others, such as Leith Hall, the end product was as fascinating as it was individual, in this case one which combined the prime interests of Mr Charles and the Hon Mrs Leith Hay. The east and west gardens together extend to approximately 8 acres, and are situated on a south-facing slope, mid-way between the entrance and the house. In the west garden the dominant feature is a curved herbaceous border, running north and south, the full length of the garden, with a border of Roses branching off at right angles from a central point. The Rose border leads to the other main feature, a rock garden, now almost completely restored and replanted with large numbers of Heaths to reduce the work of the one gardener now employed.

For a number of years the east half was leased as a market garden, before being partially restored and replanted in the 1960s as an amenity area. At the top (north) end of the east garden a Rose garden has been established on the foundations of a glasshouse which was demolished, and beyond is an open shed in which are gathered several old stones of considerable archaeological value, including some Pictish relics. The remainder of the 236 acres of grounds are now largely given over to commercial forestry.

A loch in the eastern part of the estate, which had become relatively unused and severely overgrown, was the subject of a rehabilitation programme of work designed to improve the estate. It now has a very pleasant walk around the fringe with the added advantage of a Ranger Service for those who appreciate a guided tour.

Leith Hall is one of the Trust's smaller properties, with an attractiveness quite disproportionate to its size. It is best seen in August/September when the border is really spectacular.

The gardens are open all year, 9.30 a.m. to sunset.

This is a white-harled seventeenth-century baronial mansion with a modern west wing, situated high above the right bank of the river Findhorn. The garden was laid out and developed during the seventeenth and eighteenth centuries while the house was in the ownership of the Cumming family. It is mentioned in *Memoirs of a Highland Lady,* where Elizabeth Grant of Rothiemurchus wrote:
'Logie Banks and Logie Braes! How very lovely ye were on those bright autumn days, when wandering through the Beech woods upon the rocky banks of the Findhorn, we passed hours, my cousins and I, out in the pure air, unchecked of any one'.

Reduced to a small formal garden, surrounded by Yew hedges plentifully overgrown with the Scottish Nasturtium (*Tropaeolum speciosum*), it is planted

36 LEITH HALL
Huntly
Take A96 Aberdeen to Huntly road; turn left along B9002. Leith Hall is about 32 miles from Aberdeen.
(NATIONAL TRUST FOR SCOTLAND)

37 LOGIE HOUSE
by Forres
5 miles south of Forres on A940 Forres-Grantown-on-Spey road.
(MR ALEXANDER GRANT LAING)

FIGURE 75
Euonymus hamiltonianus *at Kildrummy*

with Flowering Cherries, Rhododendrons, Azaleas and the usual herbaceous borders, all of which thrive in the kindly, though rather dry, climate.

The chief attractions are the situation, overlooking the Findhorn, and the extensive walks by the river.

38 NEWTON HOUSE
by Insch
*Insch 2½ miles. Route
A96.*
(MRS A. W. PARKIN-MOORE)

Newton House is a late seventeenth-century dwelling, and the date 1778 above the front doorway refers to the year of its extensions. A country laird's or gentleman farmer's property, it is long and narrow and dignified, standing above its forecourt and looking out across its grass parks.

Conforming to an old custom, the garden lies a little way from the house, along a woodland path, now in light, now in shadow, passing two erect Pictish stones in a clearing, both Ogham-inscribed and of exceptional interest.

The house and lands were traditional Gordon property, and the foundations of the present garden were laid by Alexander Gordon, a retired sugar-planter from Tobago. There is a stone in the garden carved with his initials and his wife's and the date 1800.

Their son, also Alexander Gordon, created the garden, and it was he who planted the magnificent trees we see today: Atlas Cedars (*Cedrus atlantica*), Japanese Red Cedars (*Cryptomeria japonica*), the great Oak and the Beeches and many of the Rhododendrons. His too was the Italian fountain, a replica of a Florentine one, carved with his initials and the date 1846.

Between the two World Wars the garden suffered much neglect. Then in 1946 the property was bought back by A. W. Parkin-Moore and his family; he was the great-great-grandson of the first-mentioned Alexander Gordon. After the end of World War II, he set himself the task of restoring the garden, working in it himself, aided by two gardeners.

Moore's paintings are still exhibited, and he was a fine amateur artist, with a sensitive eye for colour and texture. This gift manifests itself too in the garden, which shows a felicitous choice of plants, effectively placed. His main achievement was the conversion of the old walled garden, with its reddish brick walls, into a formal garden, with a raised terrace at the north end looking down a long vista between opposing Yew hedges to the Florentine fountain.

In his designs for the garden, Moore avoided straight lines, and made much play with light and shade. There are many rare and beautiful shrubs; *Clematis jackmanii* adorns the brick walls, and there are the Himalayan *Piptanthus laburnifolius,* scented Lilacs, and Tulip Trees (*Liriodendron tulipifera*).

Mr A. W. Parkin-Moore died in 1979 leaving a garden whose superlative qualities demand that it be saved for posterity.

39 THE OLD MANSE
   OF MARNOCH
Banff

The 'cold shoulder' of North-East Scotland, especially the isolated, windswept, inland reaches of Banff would seem an unlikely situation for an ornamental garden, but the Old Manse of Marnoch belongs to an old kirkton which grew up around a ford across the Deveron. This was a thriving place, before the drift of country folk to the towns; it had a church, built in 1792 at the centre of a Caledonian stone circle, its own country school and dominie's house, and the erection of the two-arched Bridge of Marnoch in 1806 recognised its importance.

THE OLD MANSE OF
MARNOCH (contd.)
On the B9117, 1 mile off the A97 Huntly to Banff road
(LIEUTENANT COLONEL & MRS
W. A. D. INNES)

The kirk's manse was built the previous year, a commodious family house entered by stone steps up to the front door on the first floor, as a precaution against floods perhaps.

Colonel and Mrs Innes acquired the property from the Church of Scotland in 1953, together with its 3 ½ acres of land, part walled garden, part glebe where the minister of Marnoch Kirk used to graze his horse and cow. A recent incumbent had provided sheltering trees, and if the garden had long lain in neglect its soil was rich alluvial loam. The new owners turned it all into a market garden, selling the produce during the 'open' months from a stall at the side of the Huntly-Banff road.

In 1974, however, when Colonel Innes reached retirement age they switched their energies towards making an ornamental garden, starting with certain advantages — the Crombie Burn running its course through their land to join the Deveron, and the existing woodland comprising Giant Firs (*Abies grandis*), Western Red Cedars (*Thuya plicata*), Lawson Cypresses (*Chamaecyparis lawsoniana*); a Western Hemlock (*Tsuga heterophylla*), Veitch's Silver Firs (*Abies veitchii*), Douglas Firs (*Pseudotsuga menziesii*), as well as Chestnuts, Poplars, Limes, Sycamores, Wych Elms and Geans. Colonel Innes's plan was to create a garden for all seasons, with 'something for everybody' — except those who like summer annuals; also, a garden of surprises where the full foliage of the young Conifers creates hidden corners and secret plantings, and where the wanderer passes from one clearing in the woodland to another, without ever retracing his steps.

This is a countryside of hard frosts, both early and late in the year, yet the Old Manse garden contains many rare and tender plants. There are some twenty different Ferns, and ten different Hostas. The Meconopses include the blue flowered *grandis* and *baileyi*, besides the yellow *M. chelidonifolia*. Primulas of different species and varieties flourish in the marshy places — Double Primroses, and *P. denticulata*, in spring, and in June *Primula bulleyana, japonica* and *pulverulenta*.

In mid June there are also Viburnums, Lilacs, Azaleas, and the first of the Roses. There is a hedge of *Rosa* 'Mundi' 33 yards long, the flowers pink splashed with white, also known as *R. gallica* 'Versicolour', named after Fair Rosamund, mistress of Henry II. There are several *R. moyesii*, including a particularly dense, arching bush of the creamy-white *R.* 'Nevada', and many *R. rugosa* hybrids.

Specimens of the Giant Himalayan Lily (*Cardiocrinum giganteum*) are growing in profusion in these woodland clearings among summer-leafing trees, including several species and hybrids of Rowan *(Sorbus)* — *S. hupehensis* with its deeply divided leaves and white or pink-tinged berries, *S. discolor*, red-berried, and *S. cashmiriana*, the largest of the white-fruited species.

Recent plantings of trees have included *Acer griseum* (the Paper-bark Maple), *Acer grosseri,* a 'Tulip Tree', *Liriodendron tulipifera*, which may reach 100 feet, and the Antarctic Beech, *Nothofagus antarctica*, which comes from southern Chile.

Against the house gable there grows a fine *Hydrangea petiolaris*, a joyful climber from Japan and China, with creamy-white heads of flowers that remain attractive over a long period, and leaves that turn golden in autumn. Its companion is *Actinidia kolomikta*, also from the Far East, with curiously-marked green and pink foliage and fragrant greenish-white flowers in June, followed by large yellowish fruits.

Mid-June is the time to see the Meconopses, Azaleas, Irises, Primulas, together with Viburnums, Lilacs and other shrubs, and the first of the Roses. Mid-July is the season for the Rose Hedge, herbaceous border, other Shrub Roses and white Foxgloves. The end of April is Daffodil time — with Dog-Tooth Violets (*Erythronium*), Double Primroses, Polyanthus and Forsythia. Yet, from Snowdrop time — and there are lots of Snowflakes (*Leucojum*) — right through spring, summer and autumn with its magnificent foliage until mid-November, there is always something of interest for the enthusiast.

40 PITMEDDEN
by Ellon
Turn off A92 Aberdeen to Ellon road onto B999; Pitmedden is about 16 miles from Aberdeen.
(NATIONAL TRUST FOR SCOTLAND)

When the National Trust for Scotland acquired the 93-acre Pitmedden Estate in 1952 from the late Major Keith, it was with an intention to restore the 3-acre walled garden as the Great Garden of Pitmedden, a formal seventeenth-century garden, and by so doing re-establish a link with the past. For many years the garden had been neglected and consequently became derelict, and it was not until Major Keith bought the estate that use was again made of the garden to grow vegetables and fruit.

The restoration was started in 1956 under the direction of Dr J. S. Richardson, formerly Inspector of Ancient Monuments in Scotland, who already had experience of this kind of work through his restoration of Edzell Castle garden for the then Ministry of Works.

Unfortunately, the plans for the original Pitmedden garden had been lost in a disastrous fire which destroyed the house in the early part of the nineteenth century, so Dr Richardson prepared a design with four parterres, three of which he knew had been in use during the early seventeenth century at the Palace of Holyrood; the fourth design was to be based upon the Coat of Arms of Sir Alexander Seton. Boxwood was used to outline the designs — about 3 miles of it was required, gleaned from several sources — and the beds were to be filled with a colourful display of annual flowers. Although historically wrong, it was considered important to have these floral additions to serve as an attraction to visitors, and also to emphasise that the original purpose such a garden served was to 'amaze and delight' those who saw it. This sophisticated and very mobile age of the twentieth century does demand the additional help of some historical inaccuracy to attract visitors; and perhaps it is none the worse for that.

During the twenty-five years which have elapsed since the restoration, the

FIGURE 76
The formal garden at Pitmedden

garden has almost reached maturity and one can but admire the forethought and planning which achieved such a splendid result. In 1975 the three-hundredth anniversary of the founding of the garden was marked by the opening of an exhibition to illustrate the evolution of the formal garden, and recently as a final addition a herb garden was made, based upon a design proposed by Dr Richardson.

Those who would like to see the garden in all its glory should aim for August or early September; but the garden is open daily, all year, from 9.30 a.m. to sunset.

41 PLUSCARDEN
ABBEY
🍀 *Vale of Pluscarden*
6 miles from both Forres and Elgin, in the Vale of Pluscarden.
(COMMUNITY OF ST BENEDICT)

'Days of my childhood in the old grey garden,
Books that engaged my green, unknown mind,
Hours spent in the haunted cloisters of Pluscarden,
How fair you seem, how faint, how far behind.'

When Andrew Lang wrote these lines over a century ago, Pluscarden Priory was a semi-ruin, owned by the 6th Earl of Fife, one in a succession of Lay Priors who held the property of the thirteenth-century building and its surrounding land at the time of the Reformation.

Over the years, there were several attempts to maintain the buildings and when James, 4th Earl of Fife, inherited the estates of Pluscarden in 1811 he made a valiant attempt at restoration. Parts of the former monks' living quarters were re-roofed and brought into use, a new road with a bridge over the Lochty Burn and the Gothic lodge and gateway were built, and the policies were planted with shrubs and trees, many of which are still in good heart today.

Through the generosity of the 3rd Marquis of Bute and his son Lord Colum Crichton-Stuart, a community of Benedictine monks from Prinknash in Gloucestershire returned to Pluscarden in September 1948 and monastic life according to the Rule of St Benedict was re-introduced.

The monk's day is more or less equally divided between worship, periods of study, prayer and meditation, and manual labour. Some of the brethren are skilled craftsmen, but all share in the routine duties of community life — household chores, vehicle maintenance, farming, beekeeping and gardening.

Of the 20 acres within the precinct wall, 9 are cultivated — lawns, woodland, ploughed fields, and a large kitchen garden. The latter, situated at the foot of the afforested Heldon Hill, and surrounded partly by high hedges and trees and the great, thick precinct wall of the Abbey, is beautifully sheltered; it faces south and fair to the sun. The produce of soft fruit, Apples and Plums and Pears, and vegetables supplies the monastery's kitchen from beginning to end of the year; the monks rarely have to buy any from outside, and this despite the fact that there are seldom less than twenty sitting down to a meal.

Set in deep boles in the thick precinct wall are straw bee skeps. The Abbot is the self-appointed bee-keeper, watching over the skeps and many other wooden hives, all called after religious houses. The bees get their nectar from the Lime trees in the abbey grounds, and from the blossom of the fruit trees (which they help to pollinate) and great stretches of Heather, Gorse and Whin, and wild flowers of the sparsely populated Vale of Pluscarden.

The honey harvest has on occasion exceeded a ton weight for the year.

Both the Old Statistical Account (1794) and George Maitland's *A Guide to the Priory of Pluscarden* (1823) make reference to a Fig tree growing against the south-facing precinct wall. Legend claims it was planted by the pre-Reformation monks, but it was most probably introduced by the Lay Prior, William Duff of Braco, who succeeded to the property in 1772 and was an ardent improver and preserver. The Fig disappeared long since, as did a vast Elm which used to obscure the east facade. A Cedar of Lebanon darkens the ancient well in an angle of the precinct wall, and there are several shady Sycamores, Elms, Copper Beeches, and Holm Oaks, as well as a single Yew, isolated in a ploughed field, where the Abbey's flock of geese — alas, no more — used to gather for the night.

A hedge of mixed Rhododendrons screens the monks' graveyard from the driveway. An alley, formed of Box on one side and Cedar trees and Rhododendrons on the other, forms a natural ambulatory. There is also a 'secret garden', hidden by Holm Oaks and banks of Laurel, with seats in the sun and borders planted with 'cottage garden' annuals — Pot Marigolds, Nasturtiums, Toadflax and *Godetia*.

Recently the Priory was given the status of an Abbey, an occasion commemorated by tree plantings. There is a new 'apple walk' formed by an 'Egremont Russet', a 'George Cave', a 'Lord Lambourne', 'Laxton's Fortune', and 'Red Ellison'. Sapling Whitebeams turn to silver in the wind by a bend in the carriageway, and, a few feet away, a *Ginkgo biloba*, regarded in the East as a sacred tree, is slowly becoming established.

Besides attending to his bees, the Abbot is frequently to be seen on his knees in the herbaceous border, ruthlessly weeding out the undesirable. In the words of St Bernard of Clairvaux, 'If you are to do the work of a prophet, you need the hoe rather than the sceptre'.

Tillypronie was built in 1867 by Sir John Clark, diplomat son of Sir James Clark, Bart., Physician to Queen Victoria. Her Majesty laid the lintel stone above the main entrance. Alterations to the house were made in 1928 by the late Lord Royden, and by the present owner in 1952.

42 TILLYPRONIE
Tarland

5 miles north-west of Tarland, off the main Ballater-Strathdon road.
(LORD ASTOR OF HEVER)

The mansion and gardens face south. They are situated on the edge of moorland, 1110-1150 feet above sea level, and the outlook across Deeside to the Vale of Cromar and the far Grampians is quite magnificent. In front, the immediate area is terraced with Rose garden, herbaceous borders, and extensive plantations of small ornamental trees and shrubs of contrasting foliages, underplanted with Potentillas, Maples, Heaths and Heathers, and two hundred and fifty different dwarf Conifers. There are also hedges of old-fashioned Shrub

Roses, a mixed colony of Barberries, and rock and alpine gardens containing choice Gentians, *Colchicum autumnale,* and *Salix reticulata*.

The closely-cropped, springy turf of the hill meadow has been laboriously planted with over a hundred different Heaths and Heathers — including the bell-flowered Cornish, Cross-Leafed and Mediterranean Ericas — in distinctive clusters, to form an enormous multi-coloured plaid of flowers and foliage.

Beyond this, the hill slopes gently down to a lake, ringed with Scots Pines, Alders and Silver Birch, and a bog garden containing pale pink Astilbes, golden yellow Ligularias, Rodgersias, Purple Loosestrife, Irises, and Primulas. The policies include a pinetum, and a kitchen garden with greenhouses.

The garden was planned and laid out in 1928 by the late Lord and Lady Royden. It has been developed further since 1953 by the present owners, Lord and Lady Astor of Hever.

43 WILLIAMSTON
by Insch
*Near Insch village. Off
A96, mid-way between
Inverurie and Huntly.*
(COMMANDER & MRS M. S. L.
BURNETT)

Williamston House, built in 1835, is the neighbour of Newton House, and the accounts of these gardens should be read together; the men who recreated them were close friends and shared their ideas on garden landscaping.

The Williamston garden was created by W. T. H. Haughton, Mrs Burnett's uncle. A professional artist, he had spent some time in Paris, and it is apparent from the style of the garden how much his tastes had been influenced by the experience. The Broad Walk, for example, with its clipped Irish Yews and a statue of St Francis feeding the birds at the terminus of the long allée, is reminiscent of the dignified formality of the park at Versailles. Parkin-Moore, proprietor of Newton House, disliked the straight line and geometrical perfection in Haughton's Yew hedges, but both men laid emphasis on the restful beauty of alternating light and shade.

Another of Haughton's allées ends beside a modern statue of St Michael leaning on his sword, close to what was once a pagan well, adopted by Christian missionaries and re-named St Michael's Well. There is also a fountain, encircled in summer by a great bed of Begonias, closely planted and of brilliant colours.

Many great trees fell in the storm of 1953, but the gardeners did not delay in clearing the ground, and within the last twenty-seven years much of the garden has been re-established. Today the owners grow and sell miniature trees, Heaths and Heathers, Azaleas and greenhouse plants. They are farmers, and the house looks out on cattle grazing in the park. There is also a lake, made by Haughton to enhance the view from the house.

MAP OF LOCATIONS:

Scale in miles

THE NORTH AND WEST

Gigha is one of the most fertile islands of the Inner Hebrides, and one of the most beautiful. The name, interpreted, means 'Isle of God'. It is only 6 miles long by 1½ miles wide.

1 ACHAMORE
GARDENS
🦋 *Isle of Gigha, Argyll*
Steamer services from West Loch Tarbert, or by ferry between Tayinloan and the island. Visitors are advised to make their own enquiries in advance.
(OLDCASTLE TRUSTEES LTD)

The Achamore Gardens on the island were created between 1944 and 1973 by Sir James Horlick, Baronet, and stocked for the most part with plants which he had either bred or propagated himself. The presence of the Gulf Stream ensures a mild climate; rainfall is moderate (45 inches) and there is an almost complete absence of frosts. The real hazard is high wind, sweeping in from the Atlantic, laden with salt spray. However, the original mixed woodland of Sycamore and Spruce, planted at the turn of the century to provide cover for game, now shelters about 50 acres of garden.

Sir James Horlick was particularly interested in Rhododendrons, for which the rich loamy soil of the Achamore Gardens is very suitable. He was also a keen breeder, and the gardens contain many of his crosses, besides species and hybrids brought to the island.

The number and variety of plants, shrubs and trees now thriving in the garden is legion: Azaleas, Camellias, Hydrangeas, Mahonias, Pieris, Viburnums, Cotoneasters, Escallonias, *Hamamelis mollis*, Embothriums, and many more, the collections of Chilean and Australasian subjects being particularly large.

Many Southern Beeches — *Nothofagus* — have been introduced from the Crarae gardens on Loch Fyne, as well as Australian Pittosporums and Rowans from America, Japan and China, Japanese Cherries, and numerous Acers and Birches.

Much space is given to Roses — Hybrid Musks, Floribundas, and *Rosa rugosa* hybrids and cultivars, the scented 'Roseraie de l'Hay' and 'Blanc Double de Coubert', and *Rosa filipes* ascending high into an old Scots Pine.

Bulbous plants have not been forgotten; there are Lilies of many kinds, Snowdrops for winter's end, and broad golden acres of Daffodils and Narcissi in spring.

2 ACHDUART OLD
SCHOOLHOUSE
🦋 *by Achiltibuie*

The house was built to accommodate the schoolmaster. It is between one hundred and a hundred and fifty years old, no one seems to know precisely, and was only recently modernised by adding a bathroom, kitchen and sun-room. 5 acres of land go with the cottage, of which 1½ acres make up the garden. Beyond lies the moor, bare, windswept and treeless.

To the north, the east and the south are great mountains and lochs. To the west lie the beautifully named 'Summer Isles' — Tanera More, Tanera Beg,

ACHDUART OLD
SCHOOLHOUSE (contd.)
*4 miles east of Achiltibuie
Post Office. Take right
hand turn after Youth
Hostel sign. Continue to
sign 'End Of Road' (1
mile). Name on gate (K. J.
MacLeod) and grid.*
(MR KENNETH J. MACLEOD &
MRS RUTH MACLEOD)

Eilean Dubh, and, across the waters of the North Minch, the Outer Hebrides.

Recognising the wind as their chief adversary, the MacLeods first enclosed the garden within a Chestnut paling, and planted sheltering Beech hedges and Sitka Spruce, Silver Birch, Willows and Alders. Today, they have a series of small gardens within a large semi-formal, woodland garden. They also created a water garden by damming two springs, originally the school's and the dominie's water suppliers.

The high winds apart, Achduart has a kindly climate, mild and wet, with some snow in winter but seldom any severe frost. The soil in the garden is similar to that of the moor, shallow and mainly peat, often saturated, but drying out rapidly in an east wind. May and June are the best summer months, transforming the bleak moorland places.

Most peat-loving plants burgeon well in the garden's little sheltered plots. There is *Olearia macrodonta*; *Olearia tomentosa*; *Desfontainea spinosa,* a shrub with Holly-like leaves and bright scarlet tubular flowers tinged with yellow, which comes from Chile and grows best by the sea; free-flowering hybrid *Camellia* × *williamsii*; Rhododendrons, Azaleas, Hydrangeas, Heaths and Heathers, and many spring bulbs. There are also Eucalyptus trees, Aspens, Dogwoods, and *Euonymus europaeus,* the common Spindle tree.

3 ACHNACLOICH
Connell
*3 miles east of Connell, off
the A85.*
(MRS T. E. NELSON)

Achnacloich is a castellated Victorian mansion occupying a promontory on the south side of Loch Etive. The frontage commands panoramic views of the mountains of Lorn to the north, Mull to the west, and Ben Cruachan to the east.

Loch Etive, a sea loch, has a moderating effect upon the climate, and the large garden on the south side gains shelter from fringes of Scots Pine and European Larch. The ground inclines steeply from a rock garden and terrace to a broad sweep of lawn, with an undulating series of ridges and open-bottomed dells on the west side. The garden complements the dignity of the house and there has obviously been a traditional interest in it. Acers, Rhododendrons and Azaleas from the inter-war period continue to flourish, and the planting area was extended during the 1950s and 60s by the late proprietor, Mr T. E. Nelson.

Mr Nelson, a well-informed plantsman, preserved the natural landscaping, deploying additional shrubs and trees in effective groups along the tops and sides of the ridges. The overall impression received is one of effortless beauty, sheltered peace, and uncluttered spaciousness.

It is a spring garden, wakening from the winter season with the flowering of early bulbs. Pale Daffodils, preferred to the bright yellow, bloom in drifts across the lawn and in the dells, already lustrous with Wind-Flowers, Wild Hyacinths and Primroses, the pale blossom of *Malus sargentii* and the delicate foliage of the 'weeping' Kilmarnock Willow (*Salix caprea* 'pendula') bearing its silky 'pussy' catkins.

FIGURE 78
An Cala

Primulas come into flower at this time in the bog garden around the pool, also the *Lysichiton*, with its highly decorative golden-yellow spathes; and from this

beginning the bog garden will go from strength to strength throughout spring, summer and autumn, producing a long succession of different Primulas, Spireas, Loosestrife, Globe Flowers, Rodgersias, and the great coarse foliage of *Gunnera manicata*, the sky blue Forget-me-not, and the deeper hue of Bugle, Irises of many different colours, and brilliant yellow Flags.

In this mild west coast climate, *Camellia × williamsii* 'Donation' flowers in the early months of the year, producing large pink semi-double blooms over a long period. Its brilliance is rivalled by the fiery young top leaves of *Pieris formosa*, preferring the woodland shade; and later by the large orange-yellow flower clusters of *Berberis linearifolia*, a hardy evergreen even though it comes from Chile.

Later, *Embothrium* (Chilean Fire Bush) is a spectacle of beauty with every twig carrying a cluster of brilliant scarlet flowers. In other parts of Britain these are often injured by sudden reversions to wintry weather, but Achnacloich is free of 'frost pockets'. About this time, or even earlier, *Enkianthus campanulatus* comes into bloom; the creamy-white flowers are bell-shaped and hang in pendulous clusters.

There are, of course, many Rhododendrons. Notable among Mrs Nelson's favourites are:

R. 'Yellow Hammer' — butter-yellow flowers with brown anthered bells, the foliage is narrowly oval, small, with a touch of bronze, it flowers quite freely in November, and again in springtime; *R. crassum* — the flowers are long and funnel-shaped, scented, and white with a distinctive yellow eye, the leaves are very handsome, apart from Cornwall and Ireland and in Argyll, it needs protection from frost; and *R. concatenans* — bell-shaped flowers, either apricot or bronze in colour, the leaves are a striking blue-green.

There is no attempt to provide ground-cover plants, except among the Rhododendrons of the *triflorum* series, where the Partridge Berry (*Gaultheria shallon*) is used. Although an attractive plant in itself, with apple-green leaves and rosy flowers giving edible purple berries, it is a robust coloniser and needs frequent checking.

The Magnolias in the Achnacloich garden are superb, some of them having the proportion of trees, to be admired from below. *M. wilsonii*, from China, is sweet scented, its flowers large and white, faintly tinged with pink as they fade. *M. sinensis*, also from China as the name implies, goes on flowering here throughout the summer. The cup-shaped flowers, which are white and fragrant, first appear in June.

The Japanese *M. obovata*, is the largest of these three. The creamy-white flowers, produced in June, are strongly scented and may measure as much as 8 inches in breadth. It produces bright crimson pendulous fruit in October and November.

Many of the plants in the garden have been selected for their brilliant autumn foliage and berries: *Cercidiphyllum japonicum*, with heart-shaped leaves turning from springtime purple to rich yellow and scarlet; the small Rowan, *Sorbus vilmorinii*, which has very fine autumn leaf colour and rosy-red berries; and Sorbus 'Joseph Rock', having upswept branches and leaves that turn orange, red, copper and purple — the amber-yellow berries are left untouched by birds. The spring-flowering *Enkianthus* turns to rich gold and red in the autumn weather. The best of the Acers in this respect is probably *A. pensylvanicum;* throughout the year its bark is coloured a pale jade green with silvery-white striations, and its large three-lobed leaves turn a golden yellow at the first sign of winter.

No more suitable name could be found for this island house and its garden than the Gaelic one, An Cala, the meaning of which is the haven or the place of peace. It is, nevertheless, part of the village of Easdale or, more accurately, Ellenabeich, the landward community, separated from the slate-quarrying island of Easdale by a strait, 400 yards across at the narrowest point. Old abandoned heaps of slate are much in evidence, and the land is stony with bright green tussocky meadows, few trees, and stretches of salt marsh washed over at high tide. The climate is maritime, much exposed to tearing gales, and with a high annual rainfall.

4 An Cala

Easdale

16 miles south-east of Oban, on the B844 to Easdale, Isle of Seil. (Mrs H. I. Blakeney)

None of these circumstances is really conducive to gardening, and the garden at An Cala was only achieved at great cost in money, time and hard labour. Realistically, the whole concept was a prodigal nonsense, but the creator, Colonel Arthur Murray (later to become Lord Elibank), inherited one of the original row of three cottages from his aunt. When his wife, actress Faith Celli — famed for her rôle as 'Peter Pan' and in many Shavian plays — heard of the inheritance, she exclaimed ardently and decisively, 'Good! Now I can create a garden!'

The 'but and ben' was too cramped for their use, but in time they were able to buy the other two cottages in the row and converted all three into a single dwelling.

The garden took longer to make. Looking back in 1939, Lord Elibank wrote, 'There was nothing on the site in 1931 except six tall Sycamore trees and one tall Willow. In 1934, to keep out the west and north-west gales, we built the grey brick wall, 15 feet high.'

What is now the Wild Garden was planted with a variety of evergreen trees. The little 'still' burn which had possibly been used by the cottagers for illicit whisky-making was turned to a new, purely decorative use. And what had previously been a bleaching green, strewn with fallen boulders off the hillside, received thousands of tons of imported top soil, rolled flat into smooth lawns and flowerbeds.

After forty years, the garden has a mature, long-established appearance. The firm stone stepways leading up to the Wild Garden are overhung by pink and white Flowering Cherry trees, Rowans, *Aralia elata* (the Chinese Angelica tree) and Rhododendrons, notably *R. rhabdotum* (white, striped deep pink and scented), and normally recommended for greenhouse cultivation only.

Lower down, Acers, Hydrangeas, Camellias and Crinodendrons fill the shrub borders. There are also varieties of *Ceanothus, Berberis, Daphne, Cytisus, Viburnum, Escallonia, Cotoneaster* and *Buddleia,* all of which prosper in seaside gardens.

The banks of the stream are planted with Astilbes, *Mimulus,* Hostas in variety, *Iris kaempferi,* Primulas of many different kinds, Rodgersias, *Filipendula hexapetala,* Willow Gentians (*G. asclepiadea*), and ferns.

A young *Pyrus salicifolia* 'pendula' ('Willow-leaved Pear') is reflected in the Lily pond, over which a water nymph is stooping.

Among the outcrops of rock and boulders flourish deep purple Thymes, the various Gentians, *Iberis*, rock Phloxes, the Alpine Willow *Salix reticulata*, and other rock plants that are tolerant of salt winds off the sea, such as Sedums, Sempervivums, Rock Roses, Aubretias, *Alyssum saxatile*, the dwarf and prostrate conifers, and different Saxifrages.

Many of these flower in May and June, An Cala's best summer months, and the season for its Roses — 'Albertine', that old favourite, trained up the white roughcast house walls, and beds of the carmine and light pink 'Betty Prior', and the single scarlet 'Karen Poulsen'.

The garden lies so close to the seashore that the sound of the rushing tide and the calling of seabirds is clearly audible at every point, and the foliage in the Wild Garden is nowhere so close that one cannot look out on the panoramic views of the Firth of Lorn, dotted with many islands, large and small — Easdale with its old slate quarries, begun in the seventeenth century, Luing, Scarba, Jura, the Garvellachs, Mull and — on clear days — Islay and Colonsay.

The present owner of An Cala is Mrs H. I. Blakeney.

5 ARDANAISEIG
⚜ *Taynuilt*

Turn off A85 approx. ½ mile from Taynuilt. Take B845 through Glen Nant to Kilchrennan, where a signpost points to Ardanaiseig. Road beyond lodge leads to house and gardens.
(Mr & Mrs J. M. Brown)

Ardanaiseig House is a Scottish Baronial style mansion, erected in 1834 according to plans prepared by William Burn. The original owner was a younger son of the Campbells of Inverawe, and gave it the name of New Inverawe. The Ainsworth family subsequently bought the house and its lands, and remained in possession from 1880 until World War II. The present owners converted it to a hotel in 1979-80. The house has a magnificent prospect of Loch Awe and the mountains to the east, including Ben Lui (3708 feet), while, to the north, Ben Cruachan (3689 feet) provides a striking backcloth to the gardens near at hand.

Though less favourable than that directly influenced by the Gulf Stream, the climate is mild and the soil acid. At an elevation of 250 feet, the gardens are sheltered by woodland, except from the east wind blowing across Loch Awe, and there are many magnificent trees of a considerable size and maturity.

Visitors are invited to walk around the gardens, following a route marked by arrows, and commencing beside a small stream alongside the main drive. The woodland path passes close to a Lily pond, overhung by a gnarled Oak whose mossy bark is covered with *Polypodium*. Some little way further, one enters the walled garden, about an acre in extent, and containing splendid herbaceous borders, lawns, plots of vegetables and soft fruits and a small orchard.

Growing among the wall-trained Plums and Apples and Pears can be seen a Judas Tree (*Cercis siliquastrum*), a favourite in English gardens, though rarely seen in Scotland, being regarded as unlikely to succeed here. It is, in fact, a native of the Mediterranean countries, and groves of it bloom about Eastertide on the Palatine Hill in Rome. The colour of the pea-like flowers, growing in clusters on the often bare branches, is appropriate to that season, being a deep pink or near purple.

The woodland surrounding the walled garden contains specimen trees, many planted when the house was built, or during the occupation of the Ainsworth family. Beneath these there are closely-set shrubberies of Rhododendrons, Azaleas, Eucryphias, Embothriums, and, indeed, all the accepted constituents of a West Highland garden.

At the front of the house there are tell-tale signs of a formal garden, dispensed with since such stiff formality went out of fashion. What were once smooth and velvety lawns merge on either side with wild woodland, and incline steeply towards the reed beds along the margin of Loch Awe. Yet there remains one particularly lovely shrub, flourishing here above the lochside — *Hoheria sex-stylosa,* a native of New Zealand, with inch-wide white flowers hanging in clusters, and grey-green lanceolate leaves, toothed at the edges. It is the pride of the Ardanaiseig Garden.

Ardchattan Priory was founded in 1230 for Valliscaulian monks by Sir Duncan MacDougall of the family of the then Lords of Lorn.

Robert Bruce held a parliament here in 1308; but in 1654 as a reprisal for the Laird's anti-Cromwell stance a party of troops partially burnt down the buildings, so that there remain today only the 13th-century choir and north aisle, traces of old masonry, and a few recumbent mediaeval tombstones marking the graves of once powerful Celtic families.

For some unexplained reason the Prior's Lodging escaped and became the nucleus of the present mansion house, whose Victorian front verandah looks out across Loch Etive to Ben Cruachan and the Isle of Mull.

The level of the front garden is just above the shingle of the lochside, and waves beat against the shore within 30 yards of its flower borders. The soil is sandy and stony, the situation bold and open, but the climate is mild, apart from occasional hard frosts; and the 3-acre garden, made in 1830, contains many choice and beautiful things.

About half of the area is formal, containing herbaceous borders, shrub borders a rock garden, and beds of Roses; the remainder informal, with fine Yew trees and Sycamores, which are over four hundred years old, banks of old Shrub Roses, and over two hundred varieties of shrubs.

6 ARDCHATTAN
  PRIORY GARDEN
Loch Etive
By north shore of Loch Etive.
(Mrs James Troughton)

Potentillas and Hebes flourish in the light soil, as does the Daisy Bush (*Olearia nummularifolia*), which like the Hebe is a native of New Zealand.

Among the larger shrubs, numerous *Viburnum, Mahonia bealei, Crinodendron hookeranum* (Chilean Lantern Tree), *Cotoneaster bullata, Hoheria lyallii, Neillia tibetica, Philadelphus* (Mock Orange), and the Chilean *Berberis linearifolia* make a spectacular display.

There are many Rowans, notably the Mountain Ash (*Sorbus sargentiana*), Flowering Crabs, and — outstanding amid many other Shrub Roses — 'Canary Bird', with its attractive fernlike foliage and bright yellow, lightly-scented blooms.

7 ARDTORNISH
Morvern, by Oban
Off A884, 2 miles north-north-east of Lochaline.
(ARDTORNISH ESTATE COMPANY)

The house and garden of Ardtornish take their name from an ancient stronghold of the Lord of the Isles and a meeting place of their legislative assemblies. The defences of the original castle have long since been broken down, and the present house, some short way inland, but commanding magnificent views of the Sound of Mull, is large by present-day standards and was built in 1890, to designs by Mr Ross of Inverness.

The style of the garden was altered in the 1920s, from that of a wild, rocky ravine, and changes have taken place fairly continuously until today when it can best be described as a natural glen, with extensive lawns and plantations of rare and beautiful shrubs.

The climate, fortunately, is mild and the garden sheltered, apart from its openness to west winds and occasional severe frosts. The soil is acid (between 4.9 and 5.6 on the pH scale), favourable for Azaleas and Rhododendrons, including many hybrids introduced from Pollok House, Glasgow.

The banks of the streams are planted with Primulas and other moisture-loving plants. Among the larger shrubs and trees, *Eucryphia, Hoheria* and specimen conifers predominate.

The Ardtornish garden is the main feature of John Raven's *A Botanist's Garden*, published by Collins in 1971.

8 ARDUAINE GARDENS
Loch Melfort
4 miles from Kilmelford, 10 miles from Kilmartin.
Route A816.
(MR HARRY WRIGHT & MR EDMUND WRIGHT)

Arduaine is Gaelic for 'green point' and the gardens come close to the shore of Asknish Bay. From the cliff behind one looks out across the sea to the many islands, large and small, to Shuna and Scarba and Jura.

The surrounding country is beautiful but wild and often desolate, and when James A. Campbell bought the Arduaine estate in 1897 a few storm-blasted Oaks, shaggy Heather and Rushes and Bracken were the only vegetation on the promontory where the gardens now lie.

Campbell first built Arduaine House, embarking on the garden many years later, in 1910. He chose an area some two hundred yards west of the house, where there was a natural hollow, sheltered by a headland, and with springs to supply it with clear water. He had as assistant and adviser in the planning his good friend Osgood Mackenzie, creator of the famous gardens at Inverewe.

Various problems interrupted progress, but the main woodland was planted in 1920. Rustic windbreaks were erected to afford the tender plants protection, some grown from seed brought back with cargoes of tea from China.

After James Campbell's death in 1929, ownership of the estate changed hands several times within the family, and progress in the creation of the gardens came to a halt at the outbreak of the 1939-45 war. The last member of the Campbell family to own Arduaine was Major Ian Campbell. His children's nurse took a keen and active interest in the garden, more so indeed than anyone else at that time, and when her charges grew up she remained to devote all her time and energies to it. She would labour on long after the daylight failed, until someone would be deputed to look for Nanny Yule with a torch.

After Miss Yule finally retired in 1964, Arduaine House was sold to the Lochmelfort Hotel Company. Thereafter the gardens were neglected, and when Edmund and Harry Wright took them over in 1971 they had to contend with a wilderness of thorns, rank weeds and fallen trees, all of which had to be cleared before systematic cultivation and replanting could begin. Much labour and care has gone into opening up the extensive woodland garden, where trees have had to be thinned to allow in more light. Besides the woodland area there are rock gardens, a water garden, a stream garden, and a cliff garden, the total area under cultivation being 24 acres.

Rhododendrons predominate over all else, especially the large-leafed species such as *R. giganteum* (the first to flower in Britain), *sinogrande, rex, fulvum, griffithianum, cinnabarinum roylei,* and the tree-like *R. arboreum.* The Wrights achieved great success and distinction for their gardens with *R. fictolacteum,* which took first prizes at the Royal Horticultural Society show in 1978, and again at Glasgow a week later. The best species in cultivation is *R. zeylanicum,* produced from seed sent from Sri Lanka.

Next in order of supremacy are the Magnolias: *M. obovata,* so sweetly scented, *M. sieboldii,* and *M. denudata,* profuse with its flowers and the 'Yulan' of Chinese temple gardens. There are several *Eucalyptus gunnii,* all of a great height. *Griselinia littoralis,* a New Zealand shrub with bright, shining, leathery green leaves, is everywhere in the woodland garden. *Berberidopsis corallina* (Coral Plant) is a creeper with a stem as thick as a man's wrist. It is to be seen here, clambering to a height of 40 feet up a Larch tree. The leaves are heart-shaped, dark green, and the flowers red on long stems. Another prize is *Trochodendron aralioides,* an evergreen native to the moist mountain woods of Japan; both leaves and flowers are shades of green.

The Wrights' *Davidia vilmoriniana,* called the Handkerchief Tree, is said to be the largest in Scotland. For sheer loveliness, however, few can excel the *Cornus kousa* var. *chinensis,* covered with creamy-white bracts in summer, its leaves turning a brilliant scarlet in autumn, or the parasitic plant, *Lathraea clandestina,* with violet flowers like an Autumn Crocus which lives parasitically on tree roots.

In spring the lawns are golden with thousands of *Narcissus cyclamineus* (miniature Daffodils), as happy here as they would be in their native Spain or Portugal.

FIGURE 79
Herbaceous border, Arduaine

It is a wonderfully tranquil garden. Goldcrests sing their high-pitched songs among the trees. Otters come to bathe in the pool. Occasionally, at dusk, a hare breaks cover to caper momentarily across the wide lawn.

Traditionally Ardullie Lodge is the home of the Chief of the Clan Munro. It is a particularly attractive small house, built in 1602 and typical of that period. The 1 acre of formal garden is also seventeenth-century in style, surrounded by hedges of an equal age.

9 ARDULLIE LODGE
🦌 *Dingwall*
4 miles Dingwall, 4 miles Evanton. Route A9.
(MR A. H. KNIGHT & MRS A. PARELIUS-KNIGHT)

House and garden are built close to the Cromarty Firth, looking across to the Black Isle. They have their own favourable micro-climate, only 50 feet above sea level. In fact, the ground is a raised beach, with a gravelly sub-soil. Rain-water drains away quickly and, having a tendency to lime, the garden is quite unsuitable for growing Rhododendrons and other calcifuges. However, bedding annuals, herbaceous plants and shrubs, vegetables and soft fruit all do well. A further 5 acres of parkland lie outwith the garden.

Barguillean farm and gardens lie in remote Glen Lonan, attained along a narrow winding road, each turn opening up new and lovely views; a wildly beautiful place, dominated by the awesome might of Ben Cruachan (3689 feet) and the mountains converging on Loch Etive. Mr and Mrs Macdonald started the garden in 1956 as a memorial to their son Angus.

10 BARGUILLEAN
🦌 *Taynuilt*
3 miles south-west of Taynuilt, on the Glen Lonan road.
(MR & MRS NEIL MACDONALD)

A rutted track leads from the farmhouse over the low, intervening meadow to the garden, situated on a wooded hillside and verging on a man-made loch. Throughout the years, it has become a host to over two hundred and fifty different varieties of Rhododendrons and an equally large collection of hybrid Azaleas. The Rhododendrons include:
'Day Dream' — wide flowers which open rose-coloured, changing to creamy yellow; 'Mrs A. T. de la Mare' — deliciously scented, with rose-pink buds opening to creamy white with greenish blotching; 'Carita' — smoky pink flowers; 'Robin Hood' — very large pink flowers, 4 inches across; 'Albatross' (Exbury hybrid) — late-flowering, pale pink blooms, which appear as extremely large flowers supported in flat-topped trusses; 'Loder's Pink Diamond' — rather large pink flowers, loosely formed, fading to a flushed white as they mature; 'Ightham Yellow'; 'Idealist' — soft pale yellow blooms with a purple brown calyx; and 'John Holmes' — red flowers in April.

Yet all these plants from foreign parts merely serve to elaborate the garden's own wild beauty and in no way alter its native spirit and character. They thrive here because the climate in this part of Argyll is usually mild, with a high annual rainfall, and the soil is acid.

Self-sown Birches, Oaks and native Conifers compose the 5-acre wood, to which the Macdonalds have introduced several varieties of *Sorbus*, like the indigenous Rowan and Whitebeam, and Lawson Cypresses with their low-reaching dense foliage, all forming effective shelter against wind, so that when the upper timbers are creaking and groaning in a storm the bottom layer of the wood may still be relatively still. Moreover, the overhead canopy mitigates the effects of summer drought, while the thick springy carpet of Heath, Heather, Moss, Blaeberry, rotting wood pulp and leafmould makes moisture-conserving ground cover. A surrounding fence was put up against the deer, which come down from the hills in search of food.

Neil Macdonald spent thirteen years digging the pond in the garden. The loch itself was created by his father in 1906, on the advice of a keeper, Angus, whose name it bears. Otherwise, the garden is a natural one; the Macdonalds work hard in it, but regard themselves as Nature's assistants. It is entirely free of factitious 'improvements'. There are no made paths, no woodland rides, no statuary, no arbours; but the Rhododendrons and Azaleas have been planted where they will best thrive, and to the best effect.

The Rhododendrons and Azaleas flower at different periods throughout eight to nine months of the year. The garden has its own native wild flowers — wild Primroses, Wild Hyacinths, Anemones, and drifts of naturalised Snowdrops and Daffodils, blooming when the hardwoods are coming into leaf. May and June are the best months for the Azaleas and Rhododendrons, followed by summer wild flowers such as the Dog Roses, Honeysuckle, Potentillas, Cranes-bill, Meadowsweet, Orchises, Heaths and Heathers, Bugle, Heart's Ease, and many others. The Azaleas provide rich autumn colour, as do the Rowans in berry and in leaf, and the Birches change from dark green to yellow to orange-brown.

The shelter of the garden and the neighbouring loch attract many birds; water fowl such as wigeon, mallard, and mute swans gather on Loch Angus, and in the woods there are many kinds of titmice, also woodpeckers, goldcrests, jays and the common birds — blackbirds, thrushes, and the occasional pheasant.

11 BRAHAN
🐚 *Conon Bridge*
(MRS A. F. MATHESON)

Brahan Castle, on the left bank of the Conon Water, was built early in the seventeenth century by the first Earl of Seaforth. It was a grand old fortress in its day, surrounded by scenery of the most magnificent kind. Brahan is the name of the house converted out of the Castle stables. It stands directly behind the Castle site and commands the same view. The house stands 100 feet above sea leavel. The climate is mild and the rainfall moderate (32 inches).

The garden was created by the last Lord and Lady Seaforth, who are buried nearby. It contains the graves of their faithful and much-loved dogs.

There are about 12 acres of garden, mainly woodland and scrub, but colourful in spring with bulbs, followed by Azaleas and Rhododendrons. Trees planted by the Seaforth family continue to flourish, and a burn runs through the garden area. The wild beauty of the garden is at its best in the late autumn months.

Brodick Castle has been the home of the Dukes of Hamilton since 1503, and stands in what must have been a fairly impenetrable position about 100 feet above the shore on the north side of Brodick bay. The building represents three stages of development. The oldest, dating from the fourteenth to the sixteenth century, has strong associations with Robert Bruce as his retreat after the Battle of Methven; the central section dates from the Cromwellian period, and the most recent addition was made in 1844, to a design by the architect James Gillespie Graham. It was acquired by the National Trust for Scotland in 1958, accepted by them in lieu of Estate Duty.

12 BRODICK CASTLE

Brodick, Isle of Arran

2 miles north of Brodick.
(NATIONAL TRUST FOR SCOTLAND)

For property which has become internationally known there is surprisingly little in the way of gardening tradition. In the most important area, the woodland, development of approximately 60 acres did not begin until 1918 when the late Duchess of Montrose began to develop a very remarkable collection of Rhododendrons and other plants in the spacious woodlands between the castle and the shore. Her interest fortunately coincided with a period of great introductions by such men as Farrer, Forrest, Kingdon-Ward and Rock, who were to realise the vast potential of the hitherto unknown treasures of the Himalayan districts of Burma, Tibet and West China. Many of these plant collections, especially Rhododendrons, found their way to Brodick, and eventually to the Royal Horticultural Society show benches in London, where they received, and continue to attract, the highest honours the Society can award.

During late March and April it is possible to see *R. giganteum* and *R. magnificum*, two of the giants of the race, in flower. In May and early June there is an abundance of the sweetly fragrant *maddenii* Rhododendrons, as well as other exotic plants from Chile, New Zealand and China. Several of these would normally require the protection of a glasshouse, although at Brodick the wet, but mild, climate, brought to the west of Scotland by the Atlantic Drift, is sufficiently warm to allow them to be grown out-of-doors. The woodland is essentially a spring and early summer garden, and the many treasures it holds are best seen in May or early June when the majority of them are in flower.

In addition to the woodland, there is a walled garden, formally designed as a Rose garden, with herbaceous borders on three sides, where the bulk of the colour comes later in the year, most notably during July and August when annual flowers, herbaceous borders and Roses make for a most colourful display. Originally this may well have served the dual purpose of vegetable flower garden, until it became too small to meet current needs. That it is the oldest part of the garden is confirmed by the date 1710 inscribed in the lintel of the north door.

FIGURE 80
Daffodils at Brodick

FIGURE 81
Autumn colours at Crarae

The gardens are open all year, from 10.00 a.m. to 5.00 p.m.

A pre-Reformation bishop built Barrogill as a grange. Then in 1556 it was acquired by George, 4th Earl of Caithness, who ten years later added a superstructure of dwelling-rooms and called it Barrogill Castle. This establishment

13 THE CASTLE OF MEY

near Thurso

THE CASTLE OF MEY
(contd.)
Just east of Mey village, off the A836 Thurso-John o' Groats road.
(HER MAJESTY QUEEN ELIZABETH THE QUEEN MOTHER)

had a garden superior to most in Caithness at that time, for when the Protestant Bishop of Caithness visited it in 1762 he remarked on there being 'plenty of Apples, Strawberries and Cherries' prospering within its bounds, and this despite the harsh climate and the wild gales that blow across the Pentland Firth with awful frequency and strength.

In 1889, the Sinclair earls relinquished their four centuries' tenure and Barrogill stood for a long period empty and ruinous, its gardens a wilderness. In 1952, however, just when it seemed that the Castle would be demolished, Her Majesty Queen Elizabeth The Queen Mother purchased it. She renamed it The Castle of Mey, and soon plans were afoot for the restoration and improvement of the property, including the gardens.

Some shelter is afforded the policies to the south by an 18-foot high stone wall, and — within recent years — by two woods of dwarf trees, laboriously planted and kept *in situ* in the clay soil by a locally evolved method of underplanting, to save the seedlings from being uprooted by the winds.

Some of the best gardens have been made on inhospitable sites, and, once within the castle walls, the flat, treeless landscape, so wildly beautiful, is forgotten. There are two walled gardens of some 2 acres in all, one on the east, one on the west side of the castle. The latter is typical of the old-fashioned, homely, generously productive Scots garden; formal in style, with gravelled paths, and plots bordered with Fuchsia hedging or flat Caithness paving stones. The herbaceous borders contain *Primula helodoxa*, the Himalayan Blue Poppy (*Meconopsis betonicifolia*), Astilbes of various colours, and the African Lily (*Agapanthus*) and brightly-coloured annuals to fill the gaps.

The greenhouse staging is loaded with pots of vivid Fuchsias, Begonias, *Impatiens* and Geraniums. Close to this there are beds of Roses, mostly modern Hybrid Teas and Floribundas.

There are several fruit trees, soft fruit bushes, and early potatoes for Her Majesty's annual visit, for her birthday on 4 August, and many other vegetables, including Sorrel for salads, and both the Globe and Jerusalem Artichokes.

14 CRARAE GARDENS
by Inveraray
On A83, about midway between Inveraray and Lochgilphead.
(THE CRARAE GARDENS CHARITABLE TRUST)

These are among the most celebrated of Scottish gardens, the delight of plantsmen, botanists, and all gardeners. Begun in 1912 by Lady Campbell of Succoth, aunt of the famous plant collector Reginald Farrer, they were enlarged and expanded by her son, Sir George Campbell, Bart. Since his death in 1967, they have been in the care of his son, Sir Ilay Campbell, who made them the subject of a charitable trust in 1978.

Lady Campbell found some remarkable trees when she came to Crarae, which lies above the west shore of Loch Fyne, a long, narrow sea loch. Among the remnants of the ancient Caledonian forest were Scots Pines and European Larches, planted in 1800 by Campbell Tate, the latter possibly derived from the famous strain of Atholl Larches.

There are now 40 acres of garden, mainly woodland in character, centred on a steep-sided ravine with a burn running down to the loch. The acid soil contains pockets of mineralised peat and some sandy loam over impermeable boulder clay.

Argyll enjoys the much vaunted 'Gulf Stream' climate, mild and wet, with an annual rainfall of 78 inches. Snow rarely lies here, although in March and April cold winds often blow out of the east, and the gardens suffered during the exceptional winters of 1976-7, 1977-8 and 1978-9.

The making of a garden in the glen began with the planting of trees, both conifer and deciduous, selected for the achievement of brilliant autumn colours. Sir George Campbell had an instinctive eye for planting the right tree or shrub in the right place. The many Rhododendrons, Azaleas, Magnolias and other flowering trees and shrubs all excel and contribute to the glory of Crarae in early summer time, but nothing equals its colour on a bright, late October day.

From the wide selection of rare and beautiful trees and shrubs, mention must be made particularly of the Chinese Beech (*Fagus englerana*); *Disanthus cercidifolius*, a rather delicate Japanese shrub, related to the Witch Hazels, which turns a lemony gold in autumn; and *Clethra delavayi,* another tender shrub from the Yunnan province of China.

There is a collection of *Sorbus*, including the superb *S.* 'Joseph Rock', and another of *Eucryphia* — *E.* 'Mt Usher', raised at a famous garden in Ireland; *E. cordifolia*, planted in 1912; *E. glutinosa*, providing fine autumn colour; *E. lucida*, with pure white flowers, and others, The Australasian *E. moorei*, which is very tender, was killed by the bad winter of 1967-8.

Reginald Farrer presented Lady Campbell with a specimen of the rare Eucalyptus, *E. urnigera*, the urn-fruited gum, which he brought back from Australia in 1912. It grew into a large tree, and after being savaged by a storm in 1968 recovered, sending out vigorous new shoots. Many more 'gums' have been introduced to the Crarae gardens, mainly from Tasmania; they thrive, because of the similarity of climate, and form a coppice above the ravine.

Near them is a Primula dell, made beneath the Eucalyptus canopy, where a spring rises.

Among the Rhododendrons are *R. fulvum,* with russet underleaves and brilliant red flowers; *R. macabeanum,* a fine yellow with large leaves; the rose-lilac *R. hodgsonii*; *R. arizelum*, with interesting foliage and pink blossoms; *R. bureavii*, well suited to the expansive garden; and some from the noble Falconeri series, with foot-long leaves and creamy-white flowers packed in trusses 6 to 9 inches across.

A tour of the Crarae gardens is necessarily a lengthy affair, with so much to study and admire; the Japanese Lantern Tree, *Criodendron hookerii*, well-named for its pendulous bells of brilliant scarlet; a fine specimen of *Osmanthus burkwoodii* (syn. *Osmanthus delavayi*), a handsome evergreen with tubular, ivory-white, slightly fragrant flowers, blooming in early summer; *Styrax obassia*, planted for autumn colour in the ravine; *Pieris taiwanensis,* useful among the

FIGURE 82
Inverewe

Rhododendrons, with its clusters of pure white flowers and evergreen foliage; and the fine ornamental Crab Apple, *Malus hupehensis,* admired for its flaking grey and brown bark and pink-in-the-bud white blossom in April.

There is a young collection of Southern Beeches (*Nothofagus*), and a splendid Monkey Puzzle (*Araucaria araucana*), once common in Victorian and Edwardian suburban gardens, and the Strawberry Tree (*Arbutus menziesii*), rarely seen except in this part of Scotland, grown for its smooth red bark, bucket-shaped white flowers, and orange-red fruit.

The walls of Crarae Lodge, which is part mid-eighteenth century, part late-nineteenth century, are clothed with the evergreen Hydrangea, *H. integerrima,* brought from Co. Down in Ireland in 1933.

The Crarae Charitable Trust was an essential foundation for the continued existence of the garden. There is a regular staff of three employees — the head gardener, an under-gardener, and the gardener's wife — to look after 40 acres, with some assistance during the school holidays. With wages continuing to rise and skilled labour in short supply, the outlook for these magnificent gardens seems gloomy.

15 DUNVEGAN CASTLE
Isle of Skye
Situated in the north-west of the Island of Skye.
(JOHN MACLEOD OF MACLEOD)

Dunvegan Castle stands on a rocky headland, washed on three sides by the sea, and approached on the fourth by a bridge across a narrow ravine. It has been in the occupation of the same family for more than seven hundred years.

The 5 acres of water and woodland garden were landscaped in the early part of the nineteenth century by the then Chief of MacLeod. The gardens are situated on the shores of Loch Dunvegan, exposed to the sea winds, although there is an adequate canopy of trees and *Rhododendron ponticum*.

The gardens have been undergoing major reconstruction during the past three years. The main area is the Water Garden, with two waterfalls and a large burn running down to the sea. The natural character of the Woodland Garden has been preserved; flowering shrubs such as Rhododendrons and Hydrangeas prosper beneath the trees. Presiding over the rehabilitation is David MacLean.

As part of the renewal, several ornamental trees have recently been added — Flowering Crab-Apples (*Malus*), the Swamp Cypress (*Taxodium distichum*), Flowering Cherries (*Prunus* in variety), and, for autumn colour, Sweet Gums (*Liquidambar*) and *Parrotia persica*. In the Water Garden, *Agapanthus*, Hostas, Meconopses, Primulas, and *Gunnera manicata* all do well. There is also a formal garden, set out with Rose beds and grass lawns.

16 EILEAN DARACH
Dundonnell

This delightful garden was created from a field by the late Mrs Alexander Maitland. In 1930 she had the foresight to plant banks of *Rhododendron ponticum* — some of the bushes are now 20 feet high — for shelter. She then skilfully sited many interesting trees and shrubs among the old Oaks which give Eilean Darach its name — 'The Island of the Oaks'. On her death, the homely 19th-century house and garden passed to her niece, the late Mrs Peter Dunphie.

The garden is typical of this area, within the influence of the Gulf Stream, a mild damp climate and peaty soil. Lying at sea level, it is only 1 mile from the head of Little Loch Broom, where shelter is essential against the sea winds.

It is a flat, tree-clad garden, with lawns about the house. In May and June, the Azaleas and Rhododendrons are at their loveliest. Nor are these the only delights — there is an unusually tall *Stewartia pseudo-camellia*, two Eucalyptus trees over 60 feet in height, a small tree of *Eucryphia glutinosa*, and bushes of *Pieris formosa* var. *forrestii*, their young foliage glowing scarlet in spring.

17 GEANIES
✿ Fearn
*3 miles east of Hill of Fearn,
on the road to
Portmahomack.*
(MR C. K. MURRAY)

Geanies House is a listed building (category 'A'), surrounded by walled gardens built over a period of time from approximately 1750 to 1850. It commands glorious views of the Moray and Dornoch Firths.

The estate underwent great improvements in the mid-nineteenth century while in the care of Kenneth Murray (1826-76), an eminent agriculturist of his time. Soon after succeeding to the ownership, he extended the arable land from 2016 acres to 4000, mainly through reclamation from bog and moss, from the open moor and from lochs.

Remarkably, the 3¼-mile long coastline rises steeply near Geanies in precipitous cliffs to a height of 200 feet above the sea, and this is where the garden lies. Twelve-foot high walls are built out from the back of the house on each side, enclosing the cultivated areas. The soil consists of an excellent light loam, the rainfall is low and the climate above the average.

A shrub garden, created around 1900 and onwards, continues to thrive. At the end of July, many of its subjects are in full bloom — *Carpenteria californica*, *Hoheria sexstylosa*, and the spectacular *Abelia floribunda*, to name only three. This is also the season for the herbaceous borders.

In autumn, colour is provided by *Enkianthus*, *Parrotia persica*, and late flowering *Eucryphia*.

Rocky paths lead down the cliffs to the shore, and walks, emerging from woodland, provide wide prospects of land and sea.

18 INVEREWE
GARDENS
✿ Poolewe
*On the A832 just north of
Poolewe.*
(NATIONAL TRUST FOR
SCOTLAND)

Inverewe gardens, in the village of Poolewe, are more than 90 miles from Inverness, the largest town of any significance. More than anything else it is the long journey through a very romantic, but barren, countryside which promotes admiration for the achievement of Osgood Mackenzie, who acquired the estate in 1862 and made a garden from what was nothing more than heather-clad moorland. He began by planting trees on 60 acres or so of the Inverewe peninsula, *Am Ploc Ard,* to provide shelter for the garden he intended to make, and then showed remarkable patience by waiting for these to grow to a reasonable height before attempting any further development. In due course sections were cleared to accommodate more precious plants. In 'Bambooselum', one of the first to be planted, one can still see some of the original planting. A very large *Magnolia campbellii, Davidia involucrata* and a very fine *Eucalyptus cordifolia* are three such plants which have now reached outstanding proportions.

On Mackenzie's death in 1922, Mairi Sawyer, his daughter, continued the work for a further thirty years before handing over the garden to The National Trust for Scotland in 1952. It was her wish that the garden should always be available to whoever wished to see it, although it is doubtful whether she ever visualised the 100,000 visitors who come each year to see the garden which she and her father had made.

Like Brodick, Inverewe owes much to the passion for Rhododendrons which was so common at the turn of the century. They still provide the back-bone of the garden, and therefore May and early June are normally the best times to visit Inverewe. However, other collections are now well established so that Primulas, Olearias, Meconopses and Heaths are among the host of plants which add to the spring and summer display. Colour in summer is provided for by the existence of two herbaceous borders and a large selection of annuals and bulbous plants which in the main decorate the area between the entrance and the house. By contrast the woodland is relatively colourless during summer and autumn periods, although the vivid blue splash of Hydrangeas, and the magnificent views of the surrounding hills seen from the garden, should encourage one to explore.

The gardens are open all year, between 9.00 a.m. and 9.00 p.m. (or dusk if earlier), daily.

19 KILARDEN

Rosneath

On B833 south of Garelochhead. Access through the 'Clachan' and on up approach road.
(MR & MRS NEIL RUTHERFORD)

The original garden at Kilarden formed part of the Church of Scotland minister's glebe, 1½ acres, purchased from the Church in 1865 when the house was built by W. C. Maughan, W.S., author of *Rosneath Past and Present* and *Annals of Garelochside*.

The name suggests that this was the site of St Modan's *Cill* or Church, and tradition has it that the house well, now lost, also belonged to St Modan.

Maughan planted many of the fine old trees and laid out a small formal garden around the dwelling. Mr and Mrs Rutherford bought the house and garden in 1941, acquiring more ground over the years, and adding to the plantings.

The policies extend to 21 acres, including 11 acres of seventeenth-century Oak and Beech plantation, 5½ acres of recently-planted mixed hard and soft woods and ornamental trees, the 'Clachan Glen', and the original 1½ acres of formal garden, all situated on a north-facing slope.

The garden soil is basically glacial drift, poor clay with fragmented rock brought down by the ice. The old wood is deeply carpeted with leafmould and loam, but the sub-soil is shallow.

At 150 feet above sea level, the climate is typical of the west coast of Scotland, mild and damp, but sheltered, and the north slope is helpful in that it drains away the cold air, encouraging tender plants to become established. Also, the garden is secluded, down by the Garelochside, and screened by its many beautiful trees — a Cedar of Lebanon (*Cedrus libani*), a large Tulip Tree (*Liriodendron tulipifera*), a majestic 'Big Tree' (*Sequoiadendron giganteum*) and several Eucryphias (including *E. cordifolia* and *E.* × *nymansensis* 'Nymansay').

The old 'Broom' plantation, containing many species and hybrid Rhododendrons, is threaded by tortuous paths, with sunny clearings and long vistas towards the Gareloch and the hills around Loch Long and Ben Ime (3319 feet) away to the north, and the unmistakable profile of The Cobbler (2891 feet).

Here and there, ponds have been created by diverting the course of the Clachan Burn, and around these a new avenue sweeps, planted on either side with Daffodils and Narcissi and massed Rhododendrons.

20 KILCOY CASTLE
✤ Muir-of-Ord
3½ miles from Muir-of-Ord, between A832 and B9162.
(MR & MRS T. I. ROBINSON)

The lands of Kilcoy, lying along the Beauly Firth, were acquired in 1611 by Alexander Mackenzie, third son of the 11th Baron of Kintail. The Castle of Kilcoy was built around this time, and is notable as the birthplace of a distinguished soldier, Lieutenant General Alex Mackenzie Fraser of Inverallochy, who died in 1809. The castle fell into ruin after years of neglect, but was eventually restored in 1890, with further improvements to the fabric in 1969. Its dramatic façade is clearly visible from the main road.

There are policies of about 12 acres, on a south-facing slope, 200 feet above sea level. The new owners cleared away the shrub and wilderness, planting instead some two hundred different trees and shrubs, selected for colour and variety; at the same time they maintained the castle's fine outlook across the open farmland to the Beauly Firth and to the hills of Glen Affric and Strath Conon.

The soil is naturally fertile and neutral and most hardy trees and shrubs quickly take root; however, no attempt is made to persevere with delicate or unwilling plants. Wide areas of rough grass have been planted with Daffodils and Narcissi to naturalise, making spring memorable for their glorious carpeting and the tree blossom and tender green of the leaves. Beds and hedges of Shrub Roses bloom from late June until late July; and autumn is a good season for brilliant foliage and berries.

21 KILDONAN GARDENS
✤ Helmsdale
In the Strath of Kildonan, 10 miles from the village of Helmsdale.
(MRS A. CLAY)

The fertile fields alongside the River Helmsdale once supported a thriving agricultural community, but with the introduction of sheep farming between 1811 and 1831 the population removed to the coast and Kildonan became a lonely valley, surrounded by empty hills, remote and wild.

Kildonan Gardens were probably first made when Kildonan Lodge was built, about 1896. They are situated in the valley of the River Helmsdale, close to where it is joined by the Kildonan Burn, though the altitude is 225 feet. A previous owner had the foresight to plant a shelter belt of trees, to break the force of strong winds blowing in over the bare land from the sea.

Summer in these parts is often warm — for this far northern area — but winter is a severe season (24°F in February being not uncommon), and only plants which are adapted to these latitudes can be expected to survive the bitter cold and cruel winds. The land outside the garden is a sea of peat; inside, however, the soil, though very acid, is fertile and free of stones.

There are just over 2 acres of garden, a flat square, rather severely formal with four terraces, long straight gravel paths running between herbaceous borders, Rose beds, a large rock garden and plots occupied each summer by bedding plants, which involve much time and labour. These are in flower in August and September, the grouse shooting and stalking season, when the owners are in residence.

Kyle House is an early nineteenth-century building, possibly by Gillespie Graham, one of the Edinburgh New Town architects. It is listed as a Class B Historic House.

There are between 2 and 3 acres of garden, partly made with soil imported by the original Mackinnon owners in the nineteenth century. The work was continued by the Seton Watsons, between 1920 and 1950, but the area has been landscaped afresh by the present owners. It is for the most part rocky outcrops and bogland, sloping mainly to the south-south-east, and lies at sea level; in fact, very close to and partly bordering the sea. The climate is mild and damp, with prevailing westerly and south-westerly winds.

There are magnificent views of the surrounding mountains and moors, the many small islands and the sea lochs: to the east, of Loch Duich with Ben Attow and the Five Sisters of Kintail; to the north and north-west of the island of Raasay and the Cuillins of Skye, wraithed in blue mists.

The acid, peaty soil is a good medium for Rhododendrons and Azaleas and Hydrangeas thrive in the dampness. Meconopses, Mahonias, and Fuchsias all delight in the seaside climate. There are Roses, Eucalyptus trees, a fine Tasmanian Laurel (*Anopterus glandulosus*) with shining green leaves and white cup-shaped flowers, a large *Rhododendron macabeanum*, one of the finest yellow-flowered big-leaved Rhododendrons, and two specimens of *Eucryphia* × *nymansensis* 'Nymansay'.

Nead-an-Eoin (Nyett-an-Yonn) — 'Nest of the Bird' — is the old name for the land. Until about forty years ago, it was worked down to the seashore as a 5-acre croft.

When Lieutenant Commander and Mrs Dalzel-Job came, the land had been abandoned for over twenty years and was almost entirely overgrown with dense furze, briar and bracken; only a few trees showed their heads above the thicket of undergrowth, and it was impossible to walk down to the shore.

For nearly ten years, until the shelter belt of evergreens became effective, very little would grow in the garden. In severe winter storms, so strong were the winds one could hardly keep one's feet outside the house, and the salt spray killed all but the toughest plants.

Now that there is shelter things are growing fast, although many trees still need support in winter gales. Apart from planting up cleared ground, much has

22 KYLE HOUSE
Kyleakin, Isle of Skye
¼ *mile out of village of Kyleakin.*
(MR & MRS COLIN MACKENZIE)

23 NEAD-AN-EOIN
by Plockton
Seaward of Plockton airstrip.
(LIEUTENANT COMMANDER & MRS DALZEL-JOB)

been achieved by the removal of unwanted growth, by trimming and encouraging what is good, and by regular mowing of grass-sown areas.

Clearing each section takes about five years. It is still in progress, but some overgrown land has been purposely left untouched as a refuge for the roedeer, pine marten and even the wild cat. Birds flock and nest among the trees, and in the woodland clearances there is a carpeting of Ling and Blaeberry where once was all Whins and Bracken.

Six rough paths lead down to the rock and heather shore of Outer Loch Carron. One beach has been cleared of rocks, and there are seats positioned here and there.

Paths through the upper woodland are very steep in parts. All this used to be completely overgrown. Now one can look out across the loch, to the Cuillins of Skye away to the west, and to the north and north-east the hills of Applecross and Torridon.

24 ROSS PRIORY
🌺 by Gartocharn
The garden is located approximately one mile north-west of the village of Gartocharn on the A811 road between Balloch and Drymen.
(UNIVERSITY OF STRATHCLYDE)

The Priory is a substantial country house with five public rooms and fifteen bedrooms. It is a listed building of historical and architectural merit, modernised in 1812 by the famous Scottish architect James Gillespie Graham.

Whilst the garden was probably established around the early nineteenth century, from the records available it is evident that the majority of the plantings of Rhododendrons, specimen trees and so on, were carried out in the mid to late 1920s.

There are 15 acres of natural garden and approximately 2 acres of walled garden. It is pleasantly undulating terrain, situated at the south end of Loch Lomond, with a ½ mile of lochside frontage and views north up the loch and its scatter of small islands, including glimpses of Ben Lomond (3192 feet).

The soil is a heavy loam type and whilst rainfall is perhaps above average for the West of Scotland, trees and shrubs do particularly well in this area where good shelter is provided by an extensive belt of mature deciduous and coniferous trees.

Since the University purchased Ross Priory in 1971, extensive re-development of the gardens has been carried out and many additional trees and shrubs planted, of which the majority are Azaleas and Rhododendrons.

25 STRONE GARDEN
🌺 by Cairndow
At Cairndow village, at the north end of Loch Fyne, on the A83 Inveraray/Arrochar road.
(LORD GLENKINGLAS)

This is a woodland garden of about 15 acres, close to the banks of the river Kinglas. The sandy loam, Gulf Stream mildness, and high annual rainfall (80-100 inches) favour its many Rhododendrons, Azaleas, and other ericaceous plants. Magnolias, Embothriums, Camellias, *Eucalyptus*, Flowering Cherries and several other rare and beautiful shrubs and ornamental trees all prosper.

However, it is for its immense trees that the Strone garden is renowned, in particular an *Abies grandis*, Giant Fir, 188 by 17 feet (in 1975), claimed to be the tallest tree in Britain. In the same plantation are several fairly close rivals, including Sawara Cypresses (*Chamaecyparis pisifera* 'Squarrosa'). Most of these

Conifers were planted between a hundred and one hundred and twenty years ago by the Callander family, who took over the land from the Campbells of Ardkinglas. The estate later became the property of Sir Andrew Noble. His son, Sir John Noble, and the present laird, Lord Glenkinglas, very largely developed the woodland.

Mid April to mid June, when Daffodils and Wild Hyacinths are in flower and the hardwood trees are freshly leafed, is the best time to visit this garden.

Torosay Castle was designed by the well known Scottish architect, David Bryce, and completed in 1858.

For many generations Mull was the clan territory of the Macleans of Duart, whose principal stronghold was the massive ancient Duart Castle. It was the scene of endless feuding between the Macleans and their rivals the Macdonalds, and in the latter half of the seventeenth century the Duart estate passed to the Campbells of Argyll.

At the beginning of the nineteenth century, the Duke of Argyll sold the parish of Torosay to his kinsman, Colonel Campbell of Possil. An old map of 1829 shows a Queen Anne house occupying the site of Torosay Castle, as well as the eighteenth-century farm square and walled garden, both of which remain unaltered.

Within ten years of the building of the castle at Torosay, the estate was bought by Charles Arbuthnot Guthrie (1825-97), younger son of David Charles Guthrie of Craigie in Fife, co-founder of the Merchant Bank of Chalmers, Guthrie, of London, who renamed it Duart House.

When Walter Murray Guthrie (1870-1911) inherited the property from his uncle in 1897, he was so appalled by its size that he at first determined to sell it. On seeing the place, however, he reversed this decision; two years later he engaged Sir Robert Lorimer to design and lay out the three Italianate Terraces and the Statue Walk which connect the Castle with the eighteenth-century Walled Garden.

In 1911 Duart Point and the ancient ruined Duart Castle were sold back to Sir Fitzroy MacLean, 10th Baronet and 26th Clan Chief of the MacLeans. He restored and occupied the Castle, so to avoid a confusion of names Torosay resumed its original name (Torosay being Gaelic for 'a hill covered with shrubs').

The relatively modern Scottish Baronial building overlooks its 11-acre garden, made on a raised beach. The style is grandly formal, with balustraded and buttressed terraces, stone stairways, belvedere, statues (ancient and modern), marble lions, etc.

The climate in these parts is typically 'Gulf Stream', that is mild, wet, and occasionally windy. This, and the peaty soil, is favourable to the cultivation of Rhododendrons, Azaleas, *Pieris formosa* 'Forrestii', *Cornus capitata* — a very beautiful sub-evergreen from India and China with white bracts tinged with

26 TOROSAY CASTLE
Mull
Two-hourly trip by steamer from Oban, on the even hours, returning on the odd hours. Voyage takes 40 minutes.
(TRUSTEES OF TOROSAY ESTATE)

pink — and the various Eucryphias. Much space is devoted to Roses and summer-bedding Begonias, and there are many fine trees, mainly *Eucalyptus*, Maples, and conifers.

27 TOURNAIG
Poolewe, Achnasheen

1 ½ miles north of Inverewe Gardens.
(SIR JOHN HORLICK)

These 5 acres of woodland close to Loch Ewe were originally Mackenzie of Gairloch property. Osgood Mackenzie, creator of the famous Inverewe gardens, lived here for a time with his daughter. The present owners have recreated the garden from the wilderness which they inherited.

The house is late nineteenth-century and Edwardian in style. The situation is magnificent, with panoramic views of the mountains and Loch Namdailthean. The gardens lie a mere 50 feet above sea level, and the climate is typically West Coast, mild but with a heavy rainfall (50 inches) and westerly winds. They are varied in character — formal areas, natural woodland, some rock gardens and ponds.

Primulas, especially Inverewe, grow magnificently in this garden, as do other plants such as Hostas and Astilbes that prefer damp sites out of the full sun. These conditions are, of course, ideal for the cultivation of Azaleas and Rhododendrons in which the garden abounds.

28 YOUNGER BOTANIC GARDEN
Benmore

On A815, 7 miles north of Dunoon, Argyllshire.
(*Owned by* DEPARTMENT OF AGRICULTURE AND FISHERIES FOR SCOTLAND (*Annexe of Royal Botanic Garden, Edinburgh*), *administered in collaboration with the Benmore Trust*)

The garden was originally laid out about the year 1820, occupying the wooded slopes and flat river valley of Strath Eachaig. As part of the original Benmore Estate and within the huge Argyll forest park, it is situated in magnificent mountain and loch scenery, particularly around Loch Eck and Loch Long.

There is a formal garden with a comprehensive collection of garden conifers but the largest area is informal woodland with a multitude of flowering shrubs and Rhododendrons. These thrive in the mild, wet climate and tree-sheltered situations; the large leaved, large flowered species are grown to particular advantage.

Some of the more mature trees date from James Duncan's occupation of Benmore House (1870-83), while the main conifer and ornamental plantings were initiated by the Younger family (1884-1925). Since then planting, especially of exotic conifers and Rhododendrons, continues under the Royal Botanic Garden, Edinburgh, in collaboration with the Benmore Trust.

Benmore House, a late Victorian castellated mansion, is now run as an Outdoor Centre by the Lothian Regional Council.

Map of Locations:

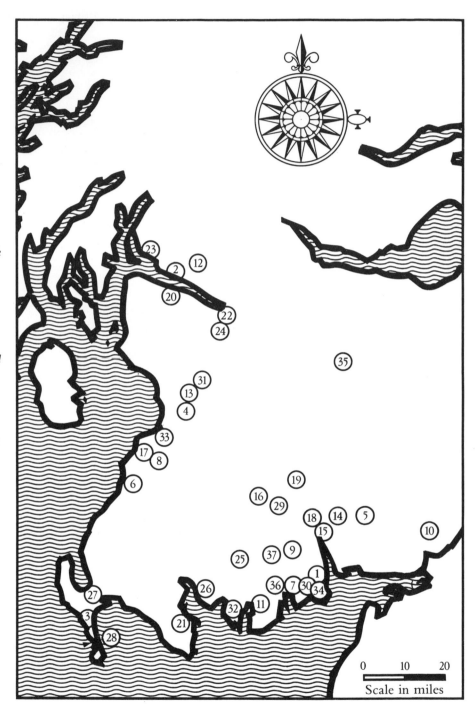

THE SOUTH WEST

John Paul Jones, the pirate, buccaneer, naval adventurer — call him what you will — was born plain John Paul on the estate of Arbigland in the year 1747. His father was the estate gardener and John Paul was brought up in a large family in the gardener's cottage. The estate owner at that time was William Craik, member of a wealthy family of Dumfries and Cumberland merchants who became highly successful agricultural improvers. They acquired Arbigland from the Earl of Southesk in 1722 for £22,000 (Scots).

When John Paul was eight years old, William Craik moved into his new mansion, an Adam style central three-storey 'Georgian Block' supported by octagonal wings, costing £4000. John Paul's father had been trained in gardening on an estate outside Edinburgh, and Craik made him responsible for landscaping his 10 acres of garden. This layout remains today without great alteration.

The 1400-acre estate is situated on a highly productive peninsula, close to the Solway Firth. The soil is neutral boulder clay over limestone, while the garden has received liberal dumpings over the centuries of leafmould and peat. The façade of the house is open to fierce winds, but 20 acres of woodland shelter the garden. The climate is typical of Kirkcudbrightshire — mild and wet with little frost, comparable, it is claimed, to that of Torquay, over 400 miles to the south.

A broad walk leads down from the mansion to the shore between dense woods of conifers and deciduous trees, underplanted with ornamental shrubs. This passes a walled kitchen garden, and, on the other side, the sunken garden, made over the foundations of the demolished old Arbigland Hall. This garden was planned and planted by the present owner's grandmother who settled at Arbigland in 1919, after the death of her husband in the 1914-18 war. Entirely self-taught in gardening, she had an instinctive judgement as to the most effective choice of plants and where to site them. Her selection included Rhododendrons, Azaleas, Camellias, *Eucryphia, Pieris, Ribes,* and *Cercis*, as well as autumn colour shrubs such as *Parrotia persica*, various Acers, *Cercidiphyllum japonicum* and *Hydrangea villosa*. Part of the sunken garden is planted with Roses, and there is also a water garden with many Primulas, Hostas, and Rodgersias.

Far removed from human habitation, this is a garden of great peace, the only sounds being the tide breaking on the shore and the cries of seabirds.

Ardoch House was built in 1780 in the Colonial Georgian style, and the garden was planned and laid out about the same time by Robert Graham of Gartmore. Close to the Clyde estuary, it lies at sea level, warmed by the Gulf stream and looking towards the hills of Argyll.

1 ARBIGLAND
Kirkbean
Signposted from Kirkbean, on A710, 14 miles south of Dumfries.
(CAPTAIN J. B. BLACKETT)

2 ARDOCH
Cardross

ARDOCH (contd.)
*On main route between
Dumbarton and Cardross.*
(ADMIRAL SIR ANGUS
CUNNINGHAME GRAHAM)

A burn flows through the garden, between areas of lawn and shrubs. Many of the *Rhododendron* species were imported from Inverewe Gardens; there are several shrubs which are native to Chile, yet they thrive in the mild, wet climate.

The garden casts aside its winter drabness in March when hundreds of Crocuses — saffron yellow, deep purple, mauve, and white — come into flower. Their only fault is that their beauty passes so quickly.

3 ARDWELL HOUSE
🐾 *Ardwell*
*10 miles south of Stranraer,
on the A716 to Drummore.*
(MR & MRS JOHN BREWIS)

The present house of Ardwell was built some time between 1720 and 1740, and remodelled in 1956 to its original Georgian proportions. The moat of a much older mansion lies to the east of it.

The 5-acre garden, lying between Luce Bay and the Irish Sea, is mostly natural in character. Many of the Tree Rhododendrons (*R. arboreum*) and some of the shrubs were planted before the 1914-18 war, but the present owners took occupation in 1949, following a neglectful period, and embarked on a necessary scheme of renewal involving clearing away areas of rank weeds and scrub and planting sapling trees.

They planned the garden so that it would regale them with a continuity of colour throughout the year, starting with Snowdrops, Winter Aconites, and the winter-flowering *Erica carnea*, followed by the main show of Daffodils, Narcissi, Azaleas, Flowering Cherries and Rhododendrons in early May.

Much of the garden is laid out with paths and courtyards of 'crazy paving', and in June these are colourful with rock plants and alpines in full flower — tiny blue Campanulas, crimson, white and pink *Dianthus,* cushion Saxifrages, Stonecrops, *Helianthemum,* the various Thymes, Aubretias in different shades of pink and purple, golden *Alyssum saxatile,* pink Thrift and so on.

These are succeeded by June's many Roses, the herbaceous borders in their summer glory, and striking plants like the Giant Hemlock (*Conium maculatum*), making way in August for Hydrangeas, many different Dahlias, the later flowering Heathers, including the true Ling, which succeed in the garden's acid soil and the mild, rather wet, climate.

Later, just as the trees are starting to assume their brilliant autumn foliage, the first Colchicums and Autumn Crocuses begin to appear, their goblet-shaped, delicate flowers all shades of mauve, deep purple, and pure white.

FIGURE 84
Ardwell

Situated as it is on The Rhinns, the garden commands expansive seascapes eastwards across Luce Bay to Port William and Whithorn, and westwards to the Irish Sea.

4 AUCHINCRUIVE
🐾 *Ayr*

Auchincruive estates originally belonged to the kinsmen of the Scottish patriot, Sir William Wallace. The present mansion, however, was built in 1764-67 for the Oswald family, with interior work by William Adam. In 1925 the estate was bought by John M. Hannah of Girvan Mains, a highly successful potato farmer. Later, he presented the land of Auchincruive to the West of Scotland College of Agriculture.

AUCHINCRUIVE
(contd.)
*3 miles from Ayr on A758.
Bus from Ayr to Arnbank
and Tarbolton stops at
College gate.*
(The Governors of the WEST OF
SCOTLAND AGRICULTURAL
COLLEGE)

There are pleasant walks by the River Ayr, and in the riverside gardens are display glasshouses, herbaceous and shrub borders; a border of Rhododendrons and other ericaceous plants, including many of Himalayan origin; and an ornamental garden containing Hybrid Tea, Floribunda, and Climbing and Rambler Roses, together with a fine collection of decorative trees. The glasshouses contain a very wide range of temperate and tropical plants. Modern glasshouses, with temperature-control apparatus, are used for producing Cucumbers, Tomatoes, Peppers and similar produce in an associated unit.

Students are trained in the amenity and commercial aspects of horticulture to Diploma and Degree level. There is also a beekeeping department owning some one hundred colonies of bees, mainly kept in outside apiaries situated between Auchincruive and Stranraer. In mid-July, these are all taken to the Heather moors at Newton Stewart and other sites in Galloway and on Arran.

5 BALGRAY
& *Lockerbie*
*3 miles north of Lockerbie
on the Boreland road
(B723) and only 1 mile off
A74.*
(M. JARDINE-PATERSON)

Balgray is a seventy-room Victorian mansion, built 1883-5 of local red sandstone. It replaced a previous dwelling.

The garden comprises 30 acres, including the walled garden and house policies. It was made over a long period, starting in the 1840s when it was owned by Robert Jardine. The walled garden was added in the late 1800s, and the pond in 1910 and the 1920s, during the time of the present owner's grandfather, Robert Jardine-Paterson.

The setting is gently undulating farming country and the gardens are contoured to the natural slopes, dipping to the river and the water garden and an island inhabited by black swans. The walled garden with its greenhouses and the many specimen trees, notably Redwoods and Limes, of mature years signify good stewardship over a long period. The garden reaches a climax of beauty in the late spring and early summer, with Daffodils and Cherry trees, Rhododendrons and Azaleas blooming by the river walks.

6 BARGANY GARDENS
& *Girvan*
*About 3 miles east of
Girvan on the B734, off the
A77 Girvan-Ayr road.*
(CAPTAIN NORTH DALRYMPLE
HAMILTON)

The Bargany estate has been in the hands of the Hamilton family since 1630. Before that it was a Kennedy property. The Kennedys lived in a fine great castle, on the banks of the river Girvan, of which unfortunately no trace now remains.

The present mansion house was built in about 1681. This date and the initials H.B., for Hamilton of Bargany, are carved above the original front door. The owner and his family welcome visitors to the gardens, which are open daily from 10 a.m. to 7 p.m. from 1 March to 31 October.

Early landscape planning, in the 18th and 19th centuries, of the park and gardens involved a series of landscape gardeners. They were William Adam, William Boutcher, Thomas White junior, George Robertson, and George Hay.

The loveliest feature of the woodland garden is the Lily pond, surrounded by 'Ponticum' Azaleas (*Rhododendron Luteum*), with splashes of other colours given by *Azalea mollis* 'Ghent', Maple, and great banks of both species and hybrid Rhododendrons.

This garden and the rock garden were laid out in about 1910 by Colonel Sir North Dalrymple-Hamilton. There is an old walled garden designed by George Hay, the centre of which is now laid down to grass. There are, however, two small gardens at either end, which in Spring are lovely with flowering cherries and Daffodils, and in summer with Kurume Azaleas and the Chilean Fire Trees (*Embothrium coccineum*) and other shrubs. Interesting trees also include the Handkerchief Tree (*Davidia involucrata*), the Maidenhair Tree (*Ginkgo biloba*) and the Fossil Tree (*Metasequoia glyptostroboides*).

The woodlands are beautiful in March with a carpet of Snowdrops, then the Daffodils in a golden mass below the house, then the summer display, and ending in the autumn with a riot of colour, Azaleas, Maples and other trees.

Miss King and Dr Paton gardened at Barnbarroch, Colvend, until seventeen years ago when they purchased Barnhourie Mill and the Miller's House, with 7 acres of land attached.

7 BARNHOURIE MILL
Colvend, by Dalbeattie
On Sandyhills Bay, on the A710 Solway coast road.
(Miss E. M. H. King & Dr M. R. Paton)

They have modernised the Miller's House, built around 1700, for their own habitation, and the property includes the seventeenth-century Mill, the machinery of which is still intact. The old mill pond, on the north-west side, has been filled in with earth and planted with rapidly growing Sitka Spruce, adding to the shelter from the prevailing west winds provided by rising hills on the south-west and north-east and thickets of old Oak trees.

The garden, on the north side of the mill, rises from that level to a mound near the centre, with the old mill lade burn tumbling in pools and falls down the east side. The soil is acid and light, with many outcrops of granite, dull-toned and lichen-covered, which embellish the garden's character.

The tides of the Solway Firth come racing in across the Merse Sands only a few hundred yards away, yet the salt winds off the sea appear not to affect the plants in the Barnhourie Mill garden, and the climate is generally very mild.

Miss King and Dr Paton are professional plant growers. They specialise in species (not hybrid) Rhododendrons, and their collection includes between two and three hundred dwarf and medium growing species — probably the largest in all Britain — besides other flowering trees and shrubs propagated by them, many of which are represented in this little jewel of a garden.

Although they are plant growers to trade, commercial aspects are entirely absent from the garden itself. Miss King designed it from the wild state in 1962, since when a place has been found for hundreds upon hundreds of plants; yet as one walks round there is no sign of crowding, but each one has been allocated a site, taking into account its flower and foliage, its texture and habit and eventual size.

Two conifers merit special mention on account of their rarity: the Korean Fir (*Abies koreana*), and the Drooping Juniper (*Juniperus recurva*) (Hu's introduction). Shrubs and trees, distinguished for their autumn colour in leaf or fruit are planted to good advantage throughout the garden — *Disanthus cercidifolius*,

FIGURE 85
*Herbaceous borders,
Broughton House*

Stewartia, Cornus in variety, *Euonymus, Photinia,* the *Sorbus* species, and *Cercidiphyllum japonicum.*

The garden is usually open to the public for one day in May, the flowering time for the Rhododendrons, Azaleas, Flowering Cherries, *Viburnum* and *Malus.*

8 BLAIRQUHAN
🐾 *Straiton, Maybole*
(MR JAMES HUNTER BLAIR)

The Blairquhan estate combines farming and forestry, and the house is in the classical style with Tudor-Gothic decorations. It was built in 1824 to plans drawn by William Burn, and still contains the original furniture. The central saloon is 60 feet in height.

The garden was entirely created between 1800 and 1820 by Sir David Hunter Blair, 3rd Baronet. He had purchased the estate in 1798 and on an old map of 1787 there is no garden shown on the present site. He was a competent landscape architect himself, and set aside plans submitted by Thomas White in 1803 in favour of his own. These involved diverting the Girvan Water in a sweeping bend round the front of the mansion, and landscaping the park and woodland.

The main approach is along a 3-mile carriageway through the park and woods, containing many of the original trees, mostly Oak, finally reaching the mansion by an avenue of stately Limes, planted about 1700.

The enclosed garden has walls on three sides only, and the bricks were made on the estate. It contains a tree nursery. The glasshouse, though new astragals have been fitted, is the original one, which was erected in 1820. A small formal garden, made at the same time, contains a sundial, while the lintels and sculptured stones from the original fortified house are incorporated in the kitchen courtyard.

The estate's arboretum contains some magnificent trees introduced about a hundred and twenty years ago; also others planted more recently, including a remarkable Southern Beech (*Nothofagus procera*).

9 BROOKLANDS
🐾 *Crocketford, by
   Dumfries*

*1½ miles from Crocketford
(A75), on New Galloway
road (A712).*
(MR & MRS N. P. MACLAREN)

Brooklands stands 560 feet above sea level, facing south, with a fine view of the gentle countryside that reaches to Screel and the hills behind Gatehouse of Fleet.

The house was built in 1830 and the garden had been long neglected when Mrs Jebb took over in 1946. She embarked on a thorough scheme of renewal which was continued by Mr and Mrs Maclaren, when they acquired the property in 1968. They retained Mrs Jebb's gardener, as much for his valuable advice as for his practical assistance in the manifold task.

Brooklands garden today contains one of the richest and most representative collections of plants, shrubs and ornamental trees in the south-west of Scotland. It is a nicely balanced collection, and the overall effect is most pleasing and harmonious.

10 BROOMHOLM
🐾 *Langholm*

Broomholm is believed to have been built about 1745, on the site of a previous property. It is, in fact, a Georgian 'C' listed house, and was once the home of the

BROOMHOLM (contd.)
*1 mile south of Langholm.
Take B6318 for Penton.
House is first property on
right-hand side.*
(CAPTAIN & MRS GERARD
HENRY)

Maxwell family, controlling appreciable estates.

There are 66 acres of land attached. The garden, unfortunately, has been somewhat neglected, probably since the turn of the century; but the setting is attractive, in typical lowland country with some fine specimen trees, including Douglas Fir. An unusual sundial, inscribed 1756, recalls the garden's old formality, and there is an island of 1 acre in extent, reached by a graceful iron bridge.

The intention of the new owners is to remake the gardens, while retaining the woodland and the riverside walks, both areas being well established with Rhododendrons, Azaleas and spring bulbs.

11 BROUGHTON
HOUSE
Kirkcudbright
*High Street,
Kirkcudbright.*
(*Trustees of the late* MR E. A.
HORNEL)

The western side of the L-shaped Kirkcudbright High Street occupies a gravelly ridge running parallel to the river Dee, and one of the 'lang rigs' belongs to Broughton House, erected in the early eighteenth century by the Murrays of Broughton (Wigtownshire) and Cally. The Murrays used it as a town house, or as a dower-house for the laird's widow following his demise, and the proportions are quite grand, with fine fenestrations, a fanlight above the main doorway, a flagged courtyard with railings around it, and broad stone steps down to the street.

Because it stands thus high above the common street level, the house is unusually private; and it was no doubt this, besides its impressive size and dignity, which commended it to E. A. Hornel (1864-1933), a highly successful artist, both professionally and in the worldly sense. A confirmed bachelor, waited on by two watch-dog maiden sisters, he did most of his work in a studio designed for him by the architect John Keppie, opening on to the seclusion of the 'lang rig' with its high walls and its flowers, and its views of the swans on the Dee and the green hills above Kirkchrist.

Hornel's pictures, still fetching high prices, are witness to his genuine love of flowers; and after his visits to Ceylon, Burma and Japan, he landscaped Broughton House garden so that it resembled a Japanese sanctuary. Although he planted it with beautiful things, none of the plants that remain there today is in fact exclusively Japanese, except the Camellias. There are Chinese Magnolias, Himalayan Honeysuckle (*Leycesteria formosa*), Chilean *Eucryphia glutinosa*, Moutans (*Paeonia suffruticosa*) — Tree Peonies — from China, and the Bush Anemone (*Carpentaria californica*) from the U.S.A. There are dwarf Japanese Stone Pines (*Pinus pinea*) planted in stone troughs, a collection of curling stones and staddles, a curious sundial, and the leaden figure of a crane, poised on one leg among the Flags and Water-Lilies of a pool.

The Japanese Garden occupies only a third of the space; the remainder is an informal Scots garden, containing beautiful but quite usual flowers, a varied collection of bulbs, early Hellebores, Primulas, *Daphne mezereum*, Winter Jasmine, and an interesting collection of ferns. There is an old *Wisteria*, covered in late May with long pendant racemes of a pale blue and silver, several Lilacs and groups of Spiraeas, including the large *Aruncus sylvester* or Goat's Beard, *Digitalis* (Foxglove), *Anemone elegans* (Japanese *hupehensis*), and collections of Floribunda and Hybrid Tea Roses.

Against the wall the gardener has trained the climbing Rose 'Albertine'; a luxuriant *Clematis* 'Jackmanii', reaching over the wall and hanging in great festoons of purple in August; and also the Chinese *Buddleia alternifolia* with its strongly scented mauve summer flowers on pendulous branches.

12 CAMERON
Loch Lomond
20 miles north of Glasgow, at Balloch on the A82.
(MR P. T. TELFER SMOLLETT)

Tobias Smollett, the Scottish novelist, expressed himself through Mr Mathew Bramble in *Humphry Clinker* when he said: 'I have seen the Lago di Gardi, Albano, De Vico, Bolsena, and Geneva, and on my honour I prefer Loch Lomond to them all.' Smollett, however, had a local interest for the Smolletts of Bonhill, who lived at Cameron House, were his kinsmen. The mansion began as a stone keep in the fourteenth century; by the eighteenth century it had been transformed into a fine Georgian house, home of Smollett's uncle, Sir James Smollett. He was host one rainy October day in 1773 to Dr Samuel Johnson and James Boswell, who stepped ashore here after sailing from Rossdhu.

Apart from the universally acknowledged beauty of Loch Lomond, Cameron is well worth visiting for its long-established gardens and woodland walks, which together cover an area of 25 acres. They were designed by the landscape gardener Lanning Roper, and also by Georgina Telfer Smollett, and cover a whole series of different gardens, including the Rhododendron and Azalea Garden, the Flower Garden, the Water Garden, the Primula Garden, the Hydrangea Walk, the Shrub Lawn, and the Pinetum.

There are many other popular attractions, such as the Wild Life Park, the Zoo Garden and the Tobias Smollett Museum, drawing thousands of visitors each year; but the botanist should discover much of interest in the gardens' extensive collections of rare and beautiful plants.

13 CARNELL
Hurlford
Kilmarnock 6 miles, Mauchline 4 miles, on A719. 1½ miles on Ayr side of A76.
(MR & MRS J. R. FINDLAY)

The mansion of Carnell, standing above the banks of the river Cessnock, was erected in 1843 to designs by the Scottish architect, William Burn. It replaced a sixteenth-century peel-tower; the tower remains part of the present building. Carnell's original masters were the Wallaces of Cairn Hill, the most famous being Sir William Wallace, gallant defender of Scotland's independence.

In 1556 John Knox preached in the old house, and received bed and board. The family's piety is expressed in lines on a marriage lintel built into the tower wall: 'Without the Lord as Maister, he bigges in vain, be he ever so strong.'

The last of the Wallaces of Cairn Hill (old name for Carnell) was Miss Lillias Wallace. From her portrait, she must have been a great beauty, and she married into the family of Hamilton of Linlithgow. Sir Walter Sandilands Hamilton of Westport, her kinsman, became aide-de-camp to John Churchill, Duke of Marlborough, victor of the battle of Blenheim in 1704, and other campaigns in the War of the Spanish Succession.

The continuing involvement of the heritors of Cairn Hill in martial affairs is evidenced by the positioning of the Lime trees in the park, planted to commemorate the squares of Scottish infantry and their officers beside them at the commencement of the battle of Dettingen (1743). This was the last occasion at which a British king (George II) was permitted to appear on the battlefield, and it brought victory over the French.

The silvan phalanxes remain unbroken, Lime trees resisting high winds. Yet spring transforms the meadow land around them into a golden carpet of Daffodils, called 'Glens' by adherents of the Scots tongue, and soon the air is sweet with Lime-flower fragrance, quickening the honey bees in their flight.

The 'Glens' and the Snowdrops that bloom in abundance in February by the banks of the Cessnock below Carnell are all picked and sold in Kilmarnock to aid local charities. The lady who organises these worthy activities now lives, with her husband Commander James B. Findlay, in the Garden House of Carnell, a short walk from the big house. Their domain forms one side of the walled garden, built in 1843. The walls of this garden have two thicknesses — stone on the outside, brick inside, the first for solidity, the second for warmth. Some excellent fruit trees ripen within this shelter, the supreme favourite being a 'Lord Lambourne' Apple, slow to ripen but of a good flavour.

The wall opposite the Garden House is lower than the other three and surmounted by railings. These are smothered in summer time with *Clematis* 'Ville de Lyon', a bright carmine red, and *C.* 'Perle d'Azur', a light blue belonging to the *C. Jackmanii* group of hybrids. They overhang the herbaceous border on the far side, measuring 100 yards by 4 yards. It was made in 1910 by Mrs Findlay's mother, and never fails. Neither has it ever been replanted in all these years. The secret, according to Commander Findlay, lies in generous applications of an organic garden compost, made to his specification.

The component plants of this border are: Delphiniums in various shades, *Galega* (Goat's Rue), *Artemisia lactiflora* (White Mugwort), Scabious, *Dictamnus fraxinella* and *D. fraxinella* 'Purpureus' (the white and the pink varieties of Burning Bush), *Gillenia trifoliata* (a neglected but valuable perennial from North America), various Potentillas, *Astrantia maxima* (Masterwort), and *Salvia pratensis*. (The last named, with its whorled blue flowers on 2-foot spikes, is sufficiently rare to prompt enquiries from nearly all visitors to the garden.)

As limestone quarries are common in this district, one does not expect to find calcifuges such as Camellias and Rhododendrons here. The exception is the ubiquitous *R. ponticum*, flourishing on a bank, giving shelter to the rock garden beneath it, and to a profusion of shade-preferring Primulas, various Meconopses, *Anemone hepatica*, and numerous Lilies, of which the gem is *Lilium szovitsianum*, raised by Mrs Findlay from seed.

FIGURE 86
Carnell – the sunken garden showing herbaceous border, water garden and part of the rockery

The greenhouse, heated by a two-circuit electric system in case of failure, produces Camellias, Cyclamen, and other 'stove plants' which are always useful for festivities in the big house.

Visits to Carnell frequently end with a glance inside the gardener's tool shed — a model of method and tidiness, each tool hanging clean and oiled and free of rust on its own hook, and the air redolent with the homely smell of onions suspended in bunches from the rafters, and rich, crumbly compost.

14 CASTLEHILL
🐝 *Kirkmahoe*
Off Duncow-Amisfield road, by windmill stump.
(SIR ARTHUR & LADY DUNCAN)

Castlehill House and its policies form part of the old barony of Duncow, and occupy a slight elevation looking out across Nithsdale and the Solway plain to the Lakeland hills. There is an earthwork behind and the area contains a wealth of tumuli, circular moats and vestiges of hill forts; there is also the stump of a windmill (1790) suggesting an old Dutch stake in the surrounding land.

The grounds and garden run to some 10 acres; the garden plan was drawn by the late Mrs Duncan and implemented by the present owners. The front is terraced with rock plants growing in the retaining walls. Much of the remainder is mature woodland, containing specimen trees, some of which overhang the pond, and waterside plantings of Maples, Primulas, Ligularias, and Rodgersias, etc.

The Cherry orchard is a delight, and the garden continues to spread outwards and develop, having new plantings of Shrub Roses, *Sorbus*, and Rhododendrons, and all despite the fact that the soil is poor and gravelly.

15 COWHILL TOWER
🐝 *Holywood*
Off A76, 1½ miles from Holywood.
(CAPTAIN & MRS A. E. WEATHERALL)

Despite the fact that Cowhill Tower was erected in 1785, it has been added to or altered by almost every generation since. The tall, beautiful red stone building stands in the solitude of its own Beech woods.

It has a spacious formal garden in front, with closely-mown lawns, and a cannon guarding ruins. Steps lead down to an intimate little garden, arranged in a delightful, stiffly formal style, containing Camellias growing against the sombre Yew hedge, a Weeping Elm, and Roses trained up pergolas. There is also a herb garden, a walled garden, greenhouses, and a Rose garden.

The trees surrounding the tower are over two hundred years old, but the main garden was reorganised by David Keswick during his retirement years, 1956-76. Woodland walks circumvent a small loch, with Azaleas about the margin, and Rhododendrons flourishing beneath the canopy of trees. Among the other ornamental shrubs are *Pieris formosa*, with its flowers like Lily-of-the-Valley and scarlet young foliage in spring, Eucryphias, Embothriums and the tall deciduous shrub from New Zealand, *Hoheria lyallii,* producing clusters of creamy-white flowers in summer. The topiary work on view is remarkable — animals, birds, and human shapes all skilfully detailed in hawthorn.

There are splendid views from the terrace of the river Nith, the Cumberland Hills, and the ruins of the original tower, with the date 1579 on the archway. Paths by the river pass an interesting collection of different varieties of *Sorbus*.

16 CRAIGDARROCH
🐝 *Moniaive*

Craigdarroch House was the marriage home of Annie Laurie, heroine of what has been called 'the world's greatest love song', composed and addressed to her by William Douglas of Fingland, her girlhood sweetheart. The romance, alas, never ripened into marriage, and Anna (*sic*), who was the daughter of Sir Robert Laurie of Maxwelton, later married Alexander Fergusson, laird of Craigdarroch. She died in 1763, having lived at Craigdarroch for over 50 years.

Fergusson actively opposed the Jacobites, and in 1726, in pursuance of a quiet countrified existence, he and his lady commissioned William Adam to build them a new house over the site of the old one, which had records going back to the fourteenth century. The new house is listed as a building of special architectural interest.

Its situation in Craigdarroch Glen is quite beautiful, amid a gentle wooded parkland of 27 acres and overlooking a 2-acre pond with wooded islands; it is at an elevation, nevertheless, of 450 feet, rising on either side to 1,000 feet, so that winds are channelled east and west. That apart, the climate is mild and damp, and the soil is a mixture of Silurian clay and loam.

The gardens were probably at their best in the 1930s. They are now being gradually re-developed, but without any intention of returning to the old formality. Instead, Nature is being assisted with plantings of ornamental trees and shrubs; thousands of Daffodils form gold carpets throughout the parks and woods in spring, and there are many fine Rhododendrons and Azaleas.

Although the title 'Country Park' may be confusing, in effect the Park embraces what were Culzean Castle gardens and policies, and they are still maintained by the National Trust for Scotland for the Country Park Joint Committee. The castle itself is not included. It was the first Country Park to be established in Scotland and was atypical of the many which have come into being since, in that it sought as far as possible to conserve as many features and aspects of a Scottish estate, including gardens and policies.

The history of Culzean gardens is a particularly rich and colourful one, as we know from an account written by Sir Herbert Maxwell in 1909 in his book *Scottish Gardens*, as well as the many follies and other garden features which one may still see at Culzean today. It is typical of what one might imagine most prosperous Scottish estates looked like at the turn of the century. The walled garden with fruit and vegetables on either side of a centrally positioned herbaceous border, the formally designed garden near the house, with an orangery on the south side, and the many 'curious' trees scattered throughout the spacious parkland. Over the years much of the 530 acres of policy lands have been devoted to commercial forestry, due to the pressure of economic circumstances, but the outstanding trees, with which Culzean is well endowed, have been carefully preserved as a reminder of the great age of tree planting, largely inspired by such men as David Douglas.

In the existing pattern of the estate the new developments required for the Country Park were carefully incorporated, as far as possible, in existing buildings. The former home farm, like the castle itself, was designed by Robert

CRAIGDARROCH (contd.)
2 miles north-west of Moniaive, off B729 Moniaive-Carsphairn road.
(Major H. H. Sykes)

17 CULZEAN COUNTRY PARK
Maybole
11 miles south of Ayr, on the A719.
(National Trust for Scotland)

FIGURE 87
The woodland garden, Culzean Castle

Adam, and was adapted to form a Reception Centre, with restaurant, shop and other facilities. A Ranger Service was established to allow the considerable educational potential of the property to be realised and made available to visitors. This proved successful enough to be included as an activity in the outdoor curriculum of several local schools.

The policy at Culzean has been to develop a number of areas throughout the estate so that interest could be spread over a larger area. The terraces and fountain garden on the south side of the castle are, of course, particularly important, but no less so than the large walled garden divided centrally into glasshouses, fruit and herbaceous borders in one half and a Rose garden in the other; or the swan pond area with attractive aviaries and cottage, now converted into a most inviting tea room. It is possible to drive around the estate, or a great part of it, but it is inevitable that one will miss much of interest as well as the pleasure of hearing so much of what Culzean can offer. The Park offers many great opportunities: gardening, sea-shore studies, nature walks, and the castle itself, present a fascinating range of activities rarely found at other garden properties.

Except in the dead of winter, Culzean is good to see at any time. Spring is heralded by a carpet of Daffodils, preceded by an equally splendid display of Snowdrops and followed by a generous scattering of Wild Hyacinths. Summer has herbaceous borders, and Roses to offer, while autumn colours, although never showy or dramatic, have an attractive quality in their rusty reds and browns.

The gardens and park are open all year; the castle and other services daily from April to October.

18 DALSWINTON HOUSE
🎴 *Dalswinton*
7½ miles north-north-west of Dumfries in the Nith valley.
(THE DALSWINTON TRUST)

Dalswinton House is a large red-freestone building situated on a commanding mound about a ½ mile from the right bank of the Nith. It was erected on the site of an ancient fortress of the Comyns by Patrick Millar (1731–1815), at one time landlord of the poet Robert Burns.

The estate comprises 30 acres of woodland and lochside garden alone, including a walled garden, laid out by Patrick Millar 1780–1820. The landscaping has been tastefully accomplished and well maintained, with many fine specimen trees and much space devoted to Rhododendrons, Azaleas and other beautiful shrubs, and a bountiful crop of Daffodils in springtime.

It is claimed that the first steamboat was sailed on Dalswinton Loch in 1788 by Millar Symington Taylor. It was named *The Comet.*

19 DRUMLANRIG CASTLE
🎴 *by Thornhill*

Drumlanrig Castle is generally esteemed as one of the first and most important Renaissance buildings in the grand manner in Scottish domestic architecture. Of the local pink sandstone, it occupies the last spur of a *drum* or *lang rig* of hill on the right bank of the river Nith, commanding magnificent views of the river valley, away to the heights of Criffel.

It was build for William Douglas, 1st Duke of Queensberry, using the foundations of the ancient stronghold of his 'Black' Douglas ancestors, and was completed, at enormous expense, after twelve years' labour, in 1691.

The gardens were probably begun by James, 2nd Duke of Queensberry, after his succession in 1695. The castle archives contain engraved plans of the gardens as they then appeared, as well as garden accounts up to the year 1723. The delights of the garden are described in the writings of Rev. Peter Rae (1700-40).

The layout was altered from time to time, mainly in 1738 and again 1815-40, to include the Barbados Garden and the American Garden; both have now disappeared.

Today there are 40 acres of garden, under cultivation or in the course of being restored. The style is elegantly formal — one early seventeenth-century parterre, and another being reintegrated; a large rock garden almost entirely replanted, a new shrub border, wide lawns and terraces and woodland glades.

There are boundaries of tree plantations all around. They include the early David Douglas introductions and the first Douglas Fir (*Pseudotsuga menziesii*), the tallest Weeping Beech (*Fagus sylvatica* 'Pendula'), the largest Sycamore (*Acer pseudoplatanus*) in Britain, and an early fan-trained *Ginkgo biloba* or Maidenhair Tree.

DRUMLANRIG CASTLE (contd.)
4 miles north of Thornhill; 18 miles north of Dumfries on A76.
(THE DUKE OF BUCCLEUCH AND QUEENSBERRY, KT)

Finlaystone House stands on a gentle north-facing slope, 50-100 feet above sea level, and surrounded by woodland. There is an excellent view of the Clyde. Parts of the building date back to the fifteenth century, and it was the residence of the fifteen Earls of Glencairn throughout their generations.

In 1556, during the time of the 'good' 5th Earl, John Knox held the first Communion of the Reformed Church in the West of Scotland in the grounds of Finlaystone, and the tree under which he stood survived removal to another site, 40 yards away, in 1900.

The gardens reached their present extent of 7½ acres around 1900, when additional ground was taken in for formal Rose gardens and shrubberies. Seventy years before, vegetables that had previously been grown on the Clyde's rich alluvial plain were transplanted into the present Walled Garden.

The soil throughout is acid, varying between heavy clay and light loam, and the climate mild and wet and sheltered, favouring tall tree growth.

A burn flows through the woodland where Snowdrops, Daffodils and Wild Hyacinths sustain the long flowering period from late winter to early summer. Then, in May, there follow the Rhododendrons and Azaleas, blooming in the trees' shade and across the lawns.

After the June Roses, the brilliance of summer moves to the herbaceous borders, lingering into the autumn months and switching finally to the woodland garden and the last glorious splendour.

20 FINLAYSTONE
Langbank
Off A8, west of Langbank.
(MR GEORGE MACMILLAN)

21 GALLOWAY HOUSE
🦌 *Garlieston*
1 *mile from Garlieston*
village.
(MR & MRS E. A. STRUTT)

The large classical house was built in 1740 for the Earls of Galloway, to designs drawn by John Douglas and Lord Garlies. Additions were made by William Burn (1842) and Sir Robert Lorimer (1909-10). Among the other owners were Nial McEacharn (author of *A Scotsman's Garden in Italy*) and Lady Forteviot, step-grandmother of the present owner.

Within a ¼ mile of Cruggleton Bay, the house looks out across Wigtown Bay to the Isle of Man and the Cumberland Hills. Surrounding it are 30 acres of garden, the woodland sloping gently to the seashore. Beeches, Limes, Douglas and Silver Firs, and Cedars growing by the water's edge act as a backcloth to the wide variety of ornamental and flowering shrubs and trees — Azaras, Embothriums, and Eucryphias from Chile; *Osmanthus*, *Itea ilicifolia*, *Styrax* and *Cercidiphyllum* from China or Japan, many different Acers and Magnolias, and Mimosa (*Acacia decurrens* var. *dealbata*) from south-east Australia or Tasmania, as well as Azaleas and Rhododendrons. The 4½-acre walled garden is used as a nursery for tender plants.

Galloway House is at present being used as a local activities centre, administered by the Strathclyde Region.

22 GLASGOW
     BOTANIC GARDENS
🦌 *Glasgow*
Great Western Road, at
junction of Queen Margaret
Drive and Byres Road.
(CITY OF GLASGOW DISTRICT
COUNCIL)

The Glasgow Botanic Gardens date from 15 May 1817, when the work of laying out a botanic garden was begun on an 8-acre site at Sandyford, at the west end of Sauchiehall Street. Previously there had been a Physic Garden in the grounds of the Old College, established in 1705 for teaching purposes and maintained for about one hundred years.

The gardens were run by the Royal Botanical Institution of Glasgow, founded on the initiative of Thomas Hopkirk. Funds were raised by public subscription and the University of Glasgow made a substantial contribution on the understanding that plant material and facilities for the students were supplied by the Gardens in perpetuity.

The plants which formed the nucleus of the new Botanic Gardens came from Hopkirk's own garden at Dalbeth, within the eastern environs of Glasgow.

Sir William Hooker, one of the most outstanding botanists of all time, was appointed to the Chair of Botany at Glasgow in 1821, and the remarkable success of the Gardens in those early years is undoubtedly attributable to his enthusiasm. They were moved to their present site, together with the original range of glasshouses, in 1839. It is undulating terrain, on the south bank of the Kelvin.

When the move was completed the Gardens were opened to members of the Institution on 30 April 1842. The public were admitted on Saturdays, on payment of one shilling; and on certain days the Gardens were 'thrown open to the Working Classes on the payment of one penny each'.

The most attractive and interesting features of the Gardens today are the glasshouses, especially the large curvilinear iron Kibble Palace, one of the largest in Britain, covering an area of 23,000 square feet. It was originally a conservatory in the grounds of the estate of John Kibble at Coulport, Loch Long. It was used for concerts and public meetings besides the purposes of the Gardens; but the Royal Botanic Institution bought out the lease in 1881 and the fine collection of Tree Ferns and plants from temperate areas of the world were established under the great dome of glass. They are now grouped according to their native geographical areas. The wings on either side of the entrance dome are used for exhibitions and a Visitor Centre.

The main range of glasshouses includes a conservatory, for the colourful display of flowers throughout the year; also glasshouses for Orchids, Begonias, temperate economic plants, succulents, a Palm house, tropical economic plants, tropical Ferns, stove plants, tropical flowers, and an aquatic house.

Crowds of people are attracted to these gardens within the busy city, for their beauty and peacefulness, as a place to walk in at leisure, or just to sit in the sun. For them there are the Herb Garden, the Rock Garden with its many alpine plants, the summer bedding displays in front of the Kibble Palace, or along the terrace before the main range of glasshouses. Beyond lies the large Double Herbaceous Border, with the Systematic Garden to the south. A particular attraction is the interesting and informative plant layouts.

A particularly interesting feature is the Chronological Border, designed to show when some of our commoner garden plants were first introduced. The plants are arranged in beds, one for each century from the sixteenth to the twentieth, and the actual year of introduction is inscribed on the plant label.

The Glenarn garden, on the Clyde near Helensburgh, is widely acclaimed as one of the best Rhododendron gardens in the country, justly famous for its large-leafed Rhododendrons, a number of which have been hybridised by Mr J. F. A. Gibson. There are some old plants dating from 1850 or thereby, but most have been planted by the Gibson family since 1927.

23 GLENARN
Rhu
Rhu ¼ mile. Route A814.

The gardens slope towards the Firth of Clyde, yet there is good shelter, especially that afforded by a closely planted, small, narrow ravine. Many of the *Rhododendron* species begin flowering in March, continuing with the taller Magnolias into April, when the Daffodils are in their prime.

More *Rhododendron* species and hybrids reach through into May and June, the best months for these magnificent shrubs; and this is also the season for Embothriums, naturalised Candelabra Primulas and the various Meconopses, Lilies in variety and their near-relatives the *Nomocharis* which flower well here.

July, often a dull period in Scottish gardens, brings a start to other delights in the Glenarn garden: the Hoherias and Olearias, both natives of New Zealand, the various Eucryphias and Philesias from Chile, and the quaintly beautiful Astrantias, modestly flowering in the woodland walks.

N.B.   The garden has recently changed hands, and may no longer be open to the public.

24 GREENBANK
   GARDEN AND
   ADVICE CENTRE
Clarkston, Glasgow
From Clarkston Toll
following the Mearns Road
to Flenders Road
(signposted); the garden is
½ mile on the right.
(NATIONAL TRUST FOR
SCOTLAND)

When Mr and Mrs W. P. Blyth bought Greenbank House in 1962, the basic pattern of the garden was very much as it had been for a considerable number of years, but in a neglected state. Having restored the garden in a most sympathetic and interesting way, Mr Blyth in 1976 offered the property to the National Trust for Scotland, which it accepted with the intention of developing an Advice Centre, similar to the one the Trust had established in 1968 at Suntrap, near Edinburgh.

Greenbank had several advantages. It was already a colourful garden, and being divided internally, the 2½-acre walled garden lent itself very easily to modifications of the sort required to meet its new purpose and aims. Surrounding the walled garden there are several fields, totalling a further 18 acres, forming an essential buffer to protect the property from a rapid increase in housing, which was beginning to absorb any available land. On the other hand, of course, the quickly increasing population found in Greenbank advice and relaxation, for a great many quite literally on their doorstep.

Mr Blyth's fondness for Shrub Roses is reflected in the present garden; in fact the collection has been considerably increased since the Trust took over the garden. Vegetables were another interest of Mr Blyth's, and these have been retained, both as something of particular interest to visitors, and because there is strong historical relevance in some of the enclosed compartments being used in the way they were intended. Otherwise the garden is simply but effectively designed. On the south front an area approximately one-third of the walled garden is enclosed, and may at one time have been very formally laid out, but now houses two herbaceous borders, bordering a central path. The same central path extends the full length of the larger part of the garden, flanked by mixed borders, and remnants of Apple trees at the south end, to remind us of a former use which at least part of the garden at one time had. Throughout there are beds and borders to provide colour in late spring and summer in which annuals play an important part in making a bright and varied display.

A fairly broad strip of woodland extends along three sides outside the walled garden, principally as shelter, although no doubt the background effect and sense of enclosure must also have been in the mind of whoever planted the trees.

The gardens are open daily, all year, from 10.00 a.m. to dusk.

25 HENSOL
Mossdale
Mossdale, Castle Douglas.
4 miles south of New
Galloway on A762.
(ADMIRAL SIR NIGEL & LADY
HENDERSON)

Hensol House is an important granite building designed by the architect Lugar and completed in 1813. One of few in Scotland designed by this celebrated architect, the house is ideally situated on a sequestered bank above the river Dee.

There are walks through the woodland and along the river, and a stream garden among the Oak trees contains Primulas, Astilbes and Hostas besides Daffodils, Irises, Snowdrops and all the usual spring bulbs. There is a kitchen garden some distance from the house.

The formal garden adjoining the house was probably made in 1813, but extended in the 1920s and onwards. The rainfall is heavy (52 inches) and the soil light and acid, so that ericaceous plants tend to dominate the scene, particularly Rhododendrons and Azaleas, with ornamental trees such as Eucryphias and Embothriums on the perimeter, and many Yew trees.

The owners are keen cultivators of alpines, grown in troughs, island rockeries and expanses of gravel, so that much of the garden is open, with a paved path leading between Rose beds to the centrally placed antique sun-dial.

It is a garden of character, affording much satisfaction to the knowledgeable botanist.

Kirkdale House was built of local granite in 1787, after designs by Robert Adam, but suffered severe damage by fire in 1893. In 1967 it was converted into eight separate apartments, fortunately without alteration to its external appearance. The house and grounds were rented for over sixty years, until 1971, when the owner's family returned to live here. They have since been attempting to restore the property to what it must have been in earlier times. Many people know Kirkdale House as the house with three hundred and sixty-five windows — one for every day of the year.

Interesting relics of the ancient and more recent past include some prehistoric 'cup and ring' stones and an ice house by the entrance gate.

Close to the seashore and Dick Hatterick's Cave and one of the most beautiful coastal roads in Britain, the house looks west across Wigtown Bay towards The Machars, that broad-based, triangular peninsula of gentle, green country.

The 3-acre garden around the house is natural in style, sloping and wooded, prettily planted with an abundance of early spring bulbs, Daffodils, wild Hyacinths, Heaths and Heathers, Rhododendrons and Azaleas. Some of the trees are said to be about 150 years old, and are remarkably tall and straight.

26 KIRKDALE HOUSE *by Creetown*
Just off the A75, half-way between Dumfries and Stranraer. 6 miles west of Gatehouse of Fleet and 3 miles east of Creetown. (KIRKDALE TRUST)

Castle Kennedy used to be the seat of the Kennedys, a powerful Galloway and Ayrshire family, who obtained their first charter to the lands in the middle of the fourteenth century. John, Lord Kennedy, was appointed Keeper of the Manor Place and Loch of Inch in 1482. The Old Castle was destroyed by fire in 1716, although the walls are still standing, and it was succeeded by Lochinch Castle, erected in 1867, presently occupied by the Earl and Countess of Stair.

The gardens measure 1 mile long by ¼ mile wide. They were designed by the 2nd Earl of Stair about 1730; he had been British Ambassador to France and was much influenced by the grandeur of the gardens at Versailles. To implement his plans, he employed the Royal Scots Greys and Inniskilling Fusiliers and their horses. The area occupied is a neck of land between two lochs, formerly beneath the sea, and the various avenues converge like the spokes of a giant wheel on a circular Lily pond.

The gardens were much neglected during the early part of the nineteenth century, but, on the succession of the 8th Earl in 1840, an old plan of the grounds was consulted, and they were renewed to conform to their previous high

27 LOCHINCH AND CASTLE KENNEDY GARDENS *by Stranraer*
4 miles east of Stranraer on A75. (THE EARL & COUNTESS OF STAIR)

standards. Later, flower beds were laid out on either side of the new mansion, and new avenues were planted, each with a different species of Conifer, imported from North America.

The magnificent broad avenue of *Araucaria araucana* (Monkey Puzzle) is a century old and the trees stand 70 feet tall, with plantings of Azaleas along either side. Dettingen Avenue, leading from the Old Castle Garden to the White Loch, is composed of fine Ilex trees, with an inner avenue of alternative *Embothrium* and *Eucryphia glutinosa*. The Pinetum used to be one of the finest in the British Isles. Alas, it suffered severe damage during the great storm of 1963. Plans are afoot to plant the area anew.

The outstanding feature of the gardens is the collection of Rhododendrons; some of the hybrids were made here, and there are specimens of *R. arboreum* one hundred years old, grown from seed brought back from the Himalayas by Sir Joseph Hooker. They succeed very well in this area's mild, damp climate. There are many other beautiful flowering shrubs and trees — Azaleas, Camellias, Embothriums, Magnolias.

Visitors are encouraged to walk round the whole garden area, and a pamphlet is available drawing attention to particular places, trees, and plants of special interest.

28 LOGAN BOTANIC GARDEN
❧ by Stranraer

14 miles south of Stranraer, signposted 1 mile off B7065.
(DEPARTMENT OF AGRICULTURE AND FISHERIES FOR SCOTLAND — *an annexe of the Royal Botanic Garden, Edinburgh*)

Situated on the double peninsula of the Rinns of Galloway, the Logan estate was in the ownership of the McDoualls of Logan from the twelfth century until 1940. The mansion-house, in the Scottish Baronial style, is private and owned by Sir Ninian Buchan-Hepburn.

There are 14 acres of garden, part woodland, part walled. It was established by the McDoualls in the early part of this century. After their deaths, it passed to Mr Olaf Hambro. The Hambro Trust later gifted the garden to the Secretary of State for Scotland for the use of the Royal Botanic Garden, Edinburgh. It is maintained as an annexe for the cultivation of tender plants. Most of these are native to the southern hemisphere, but the climate in the garden is very mild, serious frosts are rare, and the predominant winds are westerly.

The striking feature of the garden is the number of evergreen Tree Ferns (*Dicksonia antarctica*), and the avenues of Cabbage Trees (*Cordyline australis*) and Chusan Palms (*Trachycarpus fortunei*).

There is also a peat garden, and a bog garden that is usurped by the coarse yet spectacular *Gunnera manicata*.

29 MAXWELTON HOUSE
❧ Moniaive

3 miles from Moniaive, 13 miles from Dumfries on B729.
(MAXWELTON HOUSE TRUST)

Maxwelton House was the home of Annie Laurie, subject of the famous song. The house, recently restored by Mrs Stenhouse and the late Mr Hugh Stenhouse, incorporates parts of the ancient castle of Glencairn and was built by Annie Laurie's great-grandfather after 1611.

The 10 acres of garden have been in existence since the 16th century. There are spacious lawns, a ha-ha, a water garden, borders of Roses and shrubs and

herbaceous plants — the best of them around the house — and walks through the woods to the private chapel. The museum of early domestic instruments contains much of interest, and there are Victorian summerhouses. There are views from the terrace of the surrounding hills, rolling countryside and the Maxwelton Braes.

30 ROUGHHILLS
Colvend, Dalbeattie
Above Sandyhills, on the
A710 Dumfries-Dalbeattie
road.
(MR L. FONTAINE & MR D. RANGECROFT)

The house and garden of Roughhills occupy a precarious site, perched high on the cliffs of Sandyhills Bay, and only 300 yards from tides flooding in across the Mersehead Sands of the Solway Firth. The garden, like the house, has been made on shelves cut out of the hill face.

This coast was once the Galloway smugglers' domain, and the place names are still reminiscent of those distant days — Port o' Warren Bay, Cow's Snout, Gutcher's Isle, and Balcary House, especially built for stowing contraband shipped ashore from the Isle of Man.

One might say that only a madman would think of making a garden on this barren, storm-lashed hillside; but the plan succeeded, and every year, one day in May, people flock in their hundreds to see this wonderful garden.

In fact, there is little evidence of concessions having been made to the situation; there are smooth lawns, herbaceous borders, and Rose beds as in any other garden, and flourishing Rhododendrons, Azaleas, and rare shrubs and trees; and a Japanese garden in a convincing oriental style, with a Lily pond fed by a stream trickling down off the hill. A dividing hedge screens another garden on the eastern side, with wide areas of lawn, island beds, and a long border made of layer upon layer of peat blocks, so planted that the profile of contents rises evenly from front to back. One tree in particular always attracts attention — a green Conifer which has assumed the shape of a Calvary cross.

31 ROWALLAN
Fenwick
Gateway on B751
Kilmaurs-Fenwick road.
(HON JOHN CORBETT)

The old Castle of Rowallan stands on the banks of the Carmel Water. It was once the residence of the Mures of Rowallan; a daughter of this family became the first wife of Robert II, from whom our Royal Family are descended.

Part of the castle dates from 1562, but the original fortlet is several centuries older. The unfinished mansion to the north was begun by Sir Robert Lorimer in 1905, and exemplifies his style of architecture. It is built at the end of a fine avenue of Beeches. There is a well-stocked kitchen garden, situated between the two properties. The site is open and sunny, with Peaches and Nectarines trained against the walls.

Choice shrubs, Roses and borders of herbaceous plants surround the perimeter of the new mansion. There is formal front terrace, part lawn, part flagged path, with a low wall between it and the grass parks.

32 SENWICK HOUSE
Borgue

This former Hope-Dunbar property is now an hotel. It was built for a farmhouse, probably in the early seventeenth century, and extended in 1903. The neighbouring small village of Borgue is known for its excellent honey, a fact that is indicative of the area's gentle, bucolic character — rolling fields of grass and clover and rocky outcrops sloping gently down to Brighouse Bay's golden sands, girt with Blackthorn and Buckthorn scrub; an area rich in wild flowers, where the Galloway artist, E. A. Hornel, painted little country girls in long-flowing dresses picking wild Roses and blue Flax against a background of sea.

Senwick House lies in a shallow dip, facing due south, with a sheltering belt of trees around, all stooped by the salt winds off the sea. The main drive runs through a wood, thickly planted with Snowdrops, spring Crocuses, Daffodils and Narcissi.

Until the property changed hands recently, the garden had been long neglected. The present owners have made great strides in its restoration; there are many new flowering shrubs and trees, new peat walls and terraced borders containing choice rock and alpine plants, and the old Apple orchard is burgeoning anew, adding its blossom to the glories of the garden in April.

Not so many years ago, when Lady Claren Hope-Dunbar and her late husband lived at Senwick, there were three gardeners, one of them a policy man, and about the same number of indoor staff. Today, the hotel and garden are run as a family business — necessarily so, as outside help is no longer obtainable.

SENWICK HOUSE (contd.)
Near Borgue village, Kircudbright, on unclassified road to Brighouse Bay.
(MR & MRS P. A. BAINES)

From the open areas of lawn and walkways bordered by Yew hedges, a path descends logwood steps to the main garden below the nineteenth-century Skeldon House.

The gardens lie in a ravine, shaded by Beeches, Oaks, Birches and Lebanese Cedars, interspersed with Eucryphias, Embothriums, and other choice ornamental trees and shrubs, including rare and beautiful Rhododendrons and Azaleas, most of which were planted here in 1926 by a firm of London contractors.

The main feature is the river Doon, twisting and turning in a rapid course through the garden. It is crossed by a bridge on which the poet Robert Burns, according to reliable authority, wrote his poem 'Ye Banks and Braes o' Bonnie Doon', inspired, no doubt, by this beautiful dene.

There are large greenhouses, heated by oil-fired boilers, and containing much of interest: a Vine with strawberry-flavoured fruit; a Ponderosa Lemon, smuggled from America; *Citrus mitis* (the Calamondin Orange); various Crinums; the Bird of Paradise plant, *Strelitzia reginae; Tibouchina urvilleana*, with its rich purple blooms; *Lapageria rosea* and *L. alba*, the particularly fine white form of this Chilean creeper with pendulous bell-like flowers; and the sweetly scented *Rhododendron fragrantissimum* and *R.* 'Lady Alice Fitzwilliam'.

Roe deer raid the garden from time to time; there are red squirrels at home in the woods; and the bird life is remarkable for herons, sparrow hawks, and the spotted flycatcher.

33 SKELDON HOUSE
Dalrymple
1 mile from Dalrymple, on the road to Ayr.
(MR WILLIAM DUCAS)

The central portion of Southwick House is early eighteenth-century, the remainder being added in 1860. The walls are built of local granite and red freestone. The situation is low-lying, at the south side of Criffel (1868 feet), about 1½ miles from the coast, where the Southwick Water loses itself in the Mersehead Sands of the Solway Firth; the climate is mild, and the garden sheltered from the prevailing west winds by Clifton Crags and Bainloch Hill and woods of Beech, Oak and Scots Pine. On a clear day, there are views across the Solway to the Cumberland coast.

Little is known of the history of the garden, except that it was much more lavishly landscaped and planted in Victorian times, when labour was cheap and easily obtained. In the necessary simplification, over seventy flower beds were eliminated and a vast shrubbery of spotted Laurel, between the house and the river, was uprooted. Now the west front looks down on the Natural or Wild Garden, made in the 1920s by the present owner's father, Mr Robert G. D. Thomas. Its special feature is a small lake, with beautiful shrubs planted round the margins to give autumn colours; together with young Magnolias, a *Eucalyptus gunnii*, a fine *Eucryphia*, and an old standard *Wisteria*. The curling ribbon border is among the few vestiges still remaining of the Victorian garden.

There are formal gardens laid out and planted by Mrs C. H. Thomas, and a vegetable garden, all enclosed by walls and Beech hedges. The soil is sandy and light and acid, but suitable for Euphorbias, Hellebores, Hostas, Hydrangeas and Japanese Anemones, all of which thrive; also the old and new Shrub Roses, (but not the Hybrid Teas), as well as Rhododendrons and Camellias, which prosper in the moist, mild climate. There is one very old *Rhododendron*, 40 feet high and 20 feet wide, with dark red flowers, thought by the Royal Horticultural Society to be one of the early hybrids.

Depredations by rabbits, hares, roe deer, and wild mink cause much havoc throughout the gardens. A small loch within the policies attracts waterfowl.

Stonypath is situated on a windswept hillside, approximately 900 feet above sea level, on the southern edge of the Pentlands. It is about 4½ acres in total with one-third of the area enclosed in a formal or semi-formal arrangement and the remainder a wild garden of trees and water.

The garden was started in 1966 by Ian Hamilton Finlay and his wife Sue and although at first it was intended as a 'test ground' for his ideas on planting and the siting of inscriptions to be used elsewhere by architects and planners it has since become valued as a work in itself.

Stonypath is sometimes referred to as a 'poetic garden' or a garden of ideas but it is not easy to summarise the novel features of this garden which is at once so traditional and so remote from present fashion.

'Whereas the eighteenth-century horticulturalists worked with large vistas, the Finlays have planned in terms of a series of small focal points, partly because this method enabled them to proceed corner by corner as time and money per-

34 SOUTHWICK HOUSE
Caulkerbush
At the Caulkerbush junction of the A710 Solway shore road with the A745 Caulkerbush-Dalbeattie road.
(MR & MRS C. H. THOMAS)

FIGURE 89
Arum lilies at Logan Gardens

35 STONYPATH GARDEN
Little Sparta
Stonypath, Little Sparta, Dunsyre, Lanark. Turn off A702 at Dolphinton for Dunsyre or off A721 at Newbigging. Stonypath is 1 mile to the west of Dunsyre; 45 minutes drive from Edinburgh.
(IAN HAMILTON FINLAY AND SUE FINLAY)

FIGURE 90
*One of Ian Hamilton
Finlay's calligraphic
inscriptions at Stonypath*

mitted, and partly because it suited Finlay's concept of a garden of "little secret places", points of deliberate meaning that evoke a response on many levels. This is done by careful placing, throughout the garden, of a series of artefacts, usually consisting of a small piece of stone, wood or calligraphy and sometimes combined with an image to produce a visual and poetic impact. These "image-poems" are an art form in which Finlay is pre-eminent and which he has developed to a high degree of refinement.' (Christopher McIntosh in *Country Life*.)

Plants are used but this is not a plant garden in the horticultural sense. There are certain innovatory aspects, for instance strawberries are substantially used as ground-cover (these are repeated in Finlay's design for the approach to the British Embassy residence in Bonn). Foxgloves and other wild flowers are also widely used.

Stonypath has a large Garden Temple which contains Finlay's publications, stone works and other collaborations with craftsmen.

The garden is open from May to October but visitors are requested to write or phone before visiting (089981 252). The best time to visit it is in June. The Garden Temple is open all the year round, by prior appointment.

36 THREAVE SCHOOL
OF GARDENING
🜨 *Castle Douglas*
*1 mile from Castle Douglas
on A75.*
(NATIONAL TRUST FOR
SCOTLAND)

Threave was presented to the National Trust for Scotland in 1948 by the late Major A. F. Garden, together with an endowment for its upkeep. The estate is quite a large one, extending to 1490 acres, and consists of several farms as well as the School, with 60 acres or so of gardens and grounds. In addition a further 301 acres was purchased at a later stage and now forms a bird sanctuary around Threave Castle.

The School opened its doors to the first six students in October 1960 and to them fell the task of initial developments of the garden; the first stages in the making of a rock garden and peat walls, and the improvement of the area surrounding the walled garden to change it from farm land to a well-planned ornamental area. In 1961 a further six came, and twelve has remained fairly consistently the number of students ever since.

The course is for a period of two years, of which eight hours are spent in the classroom and the remaining thirty-two hours of the week in practical work in the garden, which covers a very wide range of horticultural subjects. A prospectus is available on request from the School or Trust Headquarters.

Although the main aim was, and still is, to provide a training ground for potential gardeners for the future, the fact that there were so many and varied requirements to provide experience has given rise to a very interesting and colourful area. In addition to rock and peat gardens, an arboretum has been established and a woodland garden added, and, following upon the success of a heath garden, another was begun in recent years to broaden the range of plants available, as well as offering most pleasant views over the surrounding countryside. Understandably the collection of trees and shrubs is especially good, as

are the many herbaceous and alpine plants in the garden.

After twenty years Threave has developed from what was no more than a walled garden into an outstanding and very lovely garden of about 80 acres, and a most successful School of Gardening. In 1979 nearly 50,000 people came to see the gardens, and it is to be hoped that many more visitors will discover this horticultural delight in south-west Scotland.

The gardens are open all year, daily 9.00 a.m. to sunset.

FIGURE 91
The lily pond, Threave

Walton Park was built in 1816, with Victorian additions around 1890. It is situated in woods and parkland and the 3½ acre policies included a walled garden of 1½ acres and a wild garden of 2 acres.

The late General Percy Brown and Mrs Brown were keen collectors of shrubs, most of which have been planted in the long border between the walled garden and the river Urr. Among the rarer ones are *Osmarea burkwoodii, Osmarea delavayi,* the Macartney Rose (*R. bracteata*), *Viburnum carlecephalum, Kolkwitzia amabilis,* the Pea tree (*Caragana*); *Kirengeshoma palmata* (with pale yellow wax bell flowers), and the New Zealand evergreen *Corokia*.

Another interesting Walton Park shrub is the Japanese Wineberry (*Rubus phoenicolasius*), a strong-growing Bramble which thrives beside the river.

The house nestles among Scots Pine, Douglas Fir, Spanish Chestnuts and a Walnut of great age.

37 WALTON PARK
Castle Douglas
5½ miles from Castle Douglas on road to Corsock.
(MRS PERCY BROWN)

INDEX